OUTPOSTS OF CHANGE

HOW TO CREATE A MORALLY RICH SOCIALLY JUST
SOCIETY IN HARMONY WITH NATURE
AND WHY WE MUST

Benjamin R. Wiener

OUTPOSTS MEDIA

Publisher's Cataloging-in-Publication Data

Names: Wiener, Benjamin R., 1952- author.

Title: Outposts of change : how to create a morally rich socially just society
            in harmony with nature and why we must / Benjamin R. Wiener.

Description: Summerland, CA : Outposts Media, [2021]
            Includes bibliographical references.

Identifiers: ISBN: 978-1-7368035-0-9 (paperback)
             978-1-7368035-1-6 (hardcover)
             978-1-7368035-2-3 (epub)

            LCCN: 2021919026

Subjects: LCSH: 1. Social change. 2. Social justice. 3. Environmentalism.
            4. Global environmental change. 5. Environmental justice.
            6. Sustainable living. 7. Social movements. 8. Social evolution.

            BISAC: POLITICAL SCIENCE / World / General.

            SOCIAL SCIENCE / Sociology / Social Theory.

            BUSINESS & ECONOMICS / Environmental Economics.

            NATURE / Environmental Conservation & Protection.

Classification: LCC: HM831 .W54 2021 | DDC: 303.4--dc23

Cover design by David E. Chandler
Interior design and typesetting by Colleen Sheehan

Outposts Media
P. O. Box 14
Summerland, CA 93067

Contents

THIS WORK IS DEDICATED

To Everyone Who Knows That We Must Be Better,

Believes That We Can Be Better, And Is

Willing To Help Us Become Better

At Being Human

IT IS WRITTEN

For All of Earth's Children

OUTPOSTS OF CHANGE

EARTH - 2020

As the world suffers through a global pandemic that has claimed over one million lives, shut down entire economies, and brought global financial systems to the brink of collapse, Earth's ability to support life is rapidly deteriorating.

Nineteen of the 20 hottest years on record occurred within the past two decades. Antarctica just experienced the hottest days on record. The Artic is warming 3 times faster than the global average. Polar ice caps are melting 6 times faster than in the 1990s. Sea levels are rising. And the inevitable result? Four hundred million people living in coastal environments are now at risk of becoming climate refugees within 80 years.[1] Today, 1.2 billion people are at risk from flooding. Another 1.8 billion are affected by land degradation, desertification and drought.[2]

Meanwhile, heat waves and drought conditions, which claim thousands of lives annually, blanket vast areas within Australia, Africa, Europe, and the Americas causing millions to suffer extreme hardship. Adding to the calamity, locust invasions of biblical proportions have stripped barren, lands within Kenya, Ethiopia, Uganda, and Somalia creating unprecedented threats to the food security and livelihoods of millions of people.

Wildfires ripped through the Amazon, the Artic, Australia, Paraguay, the United States, and Russia destroying entire ecosystems, killing uncountable numbers of plants and animals, releasing massive amounts of planet-warming gasses, rendering the air unfit to breath, and imperiling freshwater resources.

During the first half of 2020, nearly 10 million people joined the ranks of climate refugees as they were forced to abandon their homes because of extreme weather events. A record number of storms churned through Atlantic Ocean regions during the hurricane season, while historic floodwaters swamped large swathes of land in China, India, Pakistan, South Korea, France, Spain, the UK, and Indonesia, killing hundreds, displacing thousands, and causing billions of dollars of property damage. More than 7,000 extreme weather events have been recorded within the past 20 years.

Deserts are expanding, snowpacks are shrinking, and aquifers are being sucked dry everywhere. Dead zones permeate vast expanses of Earth's warming oceans which are contaminated with carcinogenic filth and are 30% more acidic than they were a mere 200 years ago. Half of all corals of the Great Barrier Reef in Australia have perished. Plankton populations, which are largely responsible for oxygenating Earth, are plummeting. For the first time in modern history, atmospheric and oceanic oxygen levels are falling.

Forest destruction continues unabated. Fifteen billion trees are cut down every year. In total, we have eliminated nearly 50% of all Earth's trees.[3] Beyond that, within the last 50 years, 68% of all birds, amphibians, mammals, fish, and reptiles have been wiped out.[4] Globally, pollinator populations are crashing, and extinction rates are at unprecedented levels. A new epoch in Earth's long and storied timeline has been penned. The Anthropocene. It is only the 6th planetary-level extinction event within the past 500 million years. And we are the cause.

In 2019, the world's top scientists published a report titled *Nature's Dangerous Decline 'Unprecedented'; Species Extinction Rates Accelerating.* It was the most comprehensive science-based report of its kind. It concludes that:

The overwhelming evidence ... from a wide range of different fields of knowledge, presents an ominous picture ... The health of ecosystems on which we and all other species depend is deteriorating more rapidly than ever. We are eroding the very foundations of our economies, livelihoods, food security, health and quality of life worldwide.

The stark reality of these findings should lead the conversations spread across global media outlets to heighten our awareness of the necessity of changing our ways. But sadly, they are not. So, we remain trapped within the Anthropocene traveling pathways of extinction of our own making.

Our destruction of Earth's life support systems will continue unabated, to a large degree because of our failures to responsibly manage *how* we do most things, which stems from an unwillingness of the decision-making elite to elevate the interests of the many over their own. The result? Rulers everywhere unleash acts of barbarism against those of differing views with such regularity that it stuns the conscience. Adding to the climate refugee crisis, over 5 million people in 2020 were forced to flee their homelands in Africa, the Middle East and South America because of armed conflict and violence. Entire nations like Syria, the Democratic Republic of the Congo, Burkina Faso, and Yemen are unsafe places to live.

People everywhere cry out for change as authoritarian regimes expand their powers through the use of force, repression, and resource deprivation. Whether in China, Russia, the US, Saudi Arabia, Brazil, India, North Korea, or the Sudan, the people suffer as fundamental freedoms are lost and inequality builds.

Millions have joined peaceful protests in Hong Kong, Chile, the US, Iran, Belarus, Mali, Bolivia, and elsewhere in attempts to bring to light the social injustices that have become commonplace, only to be met with acts of brutality by police and military branches of the governments they oppose. Journalists have been imprisoned and assassinated in India, China, Turkey, Saudi Arabia, and Egypt, for reporting truths that repressive regimes refuse to tolerate.

Armed conflict plagues our species. Whether in Afghanistan, Ethiopia, Nigeria, Armenia, Mexico, Azerbaijan, Ukraine, Yemen, Libya, Iraq, Syria, or Mali, tens of thousands of innocent men, women, and children are killed every year and hundreds of millions live in constant fear for their lives. Elsewhere, there are far too many communities ruled by warlords, drug-lords, gangs, religious extremists, and others. Their acts of brutality and lack of tolerance have made those places unsafe.

Safety is a relative term as starvation, unemployment, and unfair employment practices expand the ranks of those experiencing unsafe living conditions. Food insecurity renders nearly 1 billion people starving and another 1.2 billion malnourished as half the human population attempts to survive on $5.50 a day or less. It is simply impossible to feel safe when your only water source is dangerous to drink and you lack the money to pay for healthy food, safe shelter, adequate education, and quality healthcare.

Safety is also a relative term for the millions of refugees forced to flee their homelands in search of safe havens. Many arrived at former safe havens only to be imprisoned, or worse. For example, as of mid-2019 in the US, over 11,000 traumatized children were separated from their parents and "caged" at immigration detention centers described by one physician as "torture facilities."[5] Why were they so inhumanely treated? Because barbaric rulers chose to make examples of them to dissuade others from coming in search of asylum.

Whether within the structures of governance, commerce, finance or religion, truth has taken a back seat to the lie. Politicians and their minions spin one lie after another to justify their acts of malfeasance. They are often joined by media outlets who propagate their lies and subvert the truth, to everyone's detriment.

The corporate elite are no better. They operate sweat shops filled with child laborers, threaten union organizers, assassinate whistleblowers, authorize violence to quell protests against their practices, mislead the public about the safety of their products, and refuse to accept responsibility for their environmentally destructive practices. They do this to secure growth in profits and management compensation, which are at record levels of disparity with that of the average worker. And they get away with it by lobbying and bribing public officials to enact laws that insulate them from liability for the harms they cause.

Grave inequality is the accepted norm of the world's elite. They demonstrate little care about the suffering of others. The list of social ills is nearly endless because obsolete structures have not changed with the times to support a global community of billions. Nearly everyone on this planet knows things are not right. Billions cry out in desperation pleading for help. Mostly, their cries go unanswered.

AUTHOR'S NOTE

For nearly 50 years I have been watching, studying, and thinking about *how* we humans do most things. I have read countless scientific articles and books about the impacts of our activities on Earth's life support systems. I have also reviewed innumerable writings discussing the nature of our social structures.

What has become abundantly clear is the fact that Earth is in big trouble. We are rapidly destroying her ability to support life. What has become equally clear, is that *we* are in big trouble. The archaic ways within which we operate our societies are both responsible for the suffering of billions, and our inability to stem our destructive ways.

We have gotten into the mess we are in because of *how* we do most things, which is determined by the nature of the four social structures created to operate our societies: governance, commerce, finance, and religion. They were built for a different era and have proven incapable of enabling the level of rapid, systemic social change at global scales needed to enable our species, as a collective whole, to thrive. So, another, better way of being must be found. *Outposts of Change* is about better ways of being human.

Most of us are aware that really big social changes are necessary. Across the globe, people have taken to the streets crying out for fundamental change; pleading with those who govern to adopt better ways. They have been unsuccessful because they attempt to force change from within existing structures, and because they lack a unifying plan designed to enable us, collectively, to be better. Within the following pages you will be introduced to such a plan, and you will be asked to consider and accept its viability.

The good news is that we already know how to do most things in far better ways. The bad news is that existing structures are not designed to enable large scale progressive change. In fact, their fundamentals pit us against each other at a time when uniting in action under a banner of commonality is what is required if we are to save ourselves from ourselves.

Whether we choose to unite as one species in pursuit of common goals, or choose not to, will determine whether we perish, or thrive as a species destined to explore the wonders of this most incredible universe. Fortunately, we have evolved the ability to fundamentally change *how* we manage our affairs. The question for you to ponder is whether or not we possess the courage and the determination to do so. No one else will do it for us. No savior. No interstellar lifeform. No god. Just us, a community of beings, human. It is our curse. It is our opportunity. And it is our time to responsibly take control of our destiny and change how we do most things.

Change, is the one life certainty. We should expect it, count on it, and embrace it. To change the world, we need certain understandings. What follows within Books I and II is a broad overview of Earth's life support systems and a select few examples of the adverse impacts our presence is having on the ability of those systems to support life, including our own. The picture is not pretty, which highlights the necessity of fundamentally changing our ways.

Book III looks at how growth, the most fundamental of human goals, is driving us deeper and deeper down pathways of extinction. We know this to be true. Our scientists have warned the global elites to fundamentally change our ways for decades. They have not. So, the obligation to change the course of humanity falls upon us. To change *how* we do most things, we need to understand the function of each structure, which is developed within Book IV.

Book V is all about change. It considers how to initiate the process of fundamentally changing our social structures, which begins by evolving new goals designed to help ignite new ways of being. Here, we both highlight the importance of adopting new foundational goals for each social structure, and then suggest what they might be. But setting new goals is not enough to break the chains of past ways that prevent us from evolving new ways of being. To accomplish that task requires a movement of change unlike any ever attempted. The concept of a global movement of change is discussed here, along with a number of actions required to transform our societies. These actions are prerequisites to making the leap forward necessary for us to both survive and thrive. They include such things as focusing on commonality, finding ways to eliminate social inequality, and breaking free of the chains that bind us to past ways incapable of enabling a global society of billions. Where to direct our efforts to expedite the process is suggested.

Within Book VI you will find a blueprint outlining how to enable fundamental social change. Change of the magnitude envisioned provides an entirely new and inherently superior way of being. Here, you will come to recognize that the changes most of us want, evolutionary levels of change in our ways of being human, are entirely possible to achieve. Every living thing changes the world. It is what we do. The results of change can be progressive, regressive or neutral. Unfortunately, we have been traveling regressive pathways of change for far too long. To survive and thrive we must change course and experience progressive change. The title of this work was chosen because Outposts of Change are places designed to foster progressive levels of change.

Outposts are communities of hope, of possibility, and of fulfillment, founded upon a higher sense of purpose within which progress for the betterment of all is the intended way. Book VII highlights life within Outposts, showcasing new ways of being. And be clear, Outposts are places that already exist. They are built upon foundations of indelible truths within which equality and commonality, family and fellowship are their ways.

Ultimately, this work is intended to reveal what evolutionary change at this stage of our existence entails as our species attempts to emerge from an irresponsible youth, operating with near total disregard for its actions, into young adulthood with eyes focused on a future of great possibility.

The depth of what follows is simply too great to fully absorb within one reading. Make a pass through once, think about the material presented, consider whether or not the guidance that follows rings true and if so, read it through again in search of deeper meaning. Think about what the future has in store for humanity if we do not change our ways. Then ask yourself if that is the future you want to send your children's children into.

If not, consider what role you would be willing to play in perhaps the most important movement of social change humanity will have ever embarked upon. To save ourselves from ourselves will require new leaders who are willing to risk all to bring us together, united to accomplish commonly held goals founded upon the most important life values. Within Outposts, you will find those leaders. And in a very real sense, you become one when you join an Outpost.

There is great goodness within each of us. It is time to bring it forth, to release the bondage of past ways that pit one against the other, and unite under a banner of commonality with the knowledge that together, we simply are better. Whether or not we succeed in solving the vast array of problems we face depends on you and billions of others like you embracing the change most of us want, and so many desperately need. It can happen. It is my most sincere and most profound hope that together, we find our way.

BR

BOOK I

ORIGINS

Some 13.8 billion years ago the universe as we know it did not exist. Everything that makes up what now appears to be an infinitely large expanse of matter pulsing with the energy of trillions upon trillions of stars was clustered at a single point of origin.[6] It has long been thought that an explosion of cosmic proportion set our universe in motion. We are unsure of the size or shape of this universe, whether it is finite or infinite. If finite, what, if anything, dwells beyond its perimeter? If infinite, well, is it possible to have had a beginning? The point of origin was Life's palace, beyond which Life's palate of creation waited to be filled. From the moment our universe was set in motion, change was established as *the* universal constant. Change is what our universe is all about.

CHANGE

Everything set in motion at the creation remains so, here one moment, there the next. Change. To be present means to be part of a universe in perpetual motion, constantly changing. Although everything is unique, each is inextricably part of a whole engaged in eternal transformation. Whether photons streaming through space as rays of light or entire galaxies adrift within the fluidity of space, everything transforms this universe by the mere fact of its presence. A single-celled organism takes up nutrients from the surrounding environment and converts them into the building blocks of its own growth and reproduction. Change. Take a breath, move a finger, eat a meal, ride a bike, text a message, everything that you do changes something. Change defines life. It is the one thing to anticipate, plan for, and ultimately, embrace.

SEEDS OF LIFE

At the origin, the seeds of life were thrust out into an ever-expanding cosmos swirling with masses of energy. Space was born to cool, transmit, and confine this energy giving birth to gravity, that force of nature whose invisible threads unite all things. With gravity came the stars. Created to energize the universe, they provide heat and light where there had been none. Then came the planets, born into perpetual motion, they formed the platform upon which life would take hold.

BOOK II

EARTH

1

LIFE

Nearly nine billion years after the origin, Earth was born, and with her came the seeds of humanity. During her earliest days, Earth was a volatile combination of hot gases. Over time, with help from space, she began to cool, and as she did her heaviest elements condensed, pulled together by invisible gravitational forces to form a molten core that provided structure and warmth in ways similar to the functions of your own skeletal and thermoregulatory systems. Electrical currents coursed through her inner being creating magnetic fields which to this day help shield planetary surfaces from intense solar radiation that would otherwise be destructive to life, giving birth to the outermost layer of Earth's skin.

For life as we know it to flow, water, energy, and food must be present. Earth's external energy source is her sun. Water appeared at approximately the same time as her surface hardened into rock,[7] and served as a medium within which elements from rock dissolved to provide food for her earliest life forms. As Earth cooled, an atmospheric zone formed transitioning Earth to space. That atmosphere now functions as a large living organ that is permeable and flexible. It helps regulate planetary temperatures and contains, enhances, and protects Earth's other life support systems, performing functions similar to those performed by your own skin.

Earth's spin and orbit ensure that change, the elixir of life, remains a constant. Like your heart, these forces move fluids from one location to another powering a circulatory system that enables life rhythms of day and night, the seasons and tides. This system delivered water, nutrients, waste products, oxygen, and carbon dioxide to Earth's other developing life support systems until the perfect combination was achieved from which life would spring. How that happened is a mystery awaiting discovery. But happen it did.

Some four billion years ago, life found its way to Earth. Springing from her oceanic womb came the phytoplankton, microscopic single-celled plants, and animals that eat carbon dioxide (CO_2) and release oxygen. Every living thing changes the environment within which it exists, some dramatically so. Over the course of billions of years, trillions upon trillions of phytoplankton helped transform Earth into the oxygen-rich, lush, blue-green planet that we so lovingly call home. They also established the foundations of her respiratory and digestive systems.

Just as many of the components within our own bodies perform multiple functions, so too do the components of Earth's life support systems. For example, although phytoplankton serve as the primary oceanic food source, they also release oxygen for others to use and they pull carbon dioxide from the atmosphere which helps keep Earth systems from overheating. And the oxygen they produce is not just used for breathing and catalyzing chemical reactions. Some of it floats to the upper regions of Earth's atmosphere to form the ozone layer where it shields her lands from harmful cosmic radiation which enables a great diversity of terrestrial life forms.

Change comes in many forms. Most environmental change happens as life forms slowly alter their environments. Leisurely changes allow a species to adapt. Rapid environmental changes tend not to. This is why diversity is essential. The greater the number of species as well as the differences within a species, the greater the chance that one of them will successfully navigate life's challenging pathways. So, as Earth's atmosphere absorbed ever more oxygen, plants and animals took to the land. They diversified and modified their environments.

Some evolved more efficient survival strategies. But most failed to ascend the evolutionary ladder and eventually perished.

With an abundant supply of oxygen and a protective layer of ozone came an explosion in terrestrial biodiversity. Land life blossomed. Plants provided the primary food source for animals. When a plant died, evolving digestive systems containing thousands of species of bacteria, fungi, and other organisms stepped in to decompose and recirculate plant nutrients, creating nutrient-rich soils, which, over millions of years, transformed barren landscapes into fertile valleys.

Land plants evolved seeds to more efficiently spread their genetic makeup, and fish moved onshore, trading gills for lungs and fins for limbs. New habitats were constantly being created. Insects appeared to feed upon plants and later upon other insects. Plants developed strategies to protect themselves from the insect world. Insects developed strategies to protect themselves from other animals. Opportunity was everywhere as Earth joyously gave birth to all kinds of new life forms.

Within maturing digestive systems, certain animals and plants became recycling specialists. Living in or on soils, they ate dead biological matter and converted it into nutrients for use by other living things in ways similar to those of the billions of beneficial microorganisms living in your own digestive tract. Healthy soils, like healthy guts, are simply teeming with life. Today, a teaspoon of healthy soil may contain a hundred meters of fungal networks, thousands of species and millions of individuals. In fact, estimates indicate that one-quarter of all Earth species live in soils.[8] So, as our story unfolds, recognize that just as maintaining a healthy matrix of beneficial organisms within our own digestive systems is critical to our overall health and well-being, maintaining a robust soil matrix full of beneficial organisms is critical to the health and well-being of planetary level life support systems.

Multiple complex life support systems that perform functions similar to those performed by our own liver, kidneys, and lymphatic systems came into existence. Soils, swamps, deltas, estuaries, and marshlands developed to filter and purify Earth waters just as plants filter her atmosphere and gravity helps purify her waters. Over time, millions of plants and animals evolved to perform specialized functions enabling more robust and efficient support systems to sustain greater, more diverse, and more complex populations of life than ever before.

That a living Earth exists within the frigidity of space is a miracle of such celestial magnitude that it should be cherished, worshiped, and above all else, understood. From the spark that ignited life on Earth billions of years ago have evolved magnificent life support systems that are interconnected and interdependent. They exist as an integral aspect of a tiny, but living, blue sphere rocketing through a cold and foreboding environment within one of trillions of galaxies awash within the fluidity of space. Some life forms have existed for eons, others for nanoseconds. Yet, it has always been Earth's ability to change, adapt, and evolve ever more sophisticated support systems that has kept life opportunities alive.

Life ebbs and flows. Billions of species come into being, billions perish. Earth has suffered through at least five major mass extinction events over the past 540 million years during which widespread loss of biological abundance and diversity occurred, the worst of which took place approximately 252 million years ago. Although there are multiple theories about what triggered that event, it appears that greenhouse gases overheated the planet, turned the oceans acidic, and caused atmospheric and oceanic oxygen levels to plummet. The result? Nearly all planetary life vanished.[9]

Extinction is one of nature's ways of clearing pathways for another's attempts to successfully navigate the ultimate challenges and ultimate opportunities of life. Evolution is the other way, the ultimate way. Evolution is that process by which a species experiences such fundamental change that it becomes something different, a more efficient and fundamentally better form of being. Evolution and extinction. They go hand in hand.

The last major extinction event occurred approximately 66 million years ago. It ended the 185-million-year reign of the dinosaurs. Only small animals survived. Many were mammals that had occupied an ecological niche below that of the great reptiles. Change ushered out one dominant animal form and made room for another, the mammals, who rapidly filled niches left vacant.

Over time, Earth would heal. Lush tropical and verdant temperate forests would again cover her lands. Animals as abundant in number and rich in diversity as ever would repopulate the world. Aquatic environments once again burst with life. And, although it would take 66 million years, a new species of mammals would evolve to become the most dominant ever to populate her lands.

2

ALONG CAME THE HUMANS

It began in Africa. A few pairs here, a few there. They spread slowly, unrestrained by rivers, mountains, oceans, or even differing climates. They ate plants. They ate animals. They hunted. They gathered. And most importantly, they adapted and innovated. With imaginations and creative abilities far exceeding all others, they grew to dominate Earth.

Most lived in small groups apart from others. For the greater part of 200,000 years their goals were simple and unspoken: to survive. And survive they would as their populations doubled again, and again, and again. Then, about 10,000 years ago, humans learned to farm the land and save seeds, instantly transforming their world. Life became easier. Nomads set down roots as systems of governance emerged to enable co-existence.

Trade was born. Family members no longer had to provide everything needed to survive. Individuals became more reliant on the community and growth became the driving force. But growth, as we will discuss at length throughout this book, is a double-edged sword. Theoretically, the larger the community the more secure it becomes. But the larger the community, the more it consumes. Local resources get used up necessitating journeys of acquisition by trade or war.

The larger the community the greater its potential for adverse environmental impacts, which turns on how the community chooses to self-govern. All societies require structure, no matter the number of individuals. Cooperative efforts in support of communal activities are necessitated. Agreements are reached, roles delegated. So, with the gathering of a small kernel of agricultural knowledge came the beginnings of fundamental social change.

Although the discovery of agriculture was the spark responsible for igniting fundamental social change, the expansion of the community is the fuel that sustains it. We simply function better, more efficiently, within the community. Today, we are a species of 7.8 billion occupying almost every Earth habitat. Soon we will be 11 billion. We have conquered nature's competitors and defeated most of her natural defenses. We compete for access to Earth resources only with ourselves, often resulting in war and hardship. For now, we seem incapable of placing reasonable restrictions on how we access and use those resources. We have become our own worst enemy and the biggest impediment to successfully navigating evolutionary pathways. As Eric Fromm recognized, we are the only animal whose existence is a problem from which we cannot escape, and of which only we can solve.

TO SOLVE THE PROBLEM OF THEIR OWN EXISTENCE

To solve the vast array of problems that imperil our very existence, let's begin by looking back at what we have done, over time, from afar. A simple snapshot won't suffice. So, imagine observing Earth from space over the past three centuries and watch the story unfold.

Three hundred years ago, Earth's life support systems were as robust as ever. Tropical and temperate forests covered much of the land and phytoplankton enjoyed vast oceanic environments. Together, they produced prodigious amounts of oxygen and locked up equally prodigious quantities of CO_2. Earth's respiratory systems were fully operational. The air was clean. The waters were pure. But we changed all that. In just over 25 years (between 1990 and 2015) there was a net loss of world forests of an area about the size of South Africa.[10] In totality, we have destroyed 50 percent of all forest lands with only 20 percent of the remainder considered intact.[11]

Our greenhouse gas emissions have warmed and acidified Earth's oceans. The result? Phytoplankton numbers are declining.[12] And alarmingly, we now know that atmospheric and oceanic oxygen levels are also declining.[13] The first study to systematically analyze changes in global oxygen levels over the past one hundred years reveals that "Human activities have caused [an] irreversible decline of atmospheric O_2." One of the scientists who conducted that study warns that "O_2 is the most crucial atmospheric component for lives on earth," and that unless we change our ways, the decline in global oxygen levels "could affect the survival of humans and most of the species directly."[14] Today, Earth's respiratory systems are compromised, endangered.

Three hundred years ago, pollinators provided uninterrupted reproductive services, free of charge. Flowering plants were every-where. Soils were packed with millions of different kinds of organisms engaged in digesting and recycling plant and animal materials, making them available for use by the next generation. Together, Earth's repro-ductive and digestive systems were functioning at peak levels. Today, pollinator numbers have plummeted everywhere. Soils have been stripped of biological diversity and essential nutrients. As a result, Earth's reproductive and digestive systems are in a state of failure.

Three hundred years ago, intact estuaries, marshlands, grasslands, and thick soils filtered and cleansed Earth waters as efficiently as they had for hundreds of millions of years, performing functions similar to those carried out within our own bodies. Today, 85 percent of wet-lands present in the year 1700 have vanished and the rate of loss is three times faster, in percentage terms, than forest losses.[15] Temper-ate grasslands are considered the "most altered terrestrial ecosystem on the planet and are recognized as the most endangered ecosystem on most continents."[16] Only 50 percent of intact temperate grasslands remain.[17] These vital support systems are endangered.

Three hundred years ago, Earth's atmosphere was pristine. It con-tained a relatively stable mixture of CO_2 and oxygen and an intact ozone layer which helped maintain optimal life support tempera-tures. Today, Earth's atmosphere is plagued by plumes of industrial wastes rendering the air toxic to breathe and inhospitable to life. Giant holes have burned through the ozone layer, exposing us to increasing doses of cosmic radiation. And CO_2 levels have spiked, igniting planetary-level fevers as Earth environments overheat at accelerating rates, impairing the functionality of numerous support systems.

Three hundred years ago, Earth's circulatory systems were stable and fully capable of delivering a constant supply of oxygen and nutrients wherever needed. Extreme weather events were rare. Most aquatic surfaces were pristine, allowing a steady exchange of oceanic and atmospheric gasses. Now, Earth's waters are contaminated with carcinogenic filth, industrial waste, and agricultural pesticides that are exterminating plant and animal life at unprecedented rates. Oil slicks and plastics overspread vast expanses of ocean surfaces. Oceanic death zones proliferate.

Three hundred years ago, Earth's immune systems were functioning well. Although their numbers were declining, predators still roamed the lands and seas, keeping most animal populations in check. Bacteria and viruses performed similar functions equally well. Today, her immune systems have been severely compromised. We have brought most of Earth's predators to the brink of extinction. Industrialized agricultural practices promote the overuse of antibiotics, herbicides, and pesticides that contaminate domestic food sources and kill beneficial as well as harmful predators at all levels, compromising the viability of Earth's immune systems.

Five hundred years ago, there were around 500 million humans. Cities were small and surrounded by farmlands. Wildlife was plentiful. Oceans were teeming with life. Then, within a geologic blink of the eye, our population exploded. Huge cities now cover vast tracts which are often a toxic mess devoid of most other life forms. Wildlife extinctions are rampant. Things have changed dramatically for the worse. Why? Because of *how* we do most things.

Changing *how* we do what we do is the problem that we must solve.

We kill most everything we encounter: sometimes as a source of food, sometimes for sport, and often as an unintended byproduct of *how* we do most things. In less than 45 years we have caused the collective populations of all vertebrates - the mammals, birds, fishes, amphibians, and reptiles - to decline by 60 percent as a result of habitat loss and degradation, unsustainable hunting and fishing practices, pollution, and climate change. In just 50 years, we have destroyed 20 percent of the Amazon and within the past 30 years we have lost almost half of the world's shallow-water corals.[18]

The 2019 UN intergovernmental panel report titled, Nature's Dangerous Decline 'Unprecedented'; Species Extinction Rates 'Accelerating', presents overwhelming evidence that humans are eroding the very foundations of planetary life support systems. From the UN Sustainable Development Blog[19] summarizing that report's findings we are told that:

> Nature is declining globally at rates unprecedented in human history - and the rate of species extinctions is accelerating, with grave impacts on people around the world now likely ...

> "The overwhelming evidence of the IPBES Global Assessment, from a wide range of different fields of knowledge, presents an ominous picture," ... said IPBES Chair, Sir Robert Watson. "The health of ecosystems on which we and all other species depend is deteriorating more rapidly than ever. We are eroding the very foundations of our economies, livelihoods, food security, health and quality of life worldwide."

"The report also tells us that it is not too late to make a difference, but only if we start now at every level from local to global," he said. "Through 'transformative change,' nature can still be conserved, restored and used sustainably - this is also key to meeting most other global goals. **By transformative change, we mean a fundamental, system-wide reorganization across technological, economic and social factors, including paradigms, goals and values."** (Emphasis added)

"The member States of IPBES Plenary have now acknowledged that, by its very nature, transformative change can expect opposition from those with interests vested in the status quo, but also that such opposition can be overcome for the broader public good," Watson said.

Sadly, the damages from our presence continue to accelerate. From the Executive Summary of the WWF Living Planet Report 2020 we learn that between 1970 and 2016, vertebrate population declines now stand at 68%, an 8% increase in just two years. This matters:

> because biodiversity is fundamental to human life on Earth, and the evidence is unequivocal - it is being destroyed by us at a rate unprecedented in history ... in the last 50 years our world has been transformed by an explosion in global trade, consumption, and human population growth, as well as an enormous move towards urbanization ...

> Biodiversity loss threatens food security and urgent action is needed to address the loss of the biodiversity that feeds the world ... making the transformation of our global food system more important than ever ... The transformation of our economic systems is also critical.[20]

We are being told in no uncertain terms that we must fundamentally change (transform) how we operate our societies and why. The 2020 report:

> provides unequivocal and alarming evidence that nature is unravelling and that our planet is flashing red warning signs of vital natural systems failure … This highlights that a deep cultural and systemic shift is urgently needed, one that so far our civilization has failed to embrace: a transition to a society and economic system that values nature, stops taking it for granted and recognizes that we depend on nature more than nature depends on us.

The above short summaries highlight from a global perspective the enormity of the issues we face and the dire consequences that will follow if we fail to address them. The following provides some additional insight.

OXYGEN AND THE ATMOSPHERE

We are rapidly destroying the habitats necessary to support human life. Earth's oceans and forests are her lungs. We have compromised their ability to function. As recently as 200 years ago, atmospheric oxygen and CO_2 mixtures were in balance. That is no longer the case. Atmospheric and oceanic oxygen levels are dropping[21], threatening not only land life but also "the survival of fisheries and the entire marine ecosystem."[22]

Phytoplankton live in the seas and produce between 50 percent and 85 percent of planetary oxygen. Every breath you take is quite literally filled with oxygen made by these tiny oceanic plants and animals.[23] And, just like every other living thing, they are sensitive to rapid environmental change.

Fossil fuel burning has changed the makeup of Earth's atmosphere which now contains 45 percent higher CO_2 concentrations than at the start of the industrial revolution.[24] Besides contributing to the global warming phenomena, a large percentage of the extra CO_2 has been absorbed by the oceans which has made them 30 percent more acidic within just 200 years. That is a rate of change "faster than any known change in ocean chemistry in the last 50 million years."[25]

And as the atmosphere has warmed, so too have the oceans, which of course affects aquatic life. Within the past 70 years as a likely combination of warmed and more acidic oceans, there has been a 40% reduction in global phytoplanktonic biomass which has been described as "a huge number" that "is severely disquieting."[26] Why should that fact be so disturbing? Because the phytoplankton serve as one of Earth's primary oxygen producers and also as the ocean's most fundamental food source. They feed everything from microscopic animal-like zooplankton to multi-ton whales. Between 50 and 80 percent of all Earth life exist in the oceans.[27] With fewer phytoplankton to feed on, logically, there will be fewer fish in the sea to feed the over 3.5 billion people who depend upon ocean life as their primary food source.[28]

However, we are not just faced with less oxygen to breathe and less food to eat. Decreasing the production of atmospheric oxygen thins an already depleted ozone layer, increasing exposure to UV radiation which over the long term "can severely damage most animals, plants and microbes, so the ozone layer protects all life on Earth."[29] Just as in our own bodies, when one planetary-level support system is damaged, it impacts the functionality of the others, which of course affects the lives of those dependent upon it.

According to the World Health Organization, as of 2019, over 90 percent of the world's population live in areas where the air quality does not meet WHO guidelines. It estimates that 9 million people die annually from exposure to polluted air.[30] And children are especially susceptible to disease from breathing polluted air which can cause respiratory, cardiovascular, neurologic diseases, and cancers.[31]

Earth's respiratory system is under fierce attack. We are literally destroying its capacity to produce oxygen and forcing it to circulate air that is unhealthy to breathe. Add up the global impacts from the failure of this one system, and the collapse of others should be recognized as not far off. We might not intend these results, but neither are we taking affirmative action to prevent them. Why not? We'll get there. For now, recognize that our destructive nature doesn't stop here.

WATER

All life depends on a simple combination of hydrogen and oxygen atoms which create an amazing substance that exists as a solid, liquid, and vapor. Water. In mammals, circulatory systems transport blood (mostly water) to every cell in the body where nutrients and oxygen are exchanged for waste by-products which are delivered to the lungs, liver, and kidneys for purification.

Earth's circulatory systems perform similar functions, delivering water and nutrients to every corner of the globe, purifying it by evaporation, percolation through soils, flowing river waters through estuaries, marshlands, deltas at the land-sea interface, and by gravity through sedimentation.

Pure water is a life necessity. Yet, wherever we go we contaminate it. With reckless disregard for the result, we flush billions of gallons of raw sewage, industrial waste, oil, fracking fluids, and mining leachates into Earth's waters which we also contaminate with acids and other airborne industrial pollutants, urban runoff, plastics, and agricultural pesticides, herbicides, and fertilizers. These are the very same waters we use every day and are totally dependent upon for our very existence. By contaminating them we jeopardize not only our own health and well-being, but the viability of all Earth's interconnected and interdependent life support systems.

FOOD

We all need food to live, and our food production systems are dependent upon nature's ways of providing it. Unfortunately, how we produce food compromises nature's ways. In February 2016, the Intergovernmental Science-Policy Platform on Biodiversity and Ecosystem Services (IPBES), a task force of internationally recognized scientists from 124 member nations established to "form a crucial intersection between international scientific understanding and public policy," issued a groundbreaking, first-ever assessment of the critical role that pollinators play within the global ecosystem.[32]

That study recognized that 75 percent of human food crops are dependent on animal pollination and that over 40 percent of invertebrate pollinator species (particularly bees and butterflies) are on the verge of extinction, putting a substantial percentage of our food supply at risk as pollinator numbers decline. Pollinators also play critical roles in the production of many other products that humanity is dependent on, such as medicines, forage for livestock, natural fibers (cotton), and construction materials.

Two-thirds of all land animals are insects. Some are pollinators that provide "keystone" reproductive services free of charge. Some serve as food for animals. Others help decompose organic matter operating within Earth's digestive systems. All are in serious trouble. Over the past thirty years approximately 80 percent of all European flying insect populations have vanished, resulting in the loss of 400 million birds dependent upon insects for food.[33]

A research paper[34] published April 2019 which reviewed 73 investigatory reports on insect declines, confirms that we are in the midst of a massive extinction event. Over the next few decades, we are told to expect "the extinction of 40% of the world's insect species." This is a really big problem because insects provide a multitude of services critical to the health and well-being of Earth's life support systems. And make no mistake, insects are imperiled because of us. We destroy their habitats through climate change, urbanization, and industrialized agricultural practices which poison their foods. And of course, we kill them directly with pesticides. Tracking the theme of this work, these authors warn that:

> Unless we change our way of producing food, insects as a whole will go down the path of extinction in a few decades … [and that] Only decisive action can avert a catastrophic collapse of nature's ecosystems.

The decisive action they speak of is fundamentally changing *how* we do most things, including *how* we produce food. The good news is that we know how to act in ways that are far less destructive to the world we live in. The bad news is that we must dramatically and rapidly change our ways, which we humans resist doing. We will discuss how to fundamentally change our ways within Books V and VI. For now, recognize that every Earth habitat and species play significant roles in maintaining the health and well-being of all Earth life.

Consider the plight of the world's forests as an example. Forests create their own unique habitats within which a great diversity of plants and animals dwell. They make a large percentage of the oxygen you breathe and the water you drink. They recycle nutrients and trap CO_2, which helps moderate global temperatures. We know that they perform multiple planetary-level support functions. And we know that we are in the midst of destroying most forest habitats, which is why scientists have warned for decades of the absolute necessity of preserving those ecosystems intact. How have we responded to these warnings? A 2018 University of Maryland study reveals that "Despite concerted efforts to reduce tropical deforestation, tree cover loss has been rising steadily in the tropics over the past 17 years."[35]

Our destruction of Earth's forest systems is not limited to her tropical forests. Boreal forests represent approximately 30% of all forest ecosystems. They capture and store more carbon dioxide than do tropical forests, playing a critical role in moderating climate change.[36] Unfortunately, they are endangered by industrial development, logging, oil and gas development, and yes, climate change. The boreal region is "warming twice as fast as other parts of the world" and their climate zones "are moving north ten times faster than forests can migrate."[37] They simply can't adapt fast enough and so, they are endangered.

As we destroy forest ecosystems, we lose clues that could cure disease, extend life, and help reveal natural processes that could facilitate interstellar travel, among many other things. Within the larger scheme, it is critical to recognize that Earth's life support systems are interdependent. Each carries out a multitude of functions that crossover between systems, so we should expect and recognize that the tremendous loss of life which accompanies the destruction of forest habitats will extend far beyond the forests. The destruction of any habitat, harms the others.

If we stay the course by promoting practices that wipe out insect populations and destroy forest habitats, know that extinctions of pollinator-dependent species will follow. Wild and domestic flowering plants play fundamental roles within planetary food production systems. They are all at grave risk of collapse as a result of our unwillingness to responsibly manage *how* we produce food and cull forest resources for commercial use. *How* we do most things imperils everything. At a time when it is critical to modify the role we play in nature; we somehow manage to perceive ourselves as separate and distinct from all that is nature. In doing so, we fail to recognize the irony of that perception. Just as nature sends forth plagues and extinction events, it has set us loose on Earth to do as we may.

EARTH'S DEFENSES

Since the dawn of our time, Earth's natural defenses, her predators, plagues, famines, and viruses limited our numbers. Even so, our population quadrupled over the past one hundred years and is expected to double again over the next hundred. What then for Earth? Does she have other defenses to throw at us or have we become so adaptable that no matter what she does, we will continue to grow, consume, and so thoroughly impair her support systems that she loses all ability to sustain life?

Predators are Earth's first defense against overpopulation. We have conquered all predators, ascending to the top of the food chain. Infectious diseases are another of Earth's natural defenses. In the third century AD, the Antonine Plague killed one-third of all Europeans. In the sixth century, the Plague of Justinian took out nearly 50 percent of all Europeans. In the 1340s, the Bubonic Plague killed between 20 percent and 50 percent of humanity. With the arrival of Europeans to the New World in 1520 came smallpox, which killed millions. It was followed by hemorrhagic fever which doubled those plowed under, taking with it almost 80 percent of indigenous peoples. In 1918, a particularly infectious flu virus killed over 100 million.

Today, we face another pandemic triggered by the Covid-19 virus. Hundreds of millions have been infected. Over four million have already died. But human ingenuity and scientific discovery have intervened to limit the efficacy of Earth's natural defenses. Other attempts to limit our numbers will certainly follow. Whether they originate within the heart of Africa or are of our own making designed and released from a secret biological-warfare lab hidden deep underground, we will again attempt to adapt.

Mother Earth gave birth to us. She supported our evolution. Yet, we think of ourselves as unique, different from all that is nature. We are not. We are a particularly virulent species: hardy, resistant, and adaptable. We may withstand most of Earth's natural defenses. What we may not be able to withstand are the consequences of our own actions. Our challenges are self-made. And as we exist this day, we are Earth's last and best defense against ourselves.

- 3 -

ENTER THE ANTHROPOCENE - THE AGE OF EXTINCTION

Earth is a delicate, living, breathing life form that over billions of years evolved sophisticated support systems that are now, within a blink of Earth time, being destroyed by us. Extinction events are part of the natural order of things. Within the last one-half billion years, there have been five major mass extinction events. All were caused by external factors, including asteroid collisions and massive volcanic eruptions. Then came the humans. And we changed everything.

Scientific evidence now confirms that a singular organism has triggered a planetary-level extinction event on par with the most severe. We have penned a new epoch on Earth's storied timeline: the Anthropocene, that period of human domination during which thousands of species have already been rendered extinct, and unless we dramatically change our ways, millions more will shortly follow.

We are one organism of relentless, indiscriminate killers. From ants to elephants, anchovies to whales, we kill everything. What we don't eat, we burn, plow under, or destroy with toxic chemicals unleashed throughout Earth's ecosystems. The result? Between 1970 and 2016, humans wiped out over 68 percent of all vertebrate animals (mammals, birds, and fish).[38] That startling fact alone should be enough to trigger a consciousness of the absolute necessity of changing how we conduct the businesses of a global society of beings. But sadly, this catastrophe has not proven sufficient to inspire coordinated global action.

In 2019, officials in the United States, Brazil, and other countries were busy reversing conservation practices, abandoning international agreements, and rewriting rules and regulations to allow rulers of industries to wantonly and recklessly destroy and contaminate pretty much everything. Instead of correcting the course of this juggernaut of reckless human behavior, we accelerate its destructiveness.

The news is full of doom and gloom about climate change. But be clear, the exigencies we face are not just about climate change. Climate change is merely a symptom of the illness. The problem is us. The human organism is destroying Earth's web of life which has taken billions of years to refine. Our misplaced priorities, the nature of our structures, and the failures of those who pretend to lead should make it clear that,

> We are sleepwalking towards the edge of a cliff ... If there was a 60% decline in the human population, [correlating to the 60% of vertebrate animals we wiped out between 1970 and 2014] that would be equivalent to emptying North America, South America, Africa, Europe, China, and Oceania. That is the scale of what we have done ... This is far more than just being about losing the wonders of nature ... This is actually now jeopardizing the future of people. Nature is not a 'nice to have' - it is our life-support system.[39]

Because it is extremely difficult to judge the cumulative effects of the things we do from a global perspective at Earth timeframes, it is easy to pass them by. How many species of plants and animals we have already forced into extinction is unknown. What is known for certain is that unlike the past mass extinction events, the current one is of our own making.

Continually at war with ourselves, we operate societies with complete disregard for the harms we cause. Although we have the ability to intelligently manage our collective activities, we refuse to do so, evidencing little foresight and near-total lack of self-control.

It is simply impossible in this work to convey the all-encompassing nature of the harms we have unleashed on Earth. Thousands of peer-reviewed studies have been published documenting the same and our scientists continue to warn us in no uncertain terms that unless we limit our population and fundamentally change how we do most things, we face a catastrophic collapse of nature's ecosystems.

FIRST DOOMSDAY WARNING

In 1992 the Union of Concerned Scientists and over 1,700 leading scientists (including the majority of living Nobel science prize-winners) issued a manifesto to all humanity titled "World Scientists' Warning to Humanity"[40] stating:

> Human beings and the natural world are on a collision course. Human activities inflict harsh and often irreversible damage on the environment and on critical resources. If not checked, many of our current practices put at risk the future that we wish for human society and the plant and animal kingdoms and may so alter the living world that we will be unable to sustain life in the manner that we know. Fundamental changes are urgent if we are to avoid the collision our present course will bring about.

Scientists, not politicians, not corporate heads, and certainly not religious pundits, are the only people capable of assessing the impacts of humanity on Earth's vital systems. That is what we employ them to do. That is what they dedicate their lives to doing. Recognizing the urgent need to change *how* we do most things, these scientists warned that:

> No more than one or a few decades remain before the chance to avert the threats we now confront will be lost and the prospects for humanity immeasurably diminished. We the undersigned, senior members of the world's scientific community, hereby warn all humanity of what lies ahead. A great change in our stewardship of earth and life on it is required if vast human misery is to be avoided and our global home on this planet is not to be irretrievably mutilated.

To save ourselves from ourselves, the best of the best implored all leaders to:

1. Stabilize population;
2. Manage resources crucial to human welfare more effectively;
3. Bring environmentally damaging activities under control to restore and protect the integrity of the earth's systems we depend on;
4. Reduce and eventually eliminate poverty; and
5. Ensure sexual equality and guarantee women control over their own reproductive decisions.

Those are the warnings and recommendations that were given to the world's leaders a generation ago. How many of you were made aware of them? Have they been elevated to daily topics of critical discussion among society and its leaders? Are they impressed upon students from their earliest days to create an awareness within the generations to come of the absolute and immediate need to fundamentally change our ways? You know the answers.

SECOND DOOMSDAY WARNING

In 2017, on the twenty-fifth anniversary of the first Warning to Humanity, a second Warning to Humanity[41] was issued, this time by more than 15,000 scientists from 184 nations. In it they warned that:

> Humanity is now being given a second notice . . . We are jeopardizing our future by not reining in . . . consumption and by . . . failing to adequately limit population growth, reassess the role of an economy rooted in growth, reduce greenhouse gases, incentivize renewable energy, protect habitat, restore ecosystems, curb pollution . . . humanity is not taking the urgent steps needed to safeguard our imperiled biosphere.

These warnings are not just about climate change. That is just one of the most obvious adverse results from our failures to regulate how we operate a global society. These warnings are expansive and encompass the totality of human impacts upon the natural world. Are you aware of these newest warnings? Have they elevated to the most important topics of this era? Are they repeated time and again in the media to stimulate the political and social awareness necessary to change our ways? You know these answers as well.

Contrary to their prior advice to stem the tide of population growth, our population grew by two billion since 1992. Two billion! Aside from "potentially catastrophic climate change," 15,000 scientists warned that "we have unleashed a mass extinction event," that is only the sixth in roughly 540 million years. And they do not equivocate about the cause of climate change, or the onset of the Anthropocene. It is us. Recognizing that leaders have not heeded prior warnings, they suggest that:

> As most political leaders respond to pressure, scientists, media influencers, and lay citizens must insist that their

governments take immediate action as a moral imperative to current and future generations of human and other
life. With a groundswell of organized grassroots efforts,
dogged opposition can be overcome and political leaders
compelled to do the right thing.

In other words, since humanity is barreling down pathways of
extinction and since world leaders will not change the course of
humanity, they call upon the people of the world to unite to force
the change so desperately needed. Anyone would be hard-pressed to
express the urgency of action needed in words more powerful than
by stating that we must take *immediate action as a moral imperative* to
change our ways. In a final plea, they state that:

> **Soon it will be too late to shift course away from our
> failing trajectory, and time is running out. We must
> recognize, in our day-to-day lives and in our govern-
> ing institutions, that Earth with all its life is our only
> home.** (Emphasis added)

Have we, the world's people, answered their calls to unite in a
global movement to change how society operates? You know the
answer. We have neither created nor implemented a globally coordinated strategy designed to fundamentally change our ways. Why
not? Because most attempts to change things are carried out within
existing structures at local and regional levels. The problem is that
fundamental change requires rewriting most of our rules and regulations. It requires changing *how* we do almost everything, which
simply cannot happen by trying to piecemeal change within existing
structures. Another approach is needed.

SO, WHAT NOW?

Are you resigned to what lies ahead as we race along pathways of extinction? Although we are each unique in our own ways, and although most of us believe ourselves to be moral beings connected in some divine way, those beliefs will not save us from ourselves; only our collective actions can.

For over twenty-eight years, the world's leading scientists have been begging those who direct society to do the right thing, to fundamentally and dramatically change our ways. But as history reveals, most in positions of leadership do not lead. They rule, and are too bound up within obsolete structures playing games of war and chance to even attempt to lead us out of the mess we have created for ourselves.

The severity of the challenges we face are so great that we must find entirely new ways of doing most things. Existing structures work against urgent action, so new structures designed to enable new ways of being that bring out the very best that society has to offer are necessary. We have a level of responsibility to our species that no previous generation has faced. Each of us have life affirming decisions to make.

Either you choose to ignore or resist the need for progressive change and remain part of the old way which promotes hatred, intolerance, war, repression, pain, hunger, sickness, and poverty; ways that doom humanity to being nothing more than a pathogenic like organism killing its host, or you dedicate some aspect of your life to creating a society that is far more humane than any we have ever created, enabling our descendants to travel evolutionary pathways. There are no guarantees of success, but if we do not try, then who will? And if not now, then when? Read on.

4

To Change Or Not To Change That, Is The Question

Billions of your brothers and sisters cry out for change knowing that things are just not right. Earth is not well. We are not well. And, even though there are millions of examples of kind people treating each other with compassion and acting more consciously in more environmentally sound ways, global conditions continue to worsen. Why? Because at a species-wide level, we resist progressive change. That fundamental societal flaw must be corrected.

To do so, to effectively address the life-threatening issues we face, we must create new structures and new systems designed to responsibly and humanely manage the affairs of a global society of beings. We need to stop growth, take a breath, look around, take stock of ourselves and what we have done to Earth, and then we have to get to work responsibly and humanely changing how we do most things.

We are an incredible species, gifted in so many ways. We have a powerful capacity for love, yet our capacity for hatred overwhelms. We laugh and we cry and burst out with the enthusiasm of a child for life, yet with equal passion we rain such death and destruction upon everything we encounter that we threaten Earth's very existence and accordingly, our own. It is love that pulls us forward and greed that holds us back. We are industrious, yet we allow industries to destroy. We have come far but remain locked within ancient structures that abhor responsibility, resist change, and declare actions to reduce or limit our population heretical.

So many changes are necessary, but greed and the lust for power cloud the judgment of those who rule. They refuse to even try to unify to usher in a new age with new ways of being. Progressive change is the one thing they should enthusiastically embrace, but it is the one thing they resist most. With billions in urgent need of assistance, it is the one thing that should pull us together because it is the very thing we are all about.

We are instruments of change. It's what we do. If we decide to do it better, more thoughtfully, within systems designed to minimize our impacts, we can enable evolutionary levels of change. Fundamental progressive change is a really big deal. It takes time, tremendous persistence and the coordinated efforts of billions. To change or not to change? To evolve or not to evolve? Those are our decisions to make and the stakes could not be higher.

EVOLUTION OR EXTINCTION

Scientists theorize that all life on Earth may have come from a single common ancestor (the "last universal common ancestor" (LUCA)) which may have arrived around four billion years ago with a set of 355 genes found in all living Earth things.[42] Whether the LUCA was thrust out into the universe at the Creation eventually making its way here, or whether it randomly sprang to life within the primordial soup of early Earth is a different story for a different time. For now, it appears that all life forms to inhabit Earth may trace their origins to the LUCA. Trillions evolved from one.

Evolution of life forms may be broadly defined as a process of change through which a new species develops from a pre-existing one. It is thought to be a movement in a particular direction over some period of time, presumably from a simpler state to a more complex or better one.[43]

For humans, think of it as a movement over generations from a less efficient state of being to a more efficient one. At this stage in our existence, evolution requires agreement among billions of individuals operating with singularity of purpose to improve *how* we treat each other and *how* we do most things. This is a together-or-nothing process. If we are to change into a species existing more harmoniously with ourselves and with the natural world, what is required of us is fundamentally changing *how* we operate almost every aspect of every society.

Evolutionary change must be systemic. To move to a higher or better state of being now requires humanity to exist as an organized, cooperative, and efficiently operating society of beings. Anything less and we face extinction.

Extinction is the death of the last of an organism or species capable of reproduction. For us humans, the extinction of our entire species is an event that is nearly impossible to comprehend. Why is that? Perhaps because in our daily lives, it just doesn't seem even remotely imminent. Yet, as our scientists warn, that is the trajectory of the pathways we travel.

Extinction events occur by the failure of an organism to adapt to changes to the environment from external forces like volcanic eruptions, competition, predation, and disease; and from internal / self-inflicted forces such as its own failure to regulate activities that render the environments it depends upon uninhabitable. That, is exactly our problem.

We have ignited the Anthropocene, a planetary-level mass extinction event that threatens Earth's ability to support life, including our own. How will this new epoch end? No alien life form, superior race, or omnipotent being is coming to Earth to save us from ourselves. That obligation is ours, and ours alone. To save ourselves we must find commonality of purpose and then unite in action to create fundamentally superior ways of being. If we do, we will have taken an evolutionary level step forward. However, should we fail at that endeavor, extinction looms large for us humans. To evolve or not to evolve? It truly is a matter of choice. Our choice.

RESPOND TO CHANGE

It is not the strongest of the species that survives, nor the most intelligent, but the one most responsive to change.
Charles Darwin, 1809

To be "responsive to change" means that we must rapidly change how we do most things if we are to both survive and thrive. We have ignited planetary-levels of change. Our scientists have made the ruling elite well aware of the fact that we are destroying Earth's ability to support life. Yet those with the power to change our ways have failed to respond. Their failures threaten the continued existence of our species.

Biological evolution moves a species from a less efficient state of being to a more efficient one. Greater efficiency means less resistance to what is, to life. Less resistance means less conflict, less wear and tear along life's journeys, which, for humans, means better health, longer lives, and greater opportunities to contribute significantly within an evolving society. Life becomes easier as we become more fulfilled and aware beings.

We can respond to the environmental changes we face by adopting new goals within our systems of commerce to incentivize efficiencies in the production and delivery of the things we use. We can respond by elevating efficiency into a state of consciousness within which everyone seeks more efficient ways of being. Why is this important? Because the more efficient our systems, the less waste they generate. Less waste equals less pollution. Less waste equals a reduction in production as more is derived from less. Efficiency turns the complex, simple. To effectively respond to a changed Earth, we must do most things more efficiently.

But be clear, the planetary-level changes that we have ignited are happening too fast to hope for change within existing institutions. They are too slow to adapt. That means we, the people, must act now to secure our evolutionary opportunities. We must *intend* to change our ways, to evolve better ways of being human. How? By implementing a plan that comes to fruition upon accepting that the search for universal truths, no matter where it leads, is what is needed to deliver humanity into a future of unlimited possibility.

INTEND TO EVOLVE

Evolution shaped our past, made us what we are, and brought us to this critical juncture where what we choose to do, or not to do, will determine whether we evolve and thrive, or fail Earth's human experiment. We have outgrown nature's ability to care for us. We are on our own. It is our turn, our obligation, and our opportunity to determine our future.

Evolution for us at this stage in our existence is change in its most fundamental and all-encompassing form. It is painstakingly difficult to come by and centuries in the making. You will not sleep one eve and awaken to the realization that humanity is something different, something better. Although, sadly, you may sleep and awaken to the realization that it has become something far worse.

To save us from ourselves requires a determination that is so strong and so pure that it spans lifetimes during which we must change how we do just about everything we do. It requires intense faith and belief that we will all be better off for it. Because it spans generations, it is a process far greater and more substantial than any one person during any one lifetime is capable of realizing. Change in the essence of being is grand, essential, transformative, and extremely rare.

Because it showcases that which is so radically different from what is, the process is difficult to comprehend and even more difficult to achieve. Why? Because for us, it requires the cooperative efforts of billions across the globe who exist within competing societies poised to impede the creation of one unified society encompassing each of us and everything that we do.

Evolution by Intention. It is so fundamental, so pervasive, and so encompassing, that to merely describe it as hard would be a grotesque understatement. It is painfully hard. It will require the greatest feat of human endurance we will ever have been called upon to achieve. But it is within our reach.

5

FROM THE INDIVIDUAL
TO THE COLLECTIVE

Acts of resistance create headlines but rarely sustainable results. Why? Because the other side has already scripted the plays, defined the rules, and appointed the referees, putting activists at extreme disadvantage. By the time enough people become aware of harmful acts of corporate or governmental elites it is usually too late to change the result. Activists are stuck playing defense in games of offense, with success sometimes measured in delay, sometimes in incremental but beneficial change. This is not the way to enable fundamental social change.

Evolutionary change requires rewriting the human playbook. More sophisticated strategies that meet the needs of a modern society of billions must be developed and overseen by experts (not strongmen) who implement and enforce new rules and regulations that efficiently, cohesively and compassionately, guide us into a future of great possibility.

The move from competitive societies which pit individual against individual, to a single society designed to enable cooperative efforts to achieve common goals, is the opportunity of this time. It is a movement from societies within which competition enables a few individuals to rule, to a single society designed to enable every individual to achieve their full potential. This is the evolutionary step of this era. It presents in disguise, being neither easy to see, comprehend, embrace, or achieve. To achieve it will require a few extraordinary individuals,

True Leaders, to escort us into a future within which commonality is celebrated and the ways of the collective cherished.

FREEDOM DWELLS WITHIN THE COLLECTIVE

People dream of being free. But what does it mean to be free and where can true freedom be found?

Freedom dwells within the collective, as unlikely as it may sound. Freedom from oppression, disease, hunger, and uncertainty, all become possible when we act together, as One, for the benefit of all. When we do, we free ourselves from the physical, psychological, and financial burdens imposed by those who rule, to create a future of limitless possibilities within which each of us is free to pursue their life interests.

To move beyond a splintered and competitive past requires that we make a leap of faith in recognition that humanity is far better served within a collective cooperatively managed as a whole. To know life, requires that we change, first by acknowledging that it is time to grow up and begin taking responsibility for the things we do, then by uniting in action to responsibly create a humane community of all Earth's people. This process makes us different, fundamentally better beings than we have ever been. This is our challenge; our responsibility; and, it is the evolutionary opportunity of this time.

Within the entirety exists a force of being that links us all; its silken threads are strong, yet invisible. Planets revolve mysteriously around stars alight within the ether of space forming galaxies flowing in ways not yet understood. Everything is wondrously connected by the essence of life through an unseen force that links each with each other. Billions are stunningly bound as individual components of one organism inseparable from the whole, whether as part of the whole of humanity, of Earth, or of this Universe; collectively, we are all One.

Collectively, we are a force of unlimited potential. To achieve that potential requires us to change by establishing new goals for the common good and then pursuing them with unwavering courage, persistence, and belief in the good that will result. Our thoughts and feelings supported by the actions of many create the bonds necessary to secure the evolutionary change we so desperately need. When there are many engaged in helping each other accomplish common goals for the common good, order evolves from chaos. The more we do to help one another, the better each of us will feel as invisible threads within our collective consciousness transform the joy experienced from helping another into feelings of well-being.

From that joy will emanate a sense of freedom heretofore never experienced within our species as we transition from competitive societies locked in perpetual conflict, into one society of liberated individuals working together to build a better humanity. Deep within, you know this to be true. So, elevate the discussion from conflict to commonality. Allow what is good and just to reveal through our actions. Teach peace and practice the art of being peaceful at every level of society and believe in its power to enable true peace.

Only through the cooperative actions of many can peace be accomplished. Peace must become a common goal. Most of us want it. So, why not band together and say no to war. Make those who want it uncomfortable. Exclude them from your communities. Refuse to allow them to control your lives. Refuse to join them in acts of hostility. Refuse to elect them or allow them to represent your interests in governance. To be successful, to achieve peace, we must want peace with an intensity beyond the hatred that foments war. Just as no individual or nation can forge evolutionary change, only when the many have united in focused pursuit of true peace does evolutionary change become possible.

Let no one force you or anyone you know to do what will make you, them, or someone else unhappy. Just Say No. Live intending to Do No Harm to another or to Mother Earth. Teach your children the same. Adopt that motto and watch a grand sense of well-being envelope society as a movement builds to make a better world, a better humanity.

Commit to the work necessary to building a better humanity. It takes work, hard work, to make a single relationship last. Imagine the work necessary to build a community experiencing true peace, which is the cornerstone of a civilized society of beings; a truly worthy goal for us all. We must work together to build peace together.

To do so means we must change our priorities. We must disincentivize conflict, disable cultures of war, and create incentives for peace that far exceed the incentives for war. Highly reward those who work to make peace our reality. This is perhaps the hardest task of all. Enable it to flourish by dedicating whatever resources are necessary to create a society at peace with itself. Together, we can do this.

Life's threads tie us together, reverberating within, unseen, unheard, and unheralded. Tap into them. See the opportunities they present. Listen closely as they reveal knowledge of something far grander than any can imagine. Stand together to realize our potential, and your potential. Allow none to divide us. Accept no boundaries, no nations, no corporations. Act together as one, to be One.

For humanity, our evolutionary leap must be intended and supported by an intense belief in the benefits to be derived from actions for the common good. It requires billions whose collective actions spread the word, emote possibility, and build powerful feelings of necessity and unity which morph into coordinated actions to bring about the changes we need.

Stand with those who act to unite us to achieve common goals that benefit us all. It will take many actions intending the same result to make light work of the process. Billions of actions to make a better humanity will create a force that reverberates throughout society and empowers The Movement. Realize the power of the collective through The Movement. Embrace it. Blend its goals with yours. Put them in writing. Place them where you will see them and repeat them aloud with such force of emotion that they meld into the very essence of all that is you.

As you drift into sleep, know there are billions building an evolutionary desire so deep, so profound, and so powerful, that it connects each subconsciously with all others. Feel the connection. Be aware of the power of the collective as it translates thoughts of better ways of being into action.

Do not dwell on all that is wrong in the world. Instead, collaborate and encourage others to join the conversation on what can be done within your community to make it a better place to be, and get to work right now to help make it so.

Do one thing every day, no matter how small, no matter how seemingly insignificant, to make a better world. Share with others what you have done or intend to do and listen carefully to understand what they are doing. When our actions match our intention to change, no matter the opposition, no matter the suffering we endure, what we intend becomes what we shall be.

Teach your children to act with intention to make a better world. Encourage them from the earliest age to be part of the solution; to be aware that each of us has a role to play; that each of us has an impact on the outcome of Earth's human experiment. Teach them well, and the fruits of your labors will help create a world of possibility, rich in the essence of life. Teach them that the flames of change must glow brightly within them, for their burden is to carry the torch into the future to light the way for the generations that follow.

Live with thoughts of a better world where the business of humanity is elevated to the gathering of knowledge and understanding. Believe passionately in the existence of a society where everyone lives untethered by debt, free of fear for personal safety, without pangs of hunger, knowing they will always receive the best society can offer.

Creating a civilized society requires an emotional commitment backed by determination and intention to make it so. The Movement magnifies the desires of billions who engage in action with singularity of purpose to make a better humanity. It brings such life and such power to our intentions, that no force can stand against.

To make the evolutionary leap from barbaric to civilized, from individual selfishness to the collective good, requires the focused intention of a movement so powerfully directed to galvanize the change we so desperately need that it reverberates throughout our very souls. By concentrating our thoughts and actions on better ways of being and coordinating our efforts to achieve goals of the commons, we enable evolutionary levels of change and the freedoms that come with it.

FREEDOM THROUGH UNIFICATION

Unification is evolutionary. It affords humanity the opportunity to forge new pathways in search of eternal knowledge. To unify for the greater good requires great persistence, great courage, and a movement so strong, so just, and so righteous, that all opposition evaporates with time.

It begins locally with coordinated actions to establish a global society within which every citizen is provided the tools and encouragement to reach their innate potential, along with the opportunity to live happy, healthy, and spiritually fulfilling lives.

No person stands alone. In so many ways, each of us helps each other through life. To unify for the greater good requires the absolute understanding that there is no whole without the individual, and, that there are no individuals without the whole. Every contribution is of value. The contributions of an Einstein, a Curie, or a Gates would be impossible without the contributions of those who provide all else. The fundamental truth is that we are all interdependent, and with that realization, comes freedom. Freedom through unification.

A MATTER OF CHOICE
A MATTER OF WILL

As difficult as change may be for us, people everywhere cry out for it. Most know things are not right. All know things can be better. The way to improve our communities and our world is by changing our social institutions. They determine how we do most things. To change them will require billions of us who choose to unite, to work together to be fundamentally better than we are. Who in their right mind doesn't want us to be better than we are? The answer, unfortunately, is that rulers of thousand-year-old structures which are inefficient, outmoded, and backward-looking, oppose dramatic social change. They chain us to the past, protecting their ways, not enhancing what is, and enabling what can be.

Social change is a matter of choice. Fundamental structural change is a matter of will. For change to be fundamental, evolutionary, it must take root in the now and extend from generation to generation. To accomplish this level of change will require each of us to act, to help chart a new course upon which our very existence so critically depends. We must choose to be better at being human. We must act with an intense desire and determination to succeed in fundamentally changing our ways so that together, we become better. What starts with a few can end with the many if the pathways are clear and the outcomes are just.

Inaction is the easier pathway to follow, we don't have to change anything. Change by intention is harder. It requires more from each of us, but it foretells a vastly superior outcome. The pathways we ultimately travel are determined by the goals we hold in common. Our current goals lead us down pathways to our own extinction. To save ourselves from ourselves, we have to set new goals and choose action over inaction. Success is both a matter of choice, and a matter of will. Stay the course, fail to act to secure the future we all deserve, and remain as travelers of extinction's pathways.

Book III

TRAVELING PATHWAYS
OF EXTINCTION

Nations claim rights to resources far beyond their physical boundaries. In a growing trend exhibiting a form of modern-day colonialism, wealthy nations such as China, India, Saudi Arabia, the United States, Malaysia, the United Kingdom, and South Korea, along with their corporate counterparts, have purchased millions of acres of foreign cultivable land "at rock bottom prices in poorer countries" to grow and export the produce home.[44] "An estimated 500 million acres ... has been bought or leased in the developing world in the last decade," and "thousands of villagers are thought to have been evicted from their farms ... to facilitate the arrival of East Asian and Gulf Arab agribusinesses."[45]

Such land grabs serve the populations of wealthy countries but deprive local and indigenous people of their native resources. Crops are grown for export. Water is diverted to irrigate the crops or supply a thirst-quenching necessity for growing population demands abroad.

When it finally becomes so clear that population growth has brought humanity to the brink of extinction, will society choose to eliminate a growing population as part of its model, or will it continue along its current pathways of extinction? Will rulers willingly adopt fundamentally new structures to guide society into a future where the good of the commons prevails, or will they act to maintain their wealth and power, no matter the consequences? Unfortunately, there are plenty of examples that answer those questions.

Easter Island, Mangareva, Pitcairn Island, and Henderson Island enabled thriving human populations until their numbers expanded beyond the capacity of their rich environments to support human life. The following is perhaps the best example of what to expect should we continue to maintain a population beyond Earth's capacity to sustain, as recounted by Jared Diamond in *Collapse*:

The parallels between Easter Island and the whole modern world are chillingly obvious. Thanks to globalization ... all countries on Earth today share resources and affect each other, just as did Easter's dozen clans. Polynesian Easter Island was as isolated in the Pacific Ocean as the Earth is today in space. When the Easter Islanders got into difficulties, there was nowhere to which they could flee, nor to which they could turn for help; nor shall we modern Earthlings have recourse elsewhere if our troubles increase.[46]

Easter Island's once-thriving population collapsed. The society of Easter Islanders vanished. As for Mangareva, Pitcairn, and Henderson Islanders, Diamond summarizes:

For a time, all the lands prospered, and their populations multiplied. But the population of the rich land eventually multiplied beyond the numbers that even its abundant resources could support. As its forests were felled and its soils eroded, its agricultural productivity was no longer sufficient to generate export surpluses, build ships, or even to nourish its own population. With that decline of trade, shortages of the imported raw materials developed. Civil war spread, as established political institutions were overthrown by a ... changing succession of local military leaders. The starving populace of the rich land survived by turning to cannibalism. Their former overseas trade partners met an even worse fate: deprived of the imports on which they had depended, they in turn ravaged their own environments until no one was left alive.[47]

Extinction. Look around. Has anything really changed in the way we go about the business of being human? We have better technologies, but we are just as nearsighted and cruel in the use of them. Today, we travel the same pathways of extinction as those of the Easter Islanders.

GROWTH TO EXTINCTION

All living things struggle at first to survive. We humans have adapted to life on Earth, relegating basic survival to a bygone era. Now, we seek a higher goal. Growth. To achieve growth, we promote growth. With growth comes increased consumption, so we promote consumption. To incentivize consumption and hence growth, we rely on an early survival strategy, greed. That word has bad connotations so now we do things for "profit," no matter the consequences.

We are the single most destructive biologic force impacting Earth's life support systems, perhaps ever. Five hundred years ago few would argue that we were capable of redefining life on Earth. Today, it's impossible to truthfully argue otherwise. With growth and consumption as our primary goals, we jeopardize all Earth life, especially our own.

Growth as an unwritten goal is one of the most basic and divinely targeted of biologic imperatives. Create new life; be plentiful. To a point, the wisdom of "biological plenty" is unmatched. Beyond that point, its continuum imperils our very existence and must be replaced by new goals more appropriate for the times.

GROWTH
THE GOAL THAT DRIVES HUMANITY

Today success, whether in the business of governance, commerce, finance, or religion, is defined by growth. The larger a society's population base, theoretically, the more powerful become systems of governance. Consumption increases as populations grow, expanding the influence of those within systems of commerce. Most religious leaders call for big families. The larger their flock, the more financially and politically empowered become their systems of religion. And finally, the Wall Street directive to "grow your business" pretty well says it all.

To avoid impending doom, we must either immediately reduce our numbers or instantaneously become highly efficient producers of consumables, neither of which is possible within profit-driven, growth-dependent structures.

Economists call us consumers, which we most certainly are. With an overarching goal of growth, consumptive activities abound and are incentivized by the lure of riches in the guise of profits. Our quest for growth in profits is both competitive and destructive. To garner profits, some rulers of industry allow the most abhorrent activities. In the process, they embrace the lie and distort or ignore the truth, at a most perilous time.

Growth is a voluntary phenomenon within all but the Financial Structure, where it is a necessity (to be discussed shortly). Although the other structures will function more efficiently and more humanely without growth driven systems, they cannot eliminate growth when they are inextricably tied to the Financial Structure which must grow to survive.

Life on Earth is dependent upon healthy support systems. Over the past two centuries, those who govern have allowed those of industry to contaminate the air we breathe, the land we grow food on, and the waters of the world. We repeat the same mistakes displayed in example after example of failed predecessor societies. Only now, the mistakes are at planetary-levels because our numbers are so great and our presence so pervasive. The result? Earth is ill. We are to blame.

With nearly one billion starving and another billion malnourished, it should be painfully obvious that current food production and delivery systems fail us. Scientists estimate that humanity already exceeds Earth's carrying capacity by 50 percent, meaning either we halve our population, or find another half Earth to farm to support existing populations.[48] From an environmental analyst described in the *Washington Post* as "one of the world's most influential thinkers" comes the following statement published ten years ago:

> We are liquidating the earth's natural assets to fuel our consumption. Half of us live in countries where water tables are falling and wells are going dry. Soil erosion exceeds soil formation on one-third of the world's cropland, draining the land of its fertility. The world's ever-growing herds of cattle, sheep, and goats are converting vast stretches of grassland to desert. Forests are shrinking by 13 million acres per year as we clear land for agriculture and cut trees for lumber and paper. Four-fifths of oceanic fisheries are being fished at capacity or overfished and headed for collapse. In system after system, demand is overshooting supply ... If we continue with business as usual, civilizational collapse is no longer a matter of whether but when ... We are dangerously close to the edge.[49]

Have things gotten better or worse since then? You know the answer. Society is not operating as it should. It is absolutely irresponsible to grow our population while we are incapable of properly feeding and managing those already here. Yet, with growth as the name of the game, another 3.2 billion will arrive shortly. Will we go from one billion starving to three billion? Is that progress? Is it a civilized society that promotes a new life doomed to perpetual starvation, poverty, and disease, or a barbaric one? Stop. Answer the questions honestly.

Religion is often used as the excuse for not limiting our numbers. But if your God is as beneficent as you would like to believe, would he or she promote self-destructive acts that from birth doom billions to lives of misery and despair? Growth to extinction. It has happened before, and it would be the height of human hubris to think it cannot happen again.

AN ATTEMPT TO LIMIT GROWTH

Although there are few leaders willing to push an agenda requiring population reduction, there is one example of such an attempt. The year was 1979. The nation? China. The act? The one-child-per-family rule that is estimated to have prevented approximately 400 million births. That rule ended in late 2015 because "too many Chinese are heading into retirement and the nation's population has too few young people entering the labor force to provide for their retirement, healthcare, and continued economic growth."[50]

China was forced to abandon its growth limiting program because of global structural dictates that necessitate "continued economic growth." The problem faced is that if population growth is eliminated, the foundations upon which all social systems are based will crumble. Society as we know it will collapse. Would that be such a bad thing? Well, that depends upon whether alternative systems have been envisioned and enabled to replace the failed ones. If not, the world will devolve and chaos will run rampant.

What would happen to humanity if we agreed to limit family size to one child for just one generation, followed by no more than two? In short order our population would be halved, as would the environmental and social pressures from our presence on Earth. Massively overcrowded cities could be eliminated, along with homelessness, poverty, and starvation. Would humanity be better or worse off? How about Earth? The answers are obvious. But, without an alternative plan any such attempt is doomed from the outset, as was the Chinese experiment.

If we are to survive, we must change our ways. We have to grow up and take responsibility for ourselves and our actions. With respect to managing our population, inoculating 50 percent of the population and then unleashing some bioweapon that kills everyone else is neither civilized nor humane, yet it is not an inconceivable act for some to consider. Doing so would not be the act of a civil society. A civil society would recognize that humanity is far better served with fewer of us to care for. It would then develop and implement plans to responsibly and humanely manage our activities by eliminating growth dictates throughout all structures and systems.

Growth has been our objective for over 3,000 years since the Old Testament directed us to "Be fruitful and multiply and fill the earth and subdue it and have dominion over the fish of the sea and over the birds of the heavens and over every living thing that moves on the earth." We have done just that.

We have overpopulated Earth and subdued every living thing on her. Now what? Do we continue to promote population growth as a fundamental human goal which can only result in lowered living standards, social stress, inequality, and grave levels of suffering for billions, or do we grow up, take responsibility for our kind and promote population reduction to enable a civilized society to evolve? The answer rests with you and billions like you.

If we are to find our way out of the mess we have created, we need to eliminate growth as the driving force of society and create new structures with higher, more time-appropriate goals. The key rests within the Financial Structure. Change how we use money, eliminate growth dictates, and change humanity. It is that simple. Until that change occurs, expect more pain and conflict as the following few examples display.

FEEDING EXTINCTION

Good governing systems set and enforce the rules and regulations necessary to make a better, safer society. They define how things are done so that theoretically, the doing does no harm. But that is not how contemporary governing systems operate. They allow, rather than responsibly govern. As a result, we are destroying everything.

Earth's reproductive and digestive systems have been severely compromised by *how* we produce food to feed an ever-growing population. Recall that insects are among Earth's primary pollinators. Approximately 80 percent of wild plants depend on insects for pollination.[51] They also provide free pollination services to farmers, thus playing a fundamental role in agricultural productivity. But, insect pollinator populations across the globe have plummeted, and the results are predictable.

> Loss of insect diversity and abundance is expected to provoke cascading effects on food webs and to jeopardize ecosystem services.[52]

> 'Insects make up about two-thirds of all life on Earth [but] there has been some kind of horrific decline,' said Professor Dave Goulson of Sussex University, UK, and part of the team behind the new study. 'We appear to be making vast tracts of land inhospitable to most forms of life and are currently on course for ecological Armageddon. If we lose the insects, then everything is going to collapse.'[53]

"Ecological Armageddon." "Collapse." Terrifyingly descriptive words of what is to come if we do not rapidly change (in this example) *how* we farm the world.

To feed an ever-growing population and to increase corporate profits, farmers are paid less to produce more, so massive factory farming operations have cropped up everywhere. Animals are often raised in such inhumane, overcrowded, and unsanitary ways that no one in their right mind would eat these foods if they saw firsthand how they are produced. To keep these animals alive until they are slaughtered and delivered to your table, they are pumped full of antibiotics. The impact? Since 2000, these practices have contributed to a nearly three-fold increase in the spread of antibiotic-resistant bacteria easily transmitted from animals to humans.[54]

And, we know that "Antimicrobial resistance is a global problem." Unfortunately, "This alarming trend shows that the drugs used in animal farming are rapidly losing their efficacy."[55] When antibiotics are rendered incapable of stopping the spread of infectious bacteria, people die. But the harm doesn't stop there.

Industrialized farming practices use genetically modified crops designed to be sprayed with certain herbicides and pesticides. Aside from contributing to the global collapse of insect populations,[56] herbicides and insecticides contaminate the food we eat and the water we drink.[57] Studies of one of the most widely used herbicides (glyphosate/roundup) indicate that it is potentially toxic in a variety of ways to humans and animals alike.[58] Another widely used chemical (chlorpyrifos) has been confirmed to cause brain damage in children. According to the European Food Safety Authority, there is "no safe level" of exposure to this herbicide.[59] Although they finally banned its use in December, 2019, it is still in use elsewhere, including in the U.S. where the Environmental Protection Agency recently ignored the same evidence when it refused a proposed ban on that chemical.[60] Who knows how many lives have been cut short because regulators have allowed the widespread use of dangerous chemicals without prior independent scientific studies confirming them safe for use?

> Someday we shall look back on this dark era of agriculture and shake our heads. How could we have ever believed that it was a good idea to grow our food with poisons?
>
> – Jane Goodall

Compounding the problem is the fact that the overuse of herbicides and pesticides is responsible for killing beneficial organisms typically abundant within a healthy soil matrix. This usage works well for Big Ag as once nutrient-rich soils have been rendered barren, they need to be supplemented with artificial nutrients to be productive. So massive amounts of inorganic fertilizers are sold, boosting ag profits as well as food production costs which are, of course, passed on to the consumer.

End of story? Nope. Those fertilizers get washed into waterways where they trigger algal blooms so massive, they are visible from space. Unfortunately, these blooms strip aquatic environments of oxygen, killing most everything within. They are happening everywhere. The problem is not that we don't know how to responsibly and sustainably farm. We do. The problem is that capitalistic systems foster irresponsible production practices to maximize profits and encourage irresponsible governance practices to protect industry from liability for the harms they trigger.

When we are forced (because we have no alternatives) to eat food contaminated with antibiotics, insecticides and herbicides, we harm ourselves. Beyond production, our food delivery systems are allowed to follow the same ugly pattern.

> Consider what you've eaten today. Perhaps you drank juice from a plastic bottle and coffee from a Keurig pod. For breakfast, you might have had fruit with yogurt. Your lunch salad may have been packed in a plastic container. There's a good chance much of what you ingested was packaged, stored, heated, lined, or served in plastic. And unfortunately, there's mounting scientific evidence that these plastics are harming our health, from as early as our time in our mother's womb.[61]

Fast-food companies often sell the lowest quality foods packed with addictive ingredients linked to obesity and diabetes.[62] We know that "Obesity negatively affects most bodily systems. It is linked to the most prevalent and costly medical problems seen in our country, including type 2 diabetes, hypertension, coronary artery disease, many forms of cancer, and cognitive dysfunction."[63] And as the current pandemic highlights, the obese are at much greater risk of suffering complications and death from Covid-19 than most others.[64]

Yet, regulators everywhere allow industry to supply foods known to be unhealthy to eat. They can make us fat, contaminate us with chemicals that sicken us, shorten our lives, and contribute to skyrocketing health care costs. Those of governance could do the responsible thing and regulate how foods are grown and delivered to us, but they do not, and you know why. The following should be self-evident: Every industry is dependent upon consumers to buy their products. Each exists in service of humanity, not the other way around. Unfortunately, and unnecessarily, every profit-based system, in a backward twist of reality, places profits ahead of humanity. If we are to survive and thrive, these destructive practices must change.

POLLUTION AND THE GROWTH PARADIGM

The more people we create, the more goods must be produced, which is what the growth paradigm mandates. Because profits incentivize production, most systems champion cheap, inefficient production practices. Inefficient systems produce waste, which over hundreds of years of mindless release into the environment now contaminate everything, including the food we eat, the water we drink, and the air we breathe. Everything is becoming more toxic by the second. So, is it any wonder that cancer rates are rising as wildlife and plant diversity plummet?

Toxic garbage is everywhere. It poisons, strangles, and suffocates most everything it contacts, creating huge death zones on land, in rivers, and at sea. The Great Pacific Garbage Patch is one such example. It is an immeasurably large area of debris containing mostly plastic washed into rivers or intentionally and illegally dumped by manufacturers into waterways that transport it to the oceans where it becomes trapped within massive, circulating currents.

Often not visible on the surface, all five of Earth's giant oceanic gyres contain tiny plastic pieces suspended within the water column making a dense plastic soup. Plastic in the environment decomposes slowly, releasing chemical toxins over hundreds of years. In 2017, marine scientists reported that "extraordinary levels of persistent organic pollutants" (chemicals that do not naturally degrade) have been found in animals inhabiting Earth's most remote areas; areas previously considered "pristine environments," "inferring that these pollutants are pervasive across the world's oceans."[65] That study found that "regardless of depth … regardless of species … [these toxins] were present in all" sea life sampled.

Persistent organic pollutants (including PCBs and flame retardants) bond with bits of plastic and other organic debris which get eaten by tiny life forms to become food for larger creatures, concentrating the toxins up the food chain until they reach the ultimate consumer, us. These contaminants are known to have "devastating effects" on "hormonal, immune, and reproductive systems," yet we persist in practices that ensure they will end up in your body.

A study published September 13, 2019, conducted by scientists at the German Environment Ministry and the Robert Koch Institute[66] found plastic by-products in 97 to 100 percent of blood and urine samples from 2,500 children tested between 2014 and 2017. Coursing through the bodies of over 20 percent of the youngest children were dangerously high levels of PFOA, an "extremely persistent, bioaccumulative, and toxic chemical frequently used in non-stick cookware and in waterproof clothing" that is known to be toxic to the liver and harmful to reproductive systems.

The good news is that effective 2020, a global ban of that chemical kicks in. The bad news is that many of us have already been exposed to this toxin, and as the chemical is "extremely persistent," meaning it lasts a long time in the environment, we will continue to be exposed to its harmful effects for a long time to come. Sadly, "most scientists agree that it is not feasible to clean up the plastic soup" in Earth's oceans. And one expert informs that "No fish monger on Earth can sell you a certified organic wild-caught fish."[67]

So, you don't eat fish. You're safe from these toxins, right? A study published in August 2019 by scientists at the Alfred Wegener Institute[68] expands our knowledge of microplastic contamination of Earth environments. The authors identified "high concentrations" of microplastic contamination near major urban areas and surprisingly, within snow of the Alps and remote regions of the Artic, indicating the atmosphere as a transport mechanism. Of course, we drink snowmelt from the mountains and breathe planetary air, so you might think that plastics and their chemical byproducts are being absorbed in our bodies. As the above German study found, you would be correct.

What about toxins in plastics we use every day? A study published in August 2019 by the American Chemical Society[69] analyzed and benchmarked for toxicity, commonly used products made from the most widely used plastics. The authors were hoping to identify which plastics to use and which to avoid. A review of this study published October 2019 in *Consumer Reports* indicated that 74 percent of the products tested were toxic in some way, stating, "Instead of pointing to a few ... types of plastic that should be avoided, the testing instead revealed that issues of toxicity were widespread - and could be found in nearly any type of plastic ... [in fact] The researchers detected more than 1,000 chemicals in these plastics, 80 percent of which were unknown."[70]

Unknown chemicals obviously have not been precleared by regulators as safe for use. The responsible approach to allowing a new chemical compound into the stream of commerce would be to require independent third-party testing for toxicity before a new product is sold, rather than allowing manufacturers to expose us to products containing chemicals that years later are found to be unsafe. But that is not how capitalistic systems of commerce work, is it?

Capitalistic systems are growth-based, profit-driven, and competitive in nature. They are incapable of putting safety ahead of profits, so they do not, and we all suffer the consequences. Capitalistic systems are outdated. They cannot responsibly serve a society of billions and need to be replaced. We will discuss how to do just that further on.

7

GROWTH INDUCED IMPACTS - GLOBAL WARMING

The by-products of unregulated industrialization have warmed the planet and acidified her waters. As our populations grow, energy demands increase, which accelerates the global warming phenomena and compromises Earth's ability to support life.

One way to think about global warming is to correlate it to what happens within your own body when it is attacked by a virus or bacteria. In some cases, it may respond by heating up. If you become warm enough for long enough and if your own life support systems are healthy enough to survive the heat, some invaders will perish being unable to survive in the overly warm environment. However, if your internal support systems have been compromised and weakened to the point that they can't filter out the toxins released by the invaders or mount strong defensive attacks to repel their increasing numbers, you may become overwhelmed and die.

This is exactly what is happening to Earth. In a very real sense, we are the invaders. Earth's systems are responding by heating up and she is rapidly becoming less hospitable to life. If her systems are strong enough, they will survive the heat. However, we have been attacking and weakening most of her support systems for hundreds of years and there is little to indicate that we will stop the onslaught anytime soon. At some point, her systems will begin to fail and life on Earth as we know it will cease to be. That process is well underway.

Global temperature record-keeping began in 1880. Since then, 18 of the 19 hottest years occurred between 2000 and 2019. The last decade was the hottest ever recorded. Global temperatures in 2019 were 1.71 degrees F above the twentieth-century average.[71] Los Angeles warmed about 5 degrees over the last century, although the averages for the months of August and September have increased by 8 to 9 degrees.[72] And new data reveals that the world's oceans in 2019 "were the warmest in recorded human history."[73] It is impossible to know how much higher her temperatures will be or for how long they will continue to rise, but most scientific models predict a significant increase within 80 years. So, what should we prepare for?

SEA LEVELS WILL RISE

As Earth warms her polar icecaps, glaciers, and snow-packs melt, releasing trillions of gallons of freshwater into her oceans which are eight inches higher than one hundred years ago. However, the melt rate over the past twenty years is nearly double what it had been.[74] Because we fail to responsibly manage our activities, global temperatures and sea levels will continue to rise.

As Earth warms, her oceans warm. The top 2,300 feet of Earth's oceans have on average warmed 4/10th degree Fahrenheit since 1969.[75] Over that same period ocean surface temperatures rose by approximately 1.3 degrees Fahrenheit.[76] Both increases are massive and dramatic considering the incredible amount of water being warmed.

Water expands as it warms, contributing to sea-level rise. Nobody knows for certain how much sea levels will rise in the future, but rise it will. Recent estimates indicate that: "By 2050 sea level rise will push average annual coastal floods higher than land now home to 300 million people."[77] Feedback loops and accelerating ice sheet melts in Antarctica and Greenland will exaggerate the process, meaning oceans will likely warm faster and rise higher than predicted. According to a NOAA 2017 report:

> Long-term sea level rise driven by global climate change presents clear and highly consequential risks ... over the coming decades and centuries ... Global mean sea level (GMSL) ... rise is a certain impact of climate change; the questions are *when*, and *how much*, rather than *if*.[78] (emphasis original)

The Paris Agreement on climate change, effective November 4, 2016, set a goal of limiting the average global temperate rise to less than 2 degrees Celsius (3.6 degrees Fahrenheit) above pre-industrial levels. Even if we somehow meet their target, recent geologic analysis indicates that when global temperatures were just 2 C degrees higher (400,000 years ago), sea levels were 42 feet higher than present.[79] The result?

Beachfront becomes seabed with cities, even whole countries, submerged. Flooding becomes commonplace. "By 2050, 26 major US cities will face an "emerging flooding crisis." Globally, storm damage could cost cities from Hong Kong to Dhaka to New York trillions annually."[80] Besides the economic impacts already being experienced, millions of people will be displaced, and many lives will be lost. Pay attention! It is happening everywhere. And of course, the relentless onslaught of sea and weather-induced flooding does not just stop after 2100. But that's not the end of the trauma.

MILLONS WILL BECOME CLIMATE REFUGEES

By the turn of the century, a one-meter sea-level rise will have forced hundreds of millions of people to flee low lying areas. Where will they go? Which country will accept them? How will housing and other necessities be provided and paid for?

Migration from coastal flooding is not the only factor that will displace millions. Extreme drought has already taken a stranglehold over massive areas often affecting the poorest people. Drought prevents crops from being grown, livestock from being raised, and eliminates water resources necessary for survival. Drought causes mass migrations. And it's already begun, but nations fail to plan positive solutions to the impending crisis.

In addition to the climate refugees, desperate millions have already created patterns of mass migration by fleeing from dictators committing genocide and hoarding resources; or from warlords inflicting terror on communities they seek to possess; and from religious factions emotionally driven by hate who rape, rob, kill, and pillage villages of differing religious factions. Whether from countries in the Middle East, Asia, Africa, and South and Central America, people are fleeing in fear for their lives.

Millions cry out for help as they are needlessly, yet hopelessly, thrust out into an uncaring world. Some travel by foot carrying everything they own. Others attempt perilous journeys by train, boat, or cargo container. If they survive, most will be turned away at borders or forced into detention camps with tens of thousands of others struggling to exist with the barest of necessities. Compounding those problems is the fact that their physical and mental health is often severely compromised. When news of their condition arrives, our hearts cry out, but there is little we can do to help because of the nature of existing systems.

Today, we can't humanely provide for the four million refugees who have been forced from their homelands in North Africa and the Middle East, so how do you suppose nations will deal with the millions more who will be displaced in the not-too-distant future? For one answer, consider that those who govern the US have known what to plan for, for decades. From a 2004 Pentagon-sponsored report they learned that:

[H]istory shows that whenever humans have faced a choice between starving or raiding, they raid ... wars over resources were the norm until about three centuries ago. When such conflicts broke out, 25% of a population's adult males usually died. As abrupt climate change hits home, warfare may again come to define human life.[81]

Well, that's encouraging, isn't it? US military planners have for decades accepted climate change as fact and have begun planning ahead for it. How? By allocating resources to solve climate associated problems and by building new communities to house climate refugees (including their own)? Nope. Instead, the political class proves yet again incapable of providing humane solutions to the problems we face. In this case, they respond by building a bigger, longer, stronger wall to keep those in great need out. And they are not the only ones doing this. India for example is building a 2500-mile border wall to keep out the millions of Bangladeshis expected to be forced from their homes by rising sea levels. Many other nations have already done the same.

Our social structures are outdated, competitive, and reactionary. They respond to problems only when they become urgent, if at all. They neither anticipate future needs nor plan generations ahead to save lives and prevent the misery that will surely follow if they do not. Why is that? Because to a large degree our structures prohibit the allocation of financial resources to proactively address these issues.

Yet, we most definitely have the ability to prevent great human and environmental catastrophes from happening. We have the ability to anticipate the needs of billions and to build state-of-the-art communities to house everyone. We will discuss doing just that a bit further on. For now, ask yourself whether doing so is likely within existing systems and structures?

When will enough of us dare to dream better ways of being into existence and then be willing to participate in creating a new society that will humanely accommodate what is surely coming? Are you ready to help? Not sure? Perhaps the following will move you into action.

DESERTS WILL EXPAND

"Desertification" is simply the expansion of deserts. Whether from climate change, over-grazing, habitat destruction, or deforestation, desertification is upon us. No matter the reason, the impacts are being experienced on nearly every continent. Almost half of Africa is affected. Many communities have already collapsed. And the calamity will only worsen as more water systems dry up and people are forced to move or perish.

Predictably, people attempt to move out of drought-prone areas to survive. As you read this, tens of thousands wander parched deserts, looking for an oasis to settle on. There are none. The destitute have no place to turn. Hope is nonexistent. Sadly, the tears of the dying are rarely felt by those with the power to prevent their suffering.

The Southeast Asia drought of 2015 to 2017 affected nine countries. The worst drought over the past ninety years in Vietnam caused saltwater intrusions extending 90 kilometers upriver rendering river water too salty for crop irrigation, consumption, or even fish farming.[82] The Somalia Drought of 2015 to 2018, which came only six years after drought-induced famine killed 250,000 people, caused large scale crop failures, livestock deaths, malnutrition, drought-related diseases, and increased competition for limited resources resulting in rising tension, conflict, and out-migration.[83]

Australia experienced the Millennium Drought between 1997 to 2009. Affecting the Southern region of the continent, researchers described its intensity as "unprecedented" over the past 400 years.[84] In the United States, as of August 2018, based upon the Palmer Drought Index, "severe to extreme drought affected about 23 percent" of the country.

Protracted droughts are not limited to rural areas. In Cape Town, South Africa, life altering water restrictions were implemented in 2018 to stave off catastrophe from a three-year drought. If the city had the money, it could have built a desalination plant powered by solar and wind energy and avoided the crisis. But it didn't. Money remains "the sole impediment" to solving not only Cape Town's water crisis, but most human-induced crises.

FOOD PRODUCTION CAPACITY WILL DECLINE

Earth's temperature rise is rapidly diminishing mountain snow-packs, which are melting earlier and building later. With less water stowed and available to vast river systems such as those originating in the Himalayan Mountains upon which over 1.5 billion people in nine Asian countries depend, severe water shortages are projected. In many areas rain comes from fall to spring and food is grown from spring to fall. As the snowpack diminishes and melts earlier, less water will be available to meet late-season agricultural needs. Massive food production systems will be severely disrupted. Many farming communities have already been abandoned as more are forced to move or die from lack of water. Less food, not more, is to be expected.[85]

As we discussed above, we should also expect food production from the sea to diminish. Our emissions have turned the oceans warmer and more acidic. Plankton numbers are declining. Plankton are the most basic oceanic food source, so assuming that their numbers continue to decline as the oceans get warmer and more acidic, we should expect that less oceanic food, not more, will be available for human consumption in the years to come. But that is not the end of the trauma to be suffered. Let's turn back to water for a moment.

WATER WILL BECOMES SCARCE, EXPENSIVE, AND PRIVATELY OWNED

Water is the essence of life, upon which everything is dependent. Throughout human history, water has always been a free and abundant resource. Communities developed near freshwater resources. As populations grew, aqueducts, pipelines, and wells were built to ensure free access to this abundant resource. But, during the twentieth century, with the advent of global finance and the multinational corporate cartel, everything changed.

Today, freshwater resources are threatened by the obvious, and the not so obvious. Human and industrial wastes contaminate clean water resources at ever-accelerating rates - the obvious. Elite financial institutions and supremely wealthy individuals are quietly buying up water resources everywhere - the not so obvious. Why do so? Because ownership of a life necessity means profits and control. Allow a necessary resource to be privatized, create monopolies of ownership, fail to protect remaining public resources from contamination, and guarantee never-ending profits to privateers and unending misery for everyone else. This is the state of water today.

Nearly all Arab countries suffer from water scarcity. By 2025, half of the world's population will be living in water-stressed areas. According to the UN 2018 World Water Development Report, by 2050 as a result of population and economic growth, nearly six billion people will suffer from clean water scarcity. Six billion! Taking immediate action to prevent this level of suffering presents an opportunity to create a more humane society. Failing to do so could not be more inhumane.

International law obligates nations to ensure that everyone has local access to safe and affordable drinking water and sanitation facilities as a basic human right.[86] Yet, one in three people use a drinking-water source contaminated with feces,[87] which causes diarrhea, cholera, dysentery, typhoid, and polio. And approximately 800 children under the age of five die every day (300,000 annually) with 842,000 people dying every year from diarrheal diseases caused by drinking contaminated water.[88]

Providing safe, clean water to everyone is not rocket science. The technologies exist to do it right now. But the people most in need cannot afford to purchase their own purification equipment and third-world nations lack the financial ability to develop community-wide purification and sanitary systems. The money for such basic services could easily be created within the Financial Structure. But, more often than not, the financial elite refuse to create money to solve humanitarian crises without draconian conditions. If they would, millions of lives and trillions of dollars in healthcare costs could be saved.

Providing clean water and modern sanitary systems to everyone is the low hanging fruit that is easily accomplishable when money is created for this purpose. How to do so in ways that enable a more humane humanity is discussed within Book VI. For now, recognize that until recently, water was a free resource for all. Unfortunately, today it is considered a commodity to be controlled by private, profiteering entities. As impacts from a warming planet compound and local governing entities are stripped of financial resources, they will lose the ability to provide water to their communities and the elite will swoop in and take over. Not possible? Think again. This plan is well underway.

Beginning around 2006, Wall Street bankers began amassing billions of dollars to acquire and control Earth's waters from source to consumer, recognizing the potential of a "forever" faucet of profits. These people consider water to be a far more profitable commodity to own than oil will ever be. Why? Because people can exist without oil but not without water. When water is scarce, people will pay whatever it takes to get it. The fewer the alternatives, the greater the profits. For the depressing details, see the article titled: The New "Water Barons": Wall Street Mega-Banks are Buying up the World's Water.[89]

The cruelty of this play is already taking its toll on the poorest people living in the worst slums on the planet. In Jakarta, Manila, Nairobi, and elsewhere, those least able pay five to ten times more for water than others living in higher-income areas in those same cities. Surprisingly, they even pay more than consumers in London or New York. Why? Because the poorest simply have no alternatives, which should provide a glimpse into the future when all water is owned and controlled by just a few.

To be blunt, any society that allows the least able to be charged ten times more than those most able, for life essentials, is backward, destructive, and not worth being a part of. Unfortunately, there are no alternatives. Yet.

The brutality of structures that support such systems is not limited to food or water deprivations. No, those structures all tie to debt-based financial systems that extract from the poorest interest rates hundreds of times higher than the richest pay, ensuring that they remain forever poverty-stricken. Once again, humanity has it backward. We embrace principles designed to keep the destitute, destitute. Instead of creating structures that pull humanity forward, rulers embrace those that hold most back, guaranteeing death as the only way out for many.

Water became a saleable commodity when municipalities could no longer afford to provide it free of charge. Initially, municipalities spread the cost of delivery systems to the public served, and the charges were reasonable. But the elite direct political agendas that financially weaken public service providers, whether local municipalities or national governments. For example, in the US, there has been a concerted effort to defund public education systems. With depleted revenues, many schools were forced to remove drinking fountains requiring parents to pay for bottled water or soda. That's good for the beverage companies but bad for our children and their parents.

In other examples, with insufficient reserves, governing entities are forced to borrow to install, operate, and update water and sanitary service systems. Overburdened with debt, some governing entities have been forced by their lenders to sell at bargain-basement prices the public service systems they have operated for centuries. The buyers? Elites, their banks, and investment funds.

For thousands of years, water has been a community asset, free to the public. But no longer. Today, it has been replaced by a profit-generating industry that inefficiently provides it in plastic bottles laced with toxins at outrageous prices. In the United States:

> The [bottled water] industry grossed a total of $11.8 billion … in 2012, making" [a gallon of] "bottled water about … 300x the cost of a gallon of tap water …" But, "If

we take into account the fact that almost 2/3 of all bottled water sales are single 16.9 oz (500 mL) bottles ... this cost is much, much higher ... almost 2,000x the cost of a gallon of tap water.[90]

Public water fountains are a thing of the past thanks to profit-driven practices of capitalistic systems. Now, water bottling companies fill the void in supply and the results are predictably not good for the consumer. Not only are the least able forced to pay excessive amounts for a life necessity, it now comes laced with harmful chemicals. Water quality studies of name brand bottled water products disturbingly reveal the presence of "potent" "endocrine-disrupting chemicals" (EDCs) found in "the majority of bottled water products" sampled. Those chemicals "significantly inhibited human estrogen as well as androgen receptors." EDC chemicals can interfere with hormone systems and contribute to birth defects, cancers, cardiovascular, metabolic, and developmental disorders.[91]

In 2010, the United Nations General Assembly through Resolution A/RES/64/292 declared that every person has the right to safe, physically accessible, and affordable water. Their intentions and declarations are well placed. Access to all life necessities, including clean air, should be intrinsic within a package of fundamental rights supplied to every Earth being. But within existing systems, they are not.

THE AIR WE BREATHE

During World War II, the city of Los Angeles experienced smog so strong that some suspected a chemical weapons attack by Japan. In the early 1950s, physicians began connecting air pollution to public health problems. Emergency rooms overflowed with patients experiencing respiratory issues on bad-air days. Parents kept their children home from school. Athletic events were canceled. Scientists studied the issue and by the mid-1950s concluded that autos burning fossil fuels were a primary cause of the unhealthy air.

Armed with science-based knowledge, local anti-smog groups grew into a movement that influenced public opinion and pushed politicians to consider adopting regulations to reduce harmful vehicle and industrial emissions. But industry rulers fought back. They paid scientists to deny conclusions of the broader scientific community, delaying implementation of needed regulations, and we suffered.

At another critical juncture, rather than acting responsibly to the communities their businesses served by modifying their products to reduce harms, industry rulers chose not to change their ways. Using the same strategies then as now, they first argued that there was no proof linking environmental degradation to their activities; then, that the proof presented by the broad scientific community was unreliable and based on bad science; and when that propaganda proved untrue, they used money as the ultimate obstacle to progressive change, arguing that new regulations would hurt consumers and the economy by increasing costs. Once again, money was the excuse used to prevent beneficial change from taking hold.

Predictably, air pollution worsened and public outcry mounted. Because air pollution was so obviously impacting everyone (including politicians and their children) and because we, the people, were persistent in demanding change in how the powerful automobile industry conducted its business, change materialized.

Although it took ten years of organized rallies and media coverage, in 1963 the US Congress passed the Clean Air Act which set the first-ever national emission standards for vehicles. But, hiding behind the corporate shield with knowledge that they had no personal liability for disobeying the law, industry rulers directed management to disregard the law, forcing the government to sue automakers to obtain compliance, delaying change and harming everyone.[92]

Back then, politicians paid somewhat more attention to the people they represented than to corporate lobbyists, so in 1970 a more effective version of the Clean Air Act was passed, resulting in smog-free cities, healthier environments, and happier people. Positive change. Everyone benefited.

Unfortunately, those same rules were not put into effect globally. Today, cities like Beijing, New Delhi, Dhaka, Ahwaz, and Moscow experience far too many days when it is unhealthy to breathe the air. Tens of millions suffer respiratory and other associated illnesses with millions dying prematurely as a result of conditions we are responsible for allowing. According to the World Health Organization:

> Nine out of ten people breathe polluted air every day. In 2019, air pollution is considered by WHO as the greatest environmental risk to health. Microscopic pollutants in the air can penetrate respiratory and circulatory systems, damaging the lungs, heart, and brain, killing 7 million people prematurely every year from diseases such as cancer, stroke, heart and lung disease. Around 90% of these deaths are in low and middle-income countries, with high volumes of emissions from industry, transport, and agriculture, as well as dirty cookstoves and fuels in homes.

> The primary cause of air pollution (burning fossil fuels) is also a major contributor to climate change which impacts people's health in different ways. Between 2030 and 2050, climate change is expected to cause 250,000 additional deaths per year, from malnutrition, malaria, diarrhea and heat stress.[93]

Most will agree that the right to breathe clean air should be a fundamental right of every Earth being. And most will agree that the realization of that and other similar rights is unlikely within consumption-based, profit-driven systems tied to a Financial Structure that dictates growth and monetary policies of limitation; so, it is up to us to design and implement alternatives.

There is great good that resides within most of us. It should not, and need not, take unrelenting tragedy to bring it out. It is time to start planning to create the future we want and deserve. There is nothing preventing us from creating it. That, in fact, is what life opportunities are about. We have the absolute ability to change, to re-envision ourselves and our societies for the betterment of everyone, not just a few.

The question becomes one of *how*, as in *how* do we make such fundamental levels of change? Fortunately, nothing new needs to be discovered. We move forward by setting new goals to guide us in designing and implementing new structures to enable transformative change. To envision how to change the structures, we need a refined understanding of the elementary purpose of each, which brings us to The Structures.

BOOK IV

THE STRUCTURES

As human communities evolved, the ways of the hunter-gatherer had to be shed. Social structures developed, enabling unrelated individuals to live and work together. Freedom to do whatever one wanted became incompatible with the advancement of the community. Respect for another's life, work, and possessions prevailed. Rules and regulations defining acceptable behavior were adopted, giving birth to the Structure of Governance.

Specialization became a hallmark and an advantage of life within the community. Families specialized in providing some product or service to others. Life became easier as more people made more things available to others, giving birth to trade and eventually, the Structure of Commerce, which entails the production and delivery of goods and services.

For commerce to proliferate, the imagination had to be stretched. A way to equalize perceived differences in the value of goods and services in trade had to be envisioned, giving birth to the concept of money and eventually, the Structure of Finance.

Prior to the advent of science, the unknown was explained by individuals claiming to understand, represent, and be conduits of other-worldly beings. These individuals drew great power and social status by attributing natural phenomena to larger-than-life beings. They proclaimed, preached, and brought together a community governed in part by gods, giving birth to The 4th Structure - religion.

These four structures enable society. They provide the boundaries, guidelines, goals, and incentives within which their respective systems operate. Each is a creature of human imagination established long ago for societies of thousands, not billions. There is nothing sacred about any of them and there is no universal law prohibiting any from being changed. In fact, those laws are quite the opposite.

For over 9,000 years, differing systems of governance, commerce, finance, and religion have been tried. None are perfect, or even close.

Conflict enshrouds them all. Wars are fought over who governs who, which religion is dominant, who claims access to which resources and, who controls money.

One structure controls them all. It both enables society and is responsible for most of our social shortcomings. If operated differently, it has the capacity to eliminate great suffering and social inequality. Change its goals and how we use it, and we can galvanize a civilization destined for the stars. Before we get to that one, let's look at the others with an eye on how to improve them for the betterment of all.

8

THE STRUCTURE OF GOVERNANCE

Every association of two or more people, whether husband and wife, business partners, corporations, religious institutions, or nations, have one thing in common: agreements, written or unwritten, that both define and limit how the people do what they do. Governance. Agreements of governance establish the structure within which all other structures and systems of a particular society operate, theoretically, to satisfy a common purpose. These agreements define boundaries of socially acceptable behavior, establish societal goals, and enforce rules and regulations intended to aid in the accomplishment of those goals.

GOVERNANCE IS THE MANAGING STRUCTURE

Today there are 196 nations, each operating a different system of governance. Globally, there are more people employed in positions of governance than any other profession. Why? Because we haven't figured out any one system of governance capable of serving a global society of billions. So, we muddle along trying but failing to successfully manage 196 different competing systems of governance.

Governments, like corporations, are not real. Neither exists without people. They should not be viewed as anything more than people working together to achieve a common purpose, which in this case is to manage the activities of the governed. There have been many different forms of governing systems, from democracies to autocracies, monarchies to republics, and dictatorships to communes. Whether with attributes of totalitarianism or communism, socialism or fascism, all remain imperfect attempts at governance. Why? Because none have fully embraced humanity.

New structures of global governance, commerce, and finance are needed to serve all people if we are to somehow avoid the inevitable result of the pathways we currently travel. How we move forward in time is a matter of choice, our choice. We can choose to keep doing most things the way we have for thousands of years, keep the existing structures as they are, or we can fundamentally change how we do most things and enable evolutionary change.

MOST SYSTEMS OF GOVERNANCE FAIL TO MEET OUR NEEDS

A large percentage of contemporary governing systems fail to meet even the most basic needs of the governed. Many of these nations are unstable places to live. Without a safe and stable society, it is difficult to attract or retain commercial enterprises that pay a fair wage and generate sufficient revenues to support systems of taxation necessary to enable a particular system of governance to function.

Without adequate revenues, governments cannot ensure the existence of modern infrastructure systems to deliver food, clean water, sewerage treatment, power, housing, or transportation. Without adequate revenues, governments are incapable of providing quality health care, education, safety, and welfare backstop programs. Without adequate revenues, most nations fail at what they are supposed to do, to serve their people, the governed.

Failing nations tend to be the unhappiest places. Lacking revenues to support good governance, war, corruption, inequality, and poverty metastasize. Political and social instability mount resulting in mistrust in those who govern, freedoms lost, bureaucratic intolerance to criticism, civil unrest, high crime rates, military coups, terrorism, death, and despair.

Conversely, there are a few governments that provide the things the governed need most. Even though they may impose high taxes, these tend to be the happiest places to live. Why? Because these systems of governance return a fair percentage of tax dollars to the governed through well-developed social services like free education, healthcare, retirement guarantees, public transportation, modern infrastructure systems, and, importantly, they enable a safe, secure and stable society within which equal employment opportunities exist.

We are told that there are two certainties in life, death and taxes. Most people if given a choice would prefer not to have to pay taxes. Yet, we do, in part because that's the way it's been for thousands of years, and in part because no other viable alternative has presented. Unfortunately, most governments fail to provide services commensurate with taxes levied, resulting in unhappy people.

Is it possible to envision and then enable a fully operational system of governance within which taxes have been eliminated, but the services necessary to secure the happiness of the people are provided? The answer is yes. We discuss how in Book VI.

It doesn't take a whole lot for most people to feel reasonably happy. Systems of governance that create and enforce rules and regulations which directly benefit the governed enable a higher quality of life and yield the happiest people. Happy people are easy to govern and don't rebel; they have little reason to. Unhappy people make governing difficult and often have every reason to revolt.

Unfortunately, humans have yet to perfect any system of governance capable of sustaining a healthy, happy, thriving society. Why? Because no form of governance has been designed to survive the challenges of inherent greed when the other structures are so adept at promoting it.

It is critical to understand that we can't change one structure and expect an evolutionary leap forward. To evolve better ways of being, we have to fundamentally change all structures. If we do not, the evolutionary opportunity that stands before us will be lost and our societies will either devolve into the dystopian future envisioned by many, or our species will perish.

EXTRACTIVE SYSTEMS OF GOVERNANCE FORCE US DOWN PATHWAYS OF EXTINCTION

History reveals that when a governing system causes great harm to a large class of people, it will fail.[94] Those types of systems typically extract far more from the governed than they return. They will also fail when they allow the destruction of the environments the governed depend upon to survive.[95] Resistance to change, grave social inequality, and lack of foresight are the fundamental reasons for both types of failures.

Nations fail when extractive economic systems are supported by extractive political systems that impair or block economic growth, and transfer wealth and power to the elite.[96] Extractive systems are those that divide society into two factions: the few (who take the most) and the many (who work for the few and receive the least). People will stand only so much deprivation or inequality before they create movements of change which either succeed, in which case the system of governance is changed (or the rulers are replaced with little change otherwise), or they fail in which case their people suffer the consequences of retribution, death, and despair from emboldened rulers.

Rulers who resist change tend to make things worse by taking ever more of the fruits of the people's labors to fortify their positions, leaving little for everyone else. Division mounts. Civil unrest, extreme deprivation, and social disorder inevitably follow. Sadly, this is the current path of humanity as pointed out by Peter Goldmark, former Rockefeller Foundation president, who stated that "The death of our civilization is no longer a theory or an academic possibility; it is the road we're on."[97]

Change implies that something new replaces something old. Most people fear the unknown, the new, preferring to remain with what they know. Big changes scare us. Rulers are no exception. They come into power within systems operating a certain way, a way they know. Because rulers tend to be short-sighted, they care little about the harms they cause, focusing on the acquisition of wealth and the retention of power, so they resist or prohibit even clearly beneficial social change. Whether in governance, commerce, finance, or religion, these same truths have plagued humanity throughout history. But things need not be this way.

Where extractive systems of a ruling elite have been replaced by more inclusive systems that benefited a broader swath of society, doors of great opportunity presented. New versions of society developed to operate more openly, more freely, more efficiently, and at times more humanely. Nations such as Great Britain and the United States succeeded (in part) because they developed systems of governance within which political rights were more broadly distributed than to a handful of elites, and because they provided "economic opportunities not just for the elite but for a broad cross-section of society."[98] Notwithstanding the above, their social systems have never been ideal, or even close. Much of their success was the result "of endless resource extraction, conquest, and cheap/free labor of slaves and the working poor."[99]

IN SERVICE OF THE FEW, NOT THE MANY

As good as they were, even the best attempts at governance fail when those who govern come to serve the few, rather than the many. For instance, in the US the electoral process has become a financial orgy that only corporations and the very wealthy are capable of attending. Today, to secure and retain an elected office, even the most well-intentioned must seek handouts at every opportunity, but handouts don't come without strings attached. The elected now must vote their pocketbooks (not their conscience) to both attain and then retain their jobs. Bribery is rampant although a bit more sublime than the term implies. It was first transformed into the lobbyists' artform, then into practice legalized by the courts.[100] The result? This democratic institution and others like it are in a state of decline the world over because morally based, ethically driven decision-making processes have been compromised.

Rulers of multinational corporations have become so powerful that they now place their own ilk in government to serve them. Consider how the Halliburton Loophole became law as just one of many such examples.[101] Dick Cheney was the Chairman and CEO of Halliburton Company (an oil and gas production company) from 1995 to 2000. In 2001, he became Vice-President of the United States. In 2005 legislation was enacted (the Halliburton Loophole) that exempted oil and gas operations from regulation and liability (under most US environmental protection laws) for the damages their practices create. Similar laws exempt corporate actors from responsibility for the harms they ignite in their never-ending quests for profits, as the once regulated become the regulators. The result? Democracy is lost, inequality reigns, and society devolves. In the US, a once noble attempt at governance has been perverted by systems that serve the few, not the many as originally hoped for.

TO GOVERN RESPONSIBLY

To govern responsibly implies governance for the common good. Whether governing a nation or a business, where rulers are incentivized to resist socially beneficial change, environmental and social collapse inevitably follow.

In the seminal book *Collapse*, Jared Diamond cites example after example over thousands of years of one societal collapse after another stemming from failures to change the things people do and the way they do them. Entire societies have vanished because those who governed failed or refused to: anticipate an environmental problem before it arrived, recognize that it has arrived, even bother to try and solve the problem once recognized, or succeed in solving it.[102] Every one of those reasons for societal failure is in play today, just look around.

From remote Amazon rainforests where multinational corporations swoop in, extract whatever resource they want and leave behind contaminated wastelands because government regulation is nonexistent, to heartland America where multinational corporations are allowed to destroy groundwater resources, contaminate food production systems, and hide critical information from the public about adverse environmental impacts from their operations, the people and their societies suffer the consequences.

In a world where 15 percent live without electricity, 1.1 billion people have inadequate access to water and nearly 2.6 billion lack basic sanitation,[103] the elite have the power to remedy these inequities, but unwisely, they choose otherwise. Regulators could, for instance, eliminate basic survival worries by setting uniform living wage standards across the globe, but they prefer operating 196 competing systems of governance rather than uniting for the common good.

According to a 2018 World Health Organization Report, world hunger is on the rise. Nearly one in nine people suffer from malnutrition.[104] Because their families are too poor to afford proper treatment, preventable disease kills two million children every year. Yet, it would take only $60 billion annually to end extreme poverty and prevent these deprivations. Regulators could, for example, require global banking cartels to create money to end extreme poverty or require banking systems to allocate a small percentage of profits to solve these and other similar problems, but they choose otherwise, to a large degree because they are owned by the financial elite.

Children who do not attend school are often the most vulnerable and marginalized. In 2015 over a quarter of a billion children did not attend school and according to the UN, as of 2014, aid for education was decreasing. With nearly 10 percent of the global population unable to read a book or sign their names, how are they supposed to exist in a modern society? From a larger perspective, consider that less than 1 percent of what the world spends on weapons every year is needed to put every child into school.[105] Regulators could allocate a small percentage of their weapons budget to solve this problem, but competition rather than cooperation is the order of this time, so they choose otherwise.

What is clear is that the structures within which society operates tie us to a past within which competition and inequality were accepted as part of the natural order of things. If we are to create a better way of being, we need to eliminate competitive societies and unite to secure the common good. World leaders have been aware of the need to do so for over a century.

TO SECURE THE COMMON GOOD

At the end of WWI, diplomats and intellectuals on both sides of the Atlantic recognized the need for a new type of organization designed to foster international cooperation, provide security for its members, and preserve the peace. In 1920, they formed the League of Nations to do just that through the use of collective security and disarmament agreements. But many nations either refused to join or were excluded. Critically, those that did join refused to empower the League to act as a global sovereign with legal and enforcement authority over its members. If it had been so enabled and if most nations had joined, the organization might have had a chance of success, but it wasn't, and they didn't, so it was disbanded in 1946.

At the end of WWII, world leaders once again recognized the necessity of changing how humanity functions, so in 1945 fifty-one nations formed the United Nations to maintain international peace and security, develop friendly relations among nations, and promote social progress, better living standards, and human rights. Its mission has changed little in over seventy-five years. But, as with the League of Nations, its ability to secure its foundational purposes has always been severely compromised by the unwillingness of its now 193 Member States to cede fundamental functions of governance to a singular global authority. If the Member States of the United Nations acted as nations united and fully empowered a global entity legally, financially, and militarily to secure its fundamental purposes to "improve the lives of poor people, conquer hunger, disease, and illiteracy, and to encourage respect for each other's rights and freedoms," the world would be a far better place. But they have not, and it is not.

Two attempts have been made by heads of state to create a limited form of world governance. Neither was successful. With an exploding population, unregulated consumptive growth, and 196 different systems of governance competing for dominion over the world's dwindling resources, what should be glaringly evident is that unless we rapidly and dramatically change how we govern ourselves; we are in big trouble.

As deprivations mount and Earth's life support systems decline at perhaps the most critical juncture in human existence, we have fundamentally important decisions to make. We can choose inaction, continue business as usual and see what happens; or we can release the shackles that bind us to past ways and join hands united in a movement to fundamentally change how we do most things. To do so, we will need a new form of global governance that is attuned to the needs of everyone. How will we move society to adopt such a global form of governance? What will it need to provide to induce the people to choose it over existing nationalistic systems?

TO CREATE A NEW FORM OF GOVERNANCE

Change at the most comprehensive level requires a movement within which new goals are set, agreements are reached, and structures redefined to better serve humanity. As governance is the structure that is tasked with establishing and enforcing the rules and regulations within which the rest of society operates, change begins by redefining it.

The act of redefining our notions of government is not accomplished by looking at how existing governing systems fail us; that's pretty obvious. Instead, we design a totally new structure to meet the needs of most people. How? How can we know what that new structure should look like? The answer is simple. Just ask.

Ask pretty much anyone, anywhere on the planet, what they most need from government and they will tell you that they need to feel safe in the streets and in their homes. They will tell you that they need equal access to reliable and safe food delivery systems, water, and sanitation services, housing, healthcare, education, transportation, and energy resources. And, they will tell you that they need employment opportunities that pay a living wage within settings that treat everyone equally and humanely.

These are foundational needs. If we agree to codify them as the goals upon which a new system of governance is based, and if we dedicate ourselves to pursuit of these goals with unerring courage and commitment, they can and will form the basis of an evolving society of civilized beings.

We have explored the concept of governance and briefly considered how existing systems of governance fail to meet the needs of a global society of beings. We know we have to change how we manage our affairs, but our structures are inexorably linked. We can't fundamentally change how one operates without changing how they all operate. As this work is less about the past and more about *how* to change, and although volumes remain to be said about the failures of modern governance, we push forward to consider *how* we conduct the affairs of commerce.

9

THE STRUCTURE OF COMMERCE

The second essential structure of human interaction is the Structure of Commerce. It began with one person trading one thing for another thing and morphed into a structure within which pretty much everything we do in the public sphere takes place. Commerce. Commerce is the production and transfer of goods and services between and among members of society. It exists to provide what we need and want.

COMMERCE IS THE PROVISION STRUCTURE

Everyday billions of people make things and deliver things and help others accomplish things. We provide goods and services to help each other survive and hopefully to thrive by making life a little easier for each other. Over the course of human history, we imagined and then created systems to more productively manufacture and distribute most things. Unfortunately, the more successful we have become in imagining and creating new things for a growing population, the more destructive we have become. We kill and consume almost everything we encounter to sustain our growth.

Is that what defines human existence? To grow our numbers and produce and consume things regardless of the harms we create, for no reason other than because that's the way we have done things for thousands of years? Is it possible for humanity to aspire to higher goals than growth, and if so, what should they be and what do we need to do differently to pursue them? To answer these questions, we need to focus on the basics of each structure to see how they work. With that knowledge we can consider how to change them to operate in fundamentally superior ways.

For orderly change to happen, new goals will need to be agreed upon for each of the structures. Then we will need to reimagine society to enable it to accomplish those new goals. Fortunately, because the foundations of each of the structures are relatively simple, the changes that need to be implemented are also relatively simple. The challenge is to stay focused; to not let the small stuff distract us from acting to accomplish big new goals ... and of course, it's all small stuff when considered within the context of what's to come if we fail to change or ways. So, let's consider how the existing structure of commerce works, remembering that it is driven to grow.

CORPORATIONS AND COMMERCE

For hundreds of thousands of years, individuals were free to do as they pleased because most were self-reliant, living apart from others. However, that freedom was shed as communities formed and people became reliant on others. Existing systems of governance and commerce developed during periods of transition from independent living conditions to the community. As such, they remain rooted in a past within which some individuals still want the absolute freedom to do as they please, even if their actions harm others or the environment. Although rules and regulations exist to hold most of us responsible for harmful actions, rulers operate under a separate set of rules within which they avoid responsibility for harms they direct when taken in the name of an imaginary entity like a nation, or within systems of commerce through another imaginary entity, the corporation.

Thousands of years ago, as the Roman Republic and Empire grew, huge public works projects were needed to support growing populations and armies. Massive road construction projects and aqueduct systems on scales never before attempted had to be built. Expanding armies needed weaponry, clothing, transportation, and provisions. Developing cities needed paved streets, water services, markets, housing, temples, and public forums. Each of these projects required a substantial workforce of professionals skilled in many disciplines. Instead of hiring thousands of new employees, Roman governments negotiated contracts with individual craftsmen to perform some public benefit service.

Over time, associations of similarly skilled craftsmen created loosely knit entities called guilds and colleges. Members held regular meetings where differences in wages offered for similar services became both apparent and points of conflict. To address this inequality, members selected a representative to negotiate contracts on their behalf. Governmental employees eventually acknowledged the efficiency of setting a uniform wage for similarly skilled tradesmen within a particular guild or college, which became recognized as legal entities. These entities were empowered to secure contracts on behalf of their members. In essence, they became the first trade unions. Equal pay for equal service was the lesson learned over 2000 years ago. Although some evidence exists to suggest that these associations and their investors received a degree of limited liability under public works contracts, that can't be confirmed. So, it can't be said that these entities were the progenitors of the modern corporation.

The Roman Empire failed about 1500 years ago and with it went the concept of legal entities empowered to act on behalf of their members. European societies entered the Dark Ages and took a deep and prolonged step backward. Urban life disappeared. Intellectual progress was nonexistent. Warfare was rampant. Brute force ruled and, over the next 1,100 years, there is little reference to the concept of the corporation in medieval law.[106]

THE RISE OF THE MODERN CORPORATION

England, 1600 AD. To compete with Dutch spice merchants bringing salt, tea, cotton, silk, opium, and other raw materials from India and China, the British government issued a charter that formed what would become one of the most powerful business ventures ever, the (British) East India Company (EIC). In 1602, the Dutch government issued a similar charter forming the Dutch East India Company (DEIC). These two companies are the progenitors of the modern corporation.

One of the most creative and enduring attributes of the corporate entity is its ability to raise substantial sums of money by selling small pieces of itself, which spreads financial risk without increasing investor liability. In anticipation of heavy demand to acquire a legally recognized ownership interest in a corporation which would be held in common with others, entrepreneurs imagined and created the first functional marketplaces to exchange ownership interests for money (the first stock exchanges). These exchanges provided open market liquidity for investors. Values were set and a piece of paper was created (the stock certificate) certifying that the holder owned a share of company assets (known as stock). The individual shareholder became entitled to share in company profits based upon whatever percentage of the entity they owned. This marked the first time in history that the average person could own a piece of a venture granted monopolistic trading opportunities.

Both the DEIC and EIC raised vast sums of money through stock and bond sales, enabling them to build huge fleets of ships, employ hundreds of thousands to conduct trade in silk, cotton, spices, and other exotic goods not available elsewhere. Each became a veritable empire.

Between 1602 and 1796, the DEIC established colonies, minted its own money, negotiated treaties, imprisoned and executed convicts, all while conducting the most profitable business venture of its time, averaging 18 percent annual dividends for over two hundred years.

Across the channel, between 1757 and 1858, utilizing a private military twice as large as that of the British Empire, the EIC also governed large areas of India while conducting half the world's trade.

Both companies became transcontinental employers operating under laws that virtually guaranteed monopolistic status in trade at global scales. Each has been credited with contributing to the perfection of the modern-day multinational corporate entity through development of corporate identities and cultures, corporate finance, and financial capitalism.

Like nations, there is nothing real about corporations. They do not exist without people working together to accomplish a common purpose. It is the name and the purpose that identifies it. Using hierarchical structures to organize workforces, each establishes rules and regulations that govern what their employees do in the name of the entity. And, like heads of state, corporate rulers have laws crafted to shield themselves from personal responsibility for harms their decisions ignite.

Corporations exist to produce and deliver the things we need and want. Their goals are to grow as large as they can as fast as they can. Growth is incentivized by the allure of profits. The bigger an entity gets, the more money it generates which is good and bad. The good is that it enables the venture to create new and more efficient ways of doing things: progress. The bad is that this activity empowers operators to influence rule-makers to craft laws that limit both corporate and management responsibility for the things they do, which inevitably hurts their workers, consumers, and the environment. And in a very real way, such laws retard human progress.

Regulating to benefit a few financially powerful interests hurts us all. Enacting rules that insulate decision-makers from liability for harmful acts promotes regressive, irresponsible business practices. Today, entities are allowed (even incentivized) to flood world markets with highly profitable products that harm the consumer. Tobacco products are the classic example. In a more responsibly run society, harmful products with little socially redeemable value would have limited availability; but ours are not responsibly run societies, are they?

Corporate mergers are the sign of this time. Bigger is better translates to growth in no uncertain terms. In capitalistic societies, allegiances of management are owed to shareholders, not to the societies which permit their existence and to whom they serve. So, whatever it takes to generate the largest profit as fast as possible is the chosen course.

Growth is a blind factor. It directs us to barrel ahead without looking ahead, blindly accepting that it is a good thing at a moment in time when it clearly is not. So, we allow the allure of profits to incentivize growth which blinds us to the results, harming us all.

ENABLED BY MONEY

Money is the tool that enables trade, delivers profits, and empowers rulers. As industries grow and profits mount, operators use their financial might to incentivize politicians to write favorable (or prevent unfavorable) rules and regulations. The result? Laws around the world grant corporate owners and executives: freedom from responsibility for harms that most others would be jailed for committing; limited exposure to socially protective controls that might reduce profits; and the ability to create zero-tax havens for corporate entities and their owners, depriving nations of tax revenues.

TO CONTROL NATIONS

"As the nation-state was the primary entity at the dawn of the modern age, so the giant corporations are all-powerful in the twentieth-century world. Unfortunately for society, far too many giant corporations have abused this power in their relations with their

workers, their stockholders, their consumers, and the public at large. They have also abused our environment, defrauded the government, and exploited the developing nations of the Third World. In their actions, they have even abused the very democratic process that has given the opportunity to achieve this power."[107]

Corporations control nations. A recent but seemingly insignificant example of just that is set out in a July 8, 2018, *New York Times* article titled: "Opposition to Breast-Feeding Resolution by US Stuns World Health Officials."[108] The resolution by Ecuador was to "encourage breast-feeding." It "was expected to be approved quickly and easily" because it was based "on decades of research" confirming "that mother's milk is healthiest for children." The resolution proposed that "countries should strive to limit the inaccurate or misleading marketing of breast milk substitutes."

This resolution was intended to protect babies by suggesting that nations prohibit corporations from misleading their parents into believing advertising that manufactured formulas were better than a mother's milk. However, rulers of the infant formula industry asserted their power over US officials who then threatened to "unleash punishing trade measures and withdraw crucial military aid" from little Ecuador if it refused to drop the resolution, which it quickly did. Fortunately, the resolution was reintroduced by too-big-to-bully Russia and quickly approved.

Unfortunately, economic systems designed to generate profits create a vicious cycle that incentivizes bad decision-making at all governing levels as exemplified above by the power wielded by just one small industry over an international governing body. Now, imagine the political sway that oil and gas, pharmaceutical, chemical, and multinational agricultural industries exercise over governing officials worldwide. It's simply overwhelming. Profits over humanity. Corporations over nations. Common themes played out the world over.

Corporations are focused mini-governments with similar hierarchical structures. They provide a workplace for coordinated efforts to solve a common problem, provide a specific service, or produce a particular product. And, for over 400 years, people working together within corporate structures have used their imaginations and collective creativity to achieve the truly extraordinary. In the process they have also abused billions to secure the highest level of profits. And they continue to do so with impunity.

Sweatshops, child labor, death squad assassinations of union leaders or vocal opponents, company towns, forced migrant labor camps, extortion, unprotected exposure to toxic chemicals, union-busting, withheld wages, unpaid overtime, unpaid labor, and modern-day slavery. The list of human rights violations carried out within corporate systems that shield the individual perpetrators from liability is nearly endless and provides more than substantial justification to fundamentally change how they operate.

Using strategies developed over centuries and the financial might that comes from operating in near monopolistic systems, corporate ruler's willingness to abuse their fellow humans is truly staggering. The International Labor Rights Forum warns that "corporations carry out some of the most horrific human rights abuses of modern times, but it is increasingly difficult to hold them to account. Economic globalization and the rise of transnational corporate power have created a favorable climate for corporate human rights abusers."[109]

But it is not the corporation that exploits humanity, is it? Nope, that trophy goes to the individuals who operate them, the rulers. They get away with it because society has been duped into accepting the corporation as a thing, which it most certainly is not.

It was long ago recognized that for societies to function, rules and regulations had to be established and adhered to. Evolved societies recognize that to maintain lasting order, rules must be applied uniformly, without exception, across the broad spectrum of society to enable the attainment of socially desirable goals founded in morality and carried out with the highest ethicality. Unfortunately, laws today follow the dictates of a bygone era. Most allow the barbarian culture to dominate a humanity that cries out for a civilized one.

THE EXCEPTIONS TO THE RULES

Corporations have neither bodies to be punished, nor souls to be condemned. They therefore do as they like.
Edward, the First Baron Thurlow

Individuals operating modern corporations have become so powerful that they have forced society to endow corporations (and by extrapolation, the people who own and operate them) with rights superior to those of everyone else. In perhaps the most perverse twist of social logic ever, we, the people, have allowed rulers to craft laws that allow decision-makers who direct harmful actions in the name of a government or corporation to do so with impunity. And worse, by allowing these people to insulate themselves from personal liability, we encourage a morally corrupt and socially irresponsible society.

They call it "sovereign immunity" to justify insulation from liability for authorizing human rights violations in the name of governance, or the "corporate shield" to justify insulation from personal liability for authorizing environmentally or socially destructive acts in the name of a corporation. These are the very individuals who should be held to the highest moral and ethical standards, not the lowest. Yet, the higher up the status ladder one elevates, the lower their level of social responsibility becomes. Theirs are the exceptions to the rules, which begs the question: how do we change the rules to create a better society? The answers follow, but first, let's look at how a few of the exceptions play out in the corporate world.

Pick up a newspaper, search the internet, read a book about corporate misbehavior, or speak with neighbors of manufacturing facilities to understand how truly harmful corporate activities can be. Nations doing the same are no different. The problems spring from operating business ventures within profit-driven systems designed for another era. For over 150 years the fossil fuel industry has provided inexpensive energy resources that helped usher in the industrial revolution and fuel tremendous growth. That was then. Today, technology provides solutions capable of transforming the world's energy infrastructure to 100 percent clean, renewable, zero-emissions systems by 2050.[110]

Simply exchanging one existing energy production system for another can be transformative. But in profit-driven capitalistic systems, rulers resist even the most beneficial change out of fear of temporary profit reductions, and the results have been devastating. There is perhaps no better example than the more than thirty-year misinformation campaign waged by fossil fuel executives to cast doubt over scientists' warnings (including their own) that fossil fuel consumption was fundamentally responsible for global warming. Theirs is one of the most harmfully deceptive campaigns ever waged.

From Exxon's own records and employee statements as reported by the *Los Angeles Times* and others, Exxon's president, CEO, Board of Directors, and managers directed and funded a massive, decades long disinformation campaign that first denied fossil fuel linkage to global warming, then blurred the issues to delay or prevent regulations forcing them to change their ways. The harms from this level of deceit are massive. Tens of thousands of lives have already been lost with millions, perhaps billions to follow. And, environmental destruction is accelerating at an unprecedented pace as Earth's ability to support life dwindles.

According to the *Los Angeles Times*, in 1989, Exxon's Manager of Science and Strategy Development put Exxon's Board of Directors on notice that: "Data confirm that greenhouse gases are increasing in the atmosphere" and that "Fossil fuels contribute most of the CO_2," and that "scientists generally agreed gases released by burning fossil fuels could raise global temperatures significantly by the middle of the twenty-first century (between 2.7 and 8.1°F) causing glaciers to melt and sea levels to rise, 'with generally negative consequences.'"[111]

Just as global consensus seemed to be taking hold that regulations were needed to reduce CO_2 emissions from fossil fuel burning, an Exxon public affairs manager prepared an "internal draft memo" titled "The Greenhouse Effect" that "laid out what he called the 'Exxon Position.'" Toward the end of the document after an analysis that noted scientific consensus on the role fossil fuels play in global warming, he wrote that the company should "emphasize the uncertainty" (*Los Angeles Times*, 10/25/15), which is exactly what Exxon did, for decades. At that critical juncture when responsible decisions should have been made, Exxon operatives chose otherwise.

> 'There was a fork in the road. They had the opportunity to make a decision to go one way or the other,' said Hoffert, an Exxon consultant in the 1980s and Prof. Emeritus of physics at New York University. 'If Exxon had listened to its scientists and endorsed our research - and not started that campaign - it would have had, in my opinion, an enormous impact.'[112]

Even as global warming climatic impacts became visibly apparent and public awareness mounted, Exxon management continued to deny responsibility. In 2015, facing mounting accusations that it had misled the public about fossil fuel induced climate change, management issued a challenge to the public to "read all of these documents and make up your own mind." Two Harvard University scientists did just that. After studying Exxon's internal and external communications, they published the results stating,

> In other words, our study showed that ExxonMobil misled the public about climate science and its implications for decades.[113]

Exxon responded by attacking the validity of their report, prompting this reply,

In sum, ExxonMobil is now misleading the public about its history of misleading the public. This is just the latest round in a long and troubling record of doubt-mongering and misdirection by the fossil fuel industry and libertarian think tanks in response to the scientific evidence of climate change. It's become a familiar pattern. We published science; ExxonMobil offered spin.[114]

But it wasn't Exxon misleading the public, was it? No, it was the people who make the decisions in the name of the entity that were. They chose pathways of deception because capitalistic systems incentivize them to do so, in part by ensuring they cannot be held responsible for the damage their deceptive practices create, and in part by offering them compensation packages that build with profits. Assuming the facts are as stated in the numerous investigatory articles and reports, the decision-makers are the ones who have harmed us. They are the ones who should be held responsible for the death, destruction, and countless misery that will follow for centuries. They chose recklessness over responsibility, as greed trumps morality within the capitalistic systems of this day.

GREED TRUMPS MORALITY

For thousands of years people have known that it is wrong to deceive others for personal benefit, but that is exactly what fossil fuel managers appear to have done for decades, even though in the US any person making or directing a material misrepresentation of a fact to induce another to act (or not) in reliance of the representation can be held liable for all losses suffered. That is the law of the land, but to date no Exxon executive has been held personally, financially, or socially responsible for the harms they ignited.

In England, it is a crime to intentionally make a false statement of fact for personal gain resulting in some harm, but no Exxon official has been prosecuted for the alleged crimes, as greed trumps morality within the barbaric structures of this time. At that proverbial fork in the road when responsible decisions could have led society down a better path, Exxon managers knowing full well that they would not be held personally responsible for associated harms, appear to have directed actions that continue to damage Earth's support systems, accelerate the rate of global extinctions and cause grave human suffering. Why do they continue to act this way? Because we allow them to.

PROFITS OVER HUMANITY

Fossil fuel companies could have chosen to invest in the development and delivery of clean energy systems in the early 1980s when they became aware of the harms from using fossil fuels as our primary energy source. They could have preserved the same long-term profit potential as source energy producers simply by changing *how* they produce energy. But instead, they kept producing energy from fossil fuels to a large degree because there was no penalty for doing so. Pick the industry: tobacco, pharmaceutical, energy, agriculture, transportation, technology, or any other; it doesn't matter which one; they are all bound up within the same structure that demands profits over humanity.

Although they bring us amazing things, they come at a cost, both socially and environmentally. To enhance profits corporate elites have swayed the regulators away from requiring them to factor environmental impact costs into profit-taking calculations. Regulations simply absolve corporate entities of the responsibility of preventing or in many cases paying to remediate the harms they caused. The game is rigged to enhance and prolong profit taking from antiquated technologies, and to limit the development of new, competing technologies.

Resource extraction industries like oil, gas, mining, and timber producers trigger extreme levels of environmental destruction. They operate the world over. Their motives are to take what they can, as fast as they can, then get out with little to no lingering financial responsibility to cure the harms they perpetuate. Legal entities are formed for the sole purpose of extracting a resource and when the resource is exhausted, operators abandon the site and escape financial liability for the harms they cause by dissolving the entity or filing bankruptcy. Profits have already been distributed to management and shareholders. Frequently, nothing remains but vast wastelands contaminated with toxic chemicals. And the burden to clean up the mess, if that's even possible, flows to the public.[115]

Innumerable examples of such irresponsible behaviors exist everywhere. Capitalism has failed us for many reasons, not the least of which is because it insulates decision-makers from personal liability from harms that they profit from.

WHEN THERE'S NO PENALTY FOR RECKLESSNESS

When the interests of the decision-making elite . . . clash with the interests of the rest of society . . . if the elite can insulate themselves from the consequences of their actions, they are likely to do things that profit themselves, regardless of whether those actions hurt everybody else . . .
Jared Diamond.[116]

Diamond cites example after example of inflexible, short-sighted societies run by rulers so inextricably tied to custom, past practices and the lure of wealth, power and prestige, that they led their cultures down the rabbit hole of collapse and in some cases, extinction. Their societies were microcosms of today's global society within which irresponsible behaviors proliferate.

Because we are a global society of beings, the consequences of our decisions are cumulative, the impacts, global. Practices that prefer profit-taking for the benefit of a few over the good of the many place decision-makers in positions of extreme conflict, and us at their mercy.

Decisions made by individuals at the upper echelons of society determine the course of humanity. Theirs are positions that demand the highest levels of social responsibility. But laws that insulate them from liability for harmful actions they direct eviscerate that responsibility. Without personal liability, decision-makers have little incentive to act with any level of social or environmental responsibility, particularly if doing so would diminish profits or restrict their powers over society.

But what if society held decision-makers responsible for the foreseeable consequences of their actions?

Would Exxon managers have made the same decisions at that proverbial fork in the road if the rules of a global society held all decision-makers to the highest levels of responsibility, rather than lowest? Would its managers have (allegedly) covered up their own scientific reports and authorized campaigns of denial and misdirection if they knew they could be jailed and lose everything for partaking in such monumental deceptions? What do you think?

It becomes a whole lot easier for those who head society to make forward-looking decisions designed to anticipate and avoid problems when conflicts of interest are removed and responsibility is imposed. Impressively, Diamond recognized what should be obvious to all, that "failures to solve perceived problems because of conflicts of interest between the elite and the masses are much less likely in societies where the elite cannot insulate themselves from the consequences of their actions."[117]

We should hold all who stand at the pinnacle of society to the highest moral and ethical standards rather than the lowest, shouldn't we? And we can, but will we? We have imagined incredible systems to facilitate commerce. But we have designed them so poorly that we seem incapable of changing them. Even with the Apocalypse staring us in the face, we can't seem to choose right over wrong. Why? Because our systems create conflicts of interests that incentive profiteering over humanity.

We use a creature of our imagination, money, to enable systems that incentivize growth, through another creature of our imagination, profits. As so aptly stated by John Maynard Keynes, "The engine that drives enterprise is not thrift but profit."[118] Another word for thrift would be efficiency. But, our systems of commerce stand upon outdated principles that incentivize profit-taking instead of efficiency. That we can change, but not until we change our goals.

As a whole, humans exhibit little purpose other than to grow, consume, and profit thereby. We are so caught up in the consumption process that is necessary to sustain growth that we have allowed the lure of profits to override the rational necessity of regulating how we do most everything. Now, we are paying the price. With little ability to self-regulate, we are destroying the very support systems that have sustained us from the beginning. We design our systems to disregard things that are either inconvenient or profit limiting. We build in planned obsolescence so that a light bulb, water heater, tech tool, car, or even clothing will be replaced sooner rather than later to generate more profits.

And, we allow companies to operate "profitably" by enabling them to disregard costs associated with preventing or cleaning up environmental impacts from inefficient production and delivery systems. We make this possible by ensuring that there are no personal penalties for the harms corporate operatives ignite. Decision-makers thus operate as freely and recklessly as they choose. The result is a global society on the verge of ruin because, as conservative commentator George Will wrote, *"When there's no penalty for recklessness, recklessness proliferates."*

And so, we charge recklessly ahead into a future certain to be less stable as resources are consumed and environments destroyed because our systems incentivize rulers to do whatever they want, however they want, to get what they want: money and power. They are enabled to do so because they control the one structure that controls them all.

10

THE FINANCIAL STRUCTURE

One brilliant concept is so fundamentally simple that it has been successfully used to enable society for 9,000 years. Money. It is its inherent simplicity that has allowed it to become so intrinsically interwoven into the fabric of society, and therein lies the problem. Because almost everything we do is dependent upon it, the few who control it have created insanely complicated systems to maintain their control over it by obscuring its true nature, making the Financial Structure, the one structure that controls them all.

THE ENABLING STRUCTURE

At its heart, the Financial Structure exists to enable society. It is the enabling structure. Money is its tool. That is all it is. Currency was originally imagined to enable trade. Enable is the operative word. Money enables society to function. Today, although it is still the enabling tool of choice, its underlying unspoken purpose has changed. It is now used as a tool to both enable and to control society.

Who gets to use money and at what cost is determined behind closed doors by a few whose acts are shrouded in secrecy. Within the gilded towers of the global financial structure, a few individuals in conjunction with heads of state and corporate elite determine the fate of humanity. Broadly speaking, theirs is the power to end all human suffering. Instead, they choose to extract nearly limitless profits while perpetuating the single largest fraud ever committed against humankind.

The concept of money is sublimely simple. Its simplicity has allowed it to remain the singular tool upon which the global financial structure is based. People lie, cheat, steal, and kill to possess it. They play with it, gamble with it, use it daily, hoard it, worry over the lack of it, and use it to control billions. It is said to be the root of all evil, yet every human structure and system relies on it, rendering each of these realms a subject of potential malfeasance.

Making money available to enable a vibrant, civilized society engaged in the quest to understand all aspects of life should be the primary function of the Financial Structure. It is not. At its heart, this is the simplest of all structures. Unfortunately, its operatives have spawned an insanely complicated and secretive set of systems from which they control the flow of money and extract enormous profits enabling a handful to become ridiculously wealthy while depriving billions of life essentials. Fortunately, this structure needs not be run this way.

Knowledge of what money is and how it is used should be commonplace. It is not. Instead, its creation and use are held secret. Knowledge is power, making it critically important to understand the basics of the existing Financial Structure so that it can be replaced by one capable of propelling humanity into a future of limitless possibility. Armed with the knowledge of what money is and a willingness to agree to use it differently, we can enable a new form of humanity, one destined for the stars in search of understanding of the wonders of this most incredible universe. So, let's gather the knowledge we need by coming to understand what money is.

MONEY

Money is a creature of human imagination. That, is all it is. It can take any form and be anything that we agree represents some level of value. Initially, it was used to facilitate the exchange of one thing for another thing. Today, it does that and more. It is used to either limit or enable certain aspects of society.

ANIMALS, CROPS, AND BEER

Some 9,000 years ago, as our ancestors were forming the first threads of modern society, domesticated animals and grains were used as a form of payment for the goods or services of another. A cow, a camel, or a goat had agreed upon values in trade.

Five thousand years ago, Egyptians used bread, beer, grain, meat, and cloth in exchange for labor and materials. To operate their society, they set standard recipes for each loaf of bread and measures of volume for beer to be used in exchange for labor. These practices lasted 2,000 years, during which a basic daily wage might consist of four loaves of bread and a jug or two of beer, which was just enough to keep a family alive. Skilled workers who brought home multiples of the standard wage might overhear a neighbor comment, "Wow, that's a lot of dough!" or "That's a lot of bread you've got there," meaning, a lot of money.

SEA SHELLS

For over 3,200 years, the beautifully polished shell of the Cowry Sea Snail was used as a form of money within certain Chinese, Indian, and African societies. The Cowry is believed to be the first advancement in the evolution of the form of money, as it had no direct use that could be made of it (being neither food nor clothing nor weaponry, although it was often used as jewelry).

The Cowry grew abundantly in the Indian Ocean and was used extensively within trading networks throughout Asia and Africa. In remote regions of western Africa, "shell money" was legal tender until the early twentieth century. Interestingly, shell money has been used for thousands of years on almost every continent, including the Americas.

METALS

Around 3,000 years ago metals began a transition into the preferred form of money. Unlike earlier forms of money, metals were neither perishable nor fragile and could be individualized. The earliest forms of metallic money came from China and were known as "tool money" because they were stylized as small knives and spades. Round coins came into circulation approximately 2,700 years ago in China, India, and other areas around the Aegean Sea. The first modern coins were struck 2,500 years ago in the Mediterranean region. These coins, made of precious metals such as gold, silver, and bronze, were stylized with gods and emperors to confirm authenticity.

Metals as money have so successfully stood the test of time because they were non-perishable and standards were easily agreed upon. Weights as a measure were set, content was readily verifiable, and supplies were limited yielding a perception of stability. Collectively, metals established a uniform and stable valuation system that would be well-recognized across broad trading markets over vast expanses of time.

Around 600 years ago, with agricultural innovations in irrigation, soil enrichment, and animal husbandry, came access to a great variety of food and fabrics which, with the help of a standard form of currency, ushered in a global trading economy. Trade routes developed across continents and oceans. Cities grew and multiplied. The Indian Ocean Basin became a focus of commercial interchange. Silk Road routes expanded across Asia, Africa, and Europe. Great caravans carried tea, spices, silk, cotton, and other products into the expanding world of commerce. Traveling ancient routes, traders established an exchange of cultural, scientific, and technological knowledge unrivaled in history. And gold became the generally accepted medium of exchange. Its value was stable and definable. Its availability, limited.

Metals remain highly valued. They trade on global markets and as always, their value is based upon perception and agreement. Until 1970, gold maintained an extremely stable and reliable measure of value because its price was regulated. That changed in 1971 when the US deregulated it. The result? Between 1971 and 1974 its trading value shot up from $39 per ounce to $184 per ounce, an increase of 470 percent. Was there anything different about the availability of the metal or the nature of its content sufficient to cause such an extreme increase in valuation? No. What changed? Our perception of how it could be used.

Modern financial systems have elevated risk and speculation to an art form. Where once metals were used simply as a medium of exchange, within modern financial systems, for some, they are gamblers tools; and their valuations fluctuate wildly as a result. After the financial system meltdown of 2008, the price of gold shot up to $1,900 per ounce only to plunge below $800 a few years later. Today, due to perceptions of financial market instabilities, gold is valued around $1,800 per ounce. Nothing about it has changed except how we use and perceive it. Where once it enabled trade, today, it enables speculators.

TREES

Paper as a form of money first arrived on the scene in China about 1,200 years ago in the form of banknotes. This currency from trees lasted about 600 years and collapsed due to "oversupply," which led to a loss of "confidence" in its stability, resulting in an inflationary spiral, devaluation, and failure as a currency (events which have repeated themselves time and again within most societies around the world).

In feudal England about 900 years ago when paper was rare, a wooden stick notched to designate the amount of taxes owed was known as a "tally stick." The tally stick (used in England for 700 years) was often sold or used as payment for services by the government, allowing the recipient to use the stick to collect taxes owed. Society recognized that a notched "stick of wood" had value beyond that of just a piece of a tree, making it a form of money.

Nearly 600 years ago in European centers of commerce, paper money emerged in the form of "bills of exchange," which facilitated trade over great distances, avoiding the extremely dangerous practice of traveling with large amounts of gold. Bills of exchange were essentially IOUs directing someone to pay a certain amount of money by a certain date or upon satisfaction of a particular condition. Payment upon presentment of the bill of exchange was guaranteed by third parties, establishing an early form of credit. To facilitate this exchange, a few people imagined something new: a "bank," which became a place where financial transactions could take place.

Approximately 400 years ago, paper took on another form of money with the advent of another creature of the human imagination, the corporation. Individuals formed imaginary entities and sold stock certificates to raise money to operate businesses. Stock certificates (writing on paper) give the impression of something real, representing ownership of some percentage of a corporation which entitles the holder to a share of profits. Stock certificates are transferable and increase in value as corporate profits increase, making them a form of money.

If a corporation has promise, owners who don't want to dilute their ownership by selling more stock may choose to raise needed money by borrowing it. Corporate borrowings are documented on paper as another form of money called a "bond," which is a transferable promissory note stating the corporation's obligation to repay a certain amount of money over a certain amount of time with interest.

To make corporate obligations in the forms of stocks and bonds liquid, "exchanges" were created (stock and bond markets) where people would "exchange" corporate obligations, solidifying stocks and bonds as nothing more than forms of tradable paper representing value: money.

Most of us think of money as the paper notes we carry around in our pockets that are issued by governments or their associated "reserve banks" as "legal tender." It is. But the predominant form of the world's modern money is created by banks via loans to consumers, corporations, and nations. Loans create debts which is the most abundant form of money today.

DEBT MONEY

Today, most money is created as if by magic when banks make loans. Let's call it what it is: "debt money." Its creation immediately ensnares the borrower in debt. Here's how the process works:

> "Banks create money. That is what they are for . . . The manufacturing process to make money consists of making an entry in a book. That is all . . . Each and every time a Bank makes a loan, new Bank credit is created - brand new money,"[119] said Graham Towers, Governor of the Bank of Canada.

> "When a bank makes a loan, it simply adds to the borrower's deposit account in the bank by the amount of the loan. The money is not taken from anyone else's deposit; it was not previously paid into the bank by anyone. It's new money, created by the bank for the use of the borrower," said Robert B. Anderson, Secretary of the Treasury under President Eisenhower.[120]

The art of the deal is baked into the process. The financial elite first had to gain control over the right to manufacture money, which they most certainly have. Then, they had to make it seem like a privilege to "qualify" to borrow money, which by their terms, it most certainly appears to be. Finally, they had to create vast networks for loan deployment which the banks and their banking systems most certainly are.

To ensure their scheme for global domination of the money supply remains successful, the elites made the borrowing seem like something really serious is taking place, so bankers make a big fuss about the process, enshrouding it in mystery and making it seem like so much more than it is. Borrowers have to qualify to borrow something that bankers make up with a few strokes on a computer keypad. Credit reports, loan committees, behind closed-door meetings, and contracts with onerous terms legally obligating borrowers to repay the money "borrowed" with "interest" are expected if one is to enter their lair.

The success of their efforts is undeniable. A substantial percentage of the human population including most governing and commercial entities have joined the ranks of a massive and growing social class: the debtors.

The Debtors

For nearly 9,000 years, money's fundamental purpose was as a store of value to enable trade. Although it still enables, most capital is now deployed in a perverse twist of the original purpose: to enslave and control.

As of the end of 2020, global debt exceeded $280 trillion dollars of which roughly 20 percent is owed by consumers, 30 percent by corporations, 25 percent by governments, and most worrisome, 25 percent by financial institutions.[121] Nearly everyone in the developed world and many in undeveloped countries contribute to the trillions of dollars of interest paid to lenders every year. The world is drowning in debt. Before we explore what that means, there is one final form of money to consider.

Digital Assets / Crypto Currencies

The newest forms of money are the exceptions to the historic rule that only governments and banks get to create it. Digital assets, including cryptocurrencies, are available to almost anyone who has access to the internet. One major attraction of the digital asset universe is that it exists solely within the ether of the internet as 'decentralized' forms of money. That means they exist on platforms independent from the centralized monetary systems historically owned and operated by financial institutions and nations. Like debt money, digital assets and crypto currencies once again confirm the fact that the form money takes is solely a creature of the human imagination.

Conceptualized in the late 1990s, crypto currencies first came on the scene in 2009 with the creation of Bitcoin. Since then, hundreds of virtual currencies have appeared. Soon, multinational corporations like Amazon, Facebook, and JP Morgan along with nations will be rolling out their own digital currencies.

In addition, smaller companies and startups have begun creating digital 'tokens' (assets) which are used to reward brand loyalty or to act as a form of early capitalization. What makes this concept interesting is that digital tokens are accessible to a broad spectrum of investors who might not otherwise qualify for or have access to venture capital funds that invest in startups. Another attraction is the fact that globally connected trading platforms are developing to enable commerce in ways never before imagined. And as these platforms mature, they are becoming safer and more secure to transact on, as blockchain technologies expand and new forms of insurance are offered. We look deeper into how iterations of these new forms of money may help form the basis of an evolved Financial Structure within Books V and VI.

MONEY - THE TAKEAWAY

You should now have a pretty good understanding of money. It can take whatever form we want it to, and be used however we agree to use it. When we consider how to enable fundamental change in the ways within which we operate society, keep this section in mind. Now, we turn our attention to *how* money is used within the Financial Structure so that we can gather a deeper sense of why this structure must change.

A STRUCTURE OF SERVITUDE

Most money exists as debt money created as loans. Loans are "obligations to pay" originating within systems of servitude little different from slavery. That may seem like a pretty harsh statement, but this is our reality. If you want to buy a house or car or furniture or clothing or food or if you must undergo a lifesaving medical procedure, you will likely have to borrow to pay for it, and when you do you become "obligated" to repay the loan with interest, often at outrageous rates stretched over decades.

It has become nearly impossible to live without debt. And most have been conditioned to be thankful for the privilege of getting it, unwittingly entering realms of financial servitude. How so? Repayment funds have to be *earned*. Suppose you borrow $200,000 to buy a home and pay it off over 30 years at 5.5 percent interest. Over that period, you will have paid the bank $410,000, which doubles the cost of purchase. You paid an extra $210,000 of 'interest money' (their profits) for the *privilege* of borrowing something made up out of thin air with a few keystrokes on a computer.

Now ask yourself how many life hours will I spend to earn $210,000 after taxes and other expenses? Your banker took a few minutes to create the money for the loan. In return, you will most likely spend thousands of hours working to repay just the interest portion of the loan. Now, add your time spent with the billions of additional hours spent by others working to pay trillions in profits to the bankers every year, and the picture clarifies. Are a few hours of some banker's time really worth thousands of your own? Of course not. This is what modern-day financial servitude looks like.

Today, salaries of the average person are held artificially low in inflationary environments (meaning everything is expected to and does cost more each year, a subject we will return to) preventing most from accumulating enough money as savings to buy most things. So, if you want or need something of substance, most of us are forced to borrow, which quite literally obligates us to the bankers by the conditions of their loans. That, is financial servitude.

Businesses borrow trillions of dollars annually passing the production and interest costs on to consumers, meaning that lenders extract profits from our labors nearly every time we purchase something.

And governments borrow trillions of dollars annually as well. Because taxes fund governments, lenders profit from our labors with every tax payment made to cover a governmental interest obligation. Those interest payments rob us of services that good systems of governance should otherwise provide. For example:

> The vast amount of money paid to Wall Street by America's cities, counties, and states has profound impacts on our lives and local economies. Most citizens don't know about these hidden costs - they just pay them. It's a staggering amount. Over 1 trillion dollars flow from US taxpayer pockets into private Wall Street hands every year in the form of interest payments on bonds, loans, fees, and financial product costs which have resulted in:
>
> - School closures
> - Lost jobs
> - Life-long student debt
> - Reduced public services and infrastructure
> - Privatized public assets, and
> - Stymied local businesses who can't get affordable funding to grow.
>
> Wall Street extractions from the public purse seriously hurt America's strength and in just a few years will consume one-third of our economy's production in interest payments.[122]

Modern banking systems are crafted to serve the financial elite. Different systems (publicly owned banks for instance) would be less predatory and better serve society, but the stranglehold the financial elite have over government officials prohibits most alternatives.

The reality is that everything we do in a productive society is done in service of each other; we fix teeth, pick up trash, remove cancerous growths, educate children, put out fires, drill wells, work on assembly lines, build solar panels, and make children's' games. We help each other by providing things people need and want. Service to help others is good. Servitude is not.

DESIGNED TO ENSLAVE

The Financial Structure is the largest, most powerfully pervasive monopolistic structure of servitude ever created. And it grows more powerful by the day.

> Banking was conceived in iniquity and was born in sin. The bankers own the earth ... take away from them the power to create money and all the great fortunes like mine will disappear and they ought to disappear, for this would be a happier and better world to live in. But, if you wish to remain the slaves of bankers and pay the cost of your own slavery, let them continue to create money.[123] Sir Josiah Stamp, director, Bank of England.

Now, lock onto this fact: The only thing in your life that is uniquely yours, is the time you are given to live your life, your Life Hours. Then, answer this question: Do the people of this world receive fair value from lenders for the billions of Life Hours given every year in exchange for the privilege of using something that they control which requires so little of them to create? Just as the slave owners of yesterday had to give a little back to their slaves to live, the financial elite do the same. This is subtle.

We are not free to use other financial systems to conduct our affairs; there are none. And everything by design is so expensive that we are forced to borrow to live, and pay profits to borrow. Interest payments come from our Life Hours burned. In exchange for use of their money, they take a hugely disproportionate percentage of our Life Hours (codified as money earned from our labors), using accounting systems with lending guidelines designed to maximize how much they can take, leaving us just enough Life Hours to otherwise earn a basic living. This may not seem like slavery because elaborate systems obscure that fact, but slavery it is.

Wherever your obligations come from, once you've become indebted to them, they own a piece of you. And because the financial elite set the borrowing rules, escape is not easy. If you fall behind in meeting your financial obligations, they will track you down and take your home, your car, your money, and even your dignity if you let them.

Under better systems, these very same Life Hours would be used for social benefit rather than banker profit. And, since it costs little to create money, why not create it to enable society as originally intended, rather than to enslave the many and enrichen a few? We will discuss how soon. For now, recognize that the financial elite are predators of the highest order, although their predation is less obvious and more sophisticated than warrior predators. For example, they fund platforms that limit government income, making it nearly impossible to provide necessary services. Strapped for cash, governments borrow to meet social needs, increasing operational costs with ever-mounting interest obligations.

Over the past ten years the US Government paid more than $2 trillion in interest on its debt. Trillions more have been paid by state and local governing entities to cover borrowing costs. In 2017, interest paid on the national debt was $458.5 billion. The US Office of Budget and Management estimated that by 2020 the Federal Government will be obligated to make annual interest payments in excess of $500 billion. Given recent tax cuts and increased borrowing, experts estimate that by 2020 "one-half of all personal income taxes will go to servicing the national debt," an amount that "would equal our Social Security obligations."[124]

We burn billions of our own Life Hours every year to earn money to pay taxes used to pay profits to debt masters who give back little in comparison to what they take. Theirs are systems of legalized theft within which they take our money without providing fair value in return, and they do it so well we barely notice. Theft by deception. For most, that is a crime. But not for the financial elite. Theft by deception is generally defined as the use of deception "to obtain control over the property or services of another."[125] That pretty much sums up how the Financial Structure operates.

But their plans run deeper still. They want to own and control most everything. They accomplish their goals in part by pushing tax reduction agendas while simultaneously promoting untethered governmental spending. Forced privatization of public assets is the result. Think Greece in 2015. Essential services - privatized. Public property - sold for pennies on the dollar to reduce debts. Severe austerity programs - implemented. And as a result, the people pay more for water, sewage, transportation, and healthcare than ever and receive less in the way of public services funded with their tax dollars.

With nations under their control, lenders see to it that laws are written that force the continued servitude of individual borrowers, even when they can no longer toil to earn money to repay debt obligations. Maybe they have grown too old, or lost their job, or became too sick to work. What follows? Foreclosures, asset seizures, bankruptcies, desperation, and despair. For some, suicide is the only way out after debt masters have taken everything. But even those extremes are not enough to meet their greed.

WHEN FAITH IS LOST

The Financial Structure exists because people have faith that the fruits of their labors, represented as money earned, will be safe when deposited within their systems and available when needed. Faith and belief are the only things that keep this structure afloat. But when faith is lost, these systems collapse and . . .

PANIC ENSUES

On 8 June, a Scottish banker ... shorted the collapsing Company's shares in the London markets. But a momentary bounce-back in the stock ruined his plans, and he skipped town £500,000 in debt. Much of this was owed to the Ayr Bank, which imploded. In less than three weeks, another 30 banks collapsed across Europe, bringing trade to a standstill. On July 15, the directors of the Company applied to the Bank of England for a £400,000 loan. Two weeks later, they wanted another £300,000. By August, the directors wanted a £1 million bailout. The news began leaking out and seemingly contrite executives, running from angry shareholders, faced furious Parliament members. By January, the terms of a comprehensive bailout were worked out ...[126]

The year was 1772 and the company was the British East India Company. Whether the year was 1772 or 2008, when faith is lost and belief in any of the financial systems crumbles, instability and fear spread rampantly throughout society. All it takes is the speculative failure of one large entity to trigger panic and extreme social disruption. Speculative systems are dangerous. Because every aspect of society is tied to and dependent on the stability of the Financial Structure, when it is allowed to operate games of chance, and when it is run by individuals whose primary contribution to society is to make money for themselves and their few wealthy clients, we are all at risk.

BILLIONS SUFFER - SOME DIE

The Financial Structure is extremely fragile. It is totally dependent upon another extremely fragile thing, the human psyche. Financial panics from stock market manipulations to failed banking practices have led to confidence lost in one system of governance after another, resulting in currency hyperinflation events that have shaken the world time and again.

In 1929 and again in 2008, financial systems and exchanges crumbled from gamblers' losses and associated psychological impacts. Natural rhythms were altered. Banks stopped making loans and money availability constricted. Production systems shut down. Goods and services stopped flowing. Cities, nations, corporations, and untold numbers suffered bankruptcies, asset seizures, and severe life upheavals. Millions became unemployed, traumatizing families. Depressions set in. Some contemplated suicide, others acted on those thoughts. Lives were destroyed. Families were devastated as negativity spread; all because the Financial Structure is inherently unstable and regulators powerless to regulate them for the public benefit.

Over the past century, fifty-five nations have experienced hyperinflation as faith in their particular form of money was lost. Time and again banks failed, stock exchanges closed, life savings, houses and businesses were lost, riots broke out and people were killed - all because of our perceptions of the value of money and how a few are allowed to manipulate it. Society depends upon the viability of the Financial Structure. When belief in money or its stability is shattered, we all suffer. The following are but a few of many such examples. In:

1914 - Worldwide financial panic led to protracted stock exchange closures & World War I.

1921 - Germany experienced a hyper-inflationary event within which prices doubled every 3.75 days causing extreme social instability and suffering.

1929 - The US Stock Market crashed. Financial panics of epic proportions were followed by the Great Depression during which 9000 banks failed.

1931 - Bank failures triggered bank runs and panic throughout Europe.

1945 - Hungary experienced a level of hyperinflation within which prices doubled every fifteen hours.

1982 - The Latin-American debt crisis struck.

1987 - The world experienced a global liquidity crisis.

1994 - The Mexican Peso crashed - hyperinflation struck.

2000 - The Dot-Com bubble burst - stock markets crashed.

2008 - Global Financial Crisis - Stock Markets crashed - resulting in rapid wealth transfers to the elites.

Did anything real happen to ignite these crashes, bank failures, and hyper-inflationary events? No meteor hit Earth. No tidal wave, fire, volcanic eruption, plague, or drought triggered the social upheaval that followed. What did take place was paralyzing fear stemming from faith lost. Faith and belief are the two necessary ingredients of the Financial Structure. Faith that bankers will honor their financial commitments to us and belief that their systems will keep our money safe. Unfortunately, the one structure that controls them all is only as solid as the people that run it.

Faith and belief exist within our psyche, our collective consciousness. They are subject to our perceptions and the perceptions of those we connect with. When things are running smoothly because people are talking up how good the markets are, our perception is that things are OK, and our money is safe. But when the talk changes because there is always an expectation, an underlying understanding, that things will inevitably change for the worse, our perceptions and how we act can change in an instant, along with our belief in the stability of the Financial Structure.

Entities of the Financial Structure owe at least 25 percent of global debt, a large percentage of which is leveraged into speculative attempts to profit from financial deals that few can understand and fewer still can responsibly justify. At some point a computerized trading program or an overly risky series of bets placed within or by a large financial entity will trigger the next collapse. When that happens, and it will, fear that we will be denied access to our money will spread. Faith in these systems will vanish. Bank runs will follow. Will your money be there when you need it?

Problematically, there is never enough money in these systems to repay all the money owed, plus interest obligations (discussed below), so new money must constantly be created. Financial institutions are steeped in debt and need to make short and long-term loans to themselves to refinance existing obligations. But when faith is lost new loans stop being made and the dominos begin to fall. Large lenders stop making loans to smaller ones who in turn stop making business and private loans. Without the ability to generate new income and thus the ability to repay their own debt obligations, banking systems freeze up, money stops being created, and this antiquated structure stops functioning. And when it does, it takes down global economies.

But that is not the worst of it. The financial elite have had laws in the US enacted that upon deposit, make your money, their money. What you get in return is a basic IOU, which, in the event of extreme financial system instability can be converted into bank stock (in financial parlance, the "bail-in") meaning that if you need immediate access to your money, you have to find a buyer for stock in a failing financial entity.[127] Good luck with that one.

Every aspect of society is dependent upon the operational stability of the Financial Structure. With over $260 trillion of global debt, when, not if, this structure experiences its next major disruption, expect extreme turmoil and suffering to follow. The Financial Structure does not need to be operated in ways that cause great harm. Instead, it can be operated to enable a humane humanity as outlined within Book VI.

GROWTH REVISITED

New loans. More debt. Like every other structure, growth is the Financial Structure's underlying goal. But this structure is different. Without inflation (the creation of more money), there is never enough money in its systems to repay all principal plus interest owed on all the debt money created. Here's how it works.

When bankers make a loan, new money enters the banking system. For the privilege of borrowing this money, you agree to repay it over time, plus interest (interest money = their profits). Recall the $200,000 home loan. By the time it was paid in full, you paid the bank $410,000. The bank created $200,000 of debt money for you to buy the house. It did not create the additional $210,000 of interest money that you repaid them over time. So, where does that interest money come from? Only one place: more loans. New debt money must continuously be added into the money supply to cover mounting interest money obligations. But making more loans creates more interest money obligations, not less. This structure must constantly find ways to grow the money supply otherwise it will fail, making it the mother of all Ponzi Schemes.

If you learn nothing else from this work, learn that "growth" is not something preordained by any deity, nation, or structure, with the exception of the Financial Structure. Governments can exist without growth. Commerce can exist without growth. Religion can exist without growth. And human beings can definitely exist without growth, but not the Financial Structure.

Population growth provides the most obvious outlet for new loans, as more people need more of everything, so with population growth comes more borrowing to purchase more things, meaning more things must be produced resulting in production growth. Systems of commerce must spend more to produce more, so they borrow more. To meet the needs of a growing population, governments provide additional services, so they too borrow more. All of which helps keep the Financial Structure afloat. Growth drives the Financial Structure, and its dictates are that the other structures must grow as well.

But, if society is to gain control of itself, to act more responsibly in the things it does, it must reduce its numbers, not grow them. If that happens, then consumptive demands will decline, reducing environmental impacts. But doing so reduces borrowings, meaning, if we reduce our population the financial house of cards will collapse, revealing one of the underlying, unspoken justifications behind the widespread opposition to population control. Population growth is not a certainty. At some point it may slow and decline, so an insurance policy is needed to keep the Financial Structure afloat. Enter inflation.

INFLATION

Inflation, another creature of the human imagination, fits perfectly within the banker's web of deceit. Its concept is simple. Increase the cost of all things, limit wage increases to less than the inflation rate, and most will be unable to save to acquire.

Not long ago a car cost $500 and people could save to purchase one. No longer. Now the average new car in the US exceeds $33,500 and most have to borrow to purchase one. Houses were historically passed from generation to generation. Now they are tradable commodities priced so high that all but a few have to borrow to acquire a place to call home. The more expensive a thing becomes; the more money will have to be borrowed to buy it. In many locales, the exact same house costs multiples more today than it did fifty years ago. Real inflation kicked in beginning in about 1940 as borrowing to support the war effort escalated. It accelerated dramatically after 1970 when the US went off of the Gold Standard and the oil embargo raised energy prices.

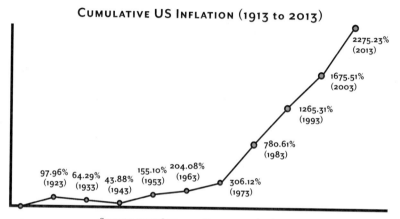

Cumulative US Inflation (1913 to 2013)

Sourced from InflationData.com, 4/15/2013

We are told that inflation is good, necessary, and to expect it. Central Banks set inflation targets. Why? To keep the global banking cartels merrily humming along. Everything must inflate to prevent the Bankers' Ponzi Scheme from unraveling. So, prices steadily increase along with borrowings.

The greater our debt burden, the more Life Hours we burn working to pay it off and the less time we have with our families, or to educate ourselves about what's truly happening around us. The less we know and the less free time we have, the easier we are to both control and take advantage of. Everyone suffers to keep this Ponzi Scheme alive. For the privilege of borrowing something they literally make up out of thin air, the financial elite take the only thing we truly have, life moments. Moments with a child, a loved one, in play or in learning are all taken from us. Unwittingly, we have become enslaved to the bankers, our masters. This is the Financial Structure of this day, but it need not be the one of a more humane tomorrow.

MASTER OR SERVANT

Pope Francis has called on the world to say: 'No to a financial system that rules rather than serves ... [stating] that the role of wealth and resources in a moral economy must be that of servant, not master.'[128]

How profoundly truthful. We imagined money to enable society and eventually built a Financial Structure to house it. Now, a few limit who can use it to those from whom they can generate profits, and they condition how they will provide it. In a moral society, those most in need would have first and easiest access to it, not the last and most burdensome. But ours is not a moral society, is it?

Finance is an industry of avarice, greed, and power to control and is, in many ways, immoral. It need not be this way. We can reimagine financial systems to fairly and humanely serve not just a few, but everyone, by creating money in abundance rather than in limitation. We'll get to how soon. Beforehand, let's gather a bit more understanding of the banking and monetary systems.

FRACTIONAL RESERVE SYSTEMS

"It is well that the people of the nation do not understand our banking and monetary system, for it they did, I believe there would be a revolution before tomorrow morning."
Henry Ford

Early on, goldsmiths realized depositors never demanded return of more than a fraction of the gold deposited with them at any time. Recognizing profit potentials from using "other people's money," goldsmiths began lending depositors' gold, keeping interest payments for themselves. This practice eventually morphed into the fractional reserve banking system, the workings of which were kept secret for centuries.

Faith in the stability of this system is critical. People must believe that when they need their money it will be available, which is its inherent flaw because financial institutions operating fractional reserve systems by definition do not maintain the depositor's money on reserve - ready for payout when needed. Inevitably, when word gets out that a financial institution is about to fail, fear strikes hard and fast. People "run" to the bank to withdraw their money while there is still some to grab, compounding the problem. The bigger the systemic failure, the worse the impact. As panic sets in, entire economies become paralyzed. That happened in 1929 and 2008, and it will happen again, only the next time the consequences will be far worse. Why? Because as George Will stated, "When there is no penalty for failure, failure proliferates."

Today, there truly is no penalty for the failures of those operating our financial institutions; in fact, in the most extreme cases, they are rewarded. Look no further than financial sector operatives who steered their industry into the 2008 financial crisis and how handsomely they have been rewarded since. Only one lower-level executive at a second-tier institution went to jail.[129] Why? Because

> [f]ederal prosecutors almost never bring criminal charges against top executives of large corporations, from banking to pharmaceuticals to technology ... As the economy limps back from the Great Recession, compensation has recovered, corporate profits are at record levels and executives see that few, if any, of their peers ever go to prison

anymore. Perhaps one reason Americans have come to begrudge the wealthy is a resentment of their culture of impunity.[130]

Governments have ceded the right to create money to financial institutions. That was a huge mistake. Those institutions have become so powerfully essential to global governance and commerce that they have strong-armed regulators into believing they are "too big to fail," so we end up bailing them out from the financial calamities they create, just as was done in 2008. And because decision-makers are not penalized for allowing recklessness to metastasize into financial system failures, recklessness proliferates within their institutions.

After the crash of 1929, the US Government enacted laws to limit risky banking practices and established "federal insurance" programs to guarantee repayment of deposited funds, providing psychological stability to an otherwise fragile system. Similar governmental programs have been established around the world, but none have the ability to guarantee the stability of a Financial Structure teetering on over $260 trillion dollars of debt. As Franklin Roosevelt stated in 1936, "We now know that government by organized money is just as dangerous as government by organized mob." He was correct. Wielding the power of money, the financial elite most certainly control politicians.

Unfortunately, laws intended to protect the public by reigning in corporate abuses have been replaced by "too big to fail" laws, solidifying control over governance in the hands of organized money. Money is so intrinsic in society that those who control it, control everything. It's been that way for a long time. As Roosevelt also stated, "The real truth of the matter is, as you and I know, that a financial element in the large centers has owned the Government ever since the days of Andrew Jackson."[131]

Most governments are in debt, many inescapably so. Debt carries interest obligations and more importantly, leverage. As FDR acknowledged almost a century ago, the financial elite own our governments, which means, they own us. How so? We work to pay financial institutions profits from our own borrowings, from the borrowings of governance paid from our tax dollars, and from industry borrowing costs passed on to us at the point of purchase. In one way or another, we all work for the financial elite. That should not be the case. Paraphrasing Pope Francis, the financial system should be used to serve us, not rule us. Money should be used to enable everyone to reach their innate potential, and it can when used differently.

Remember, the function of governance is to set and enforce the rules and regulations within which the rest of society operates. Regulatory attempts to limit risk-taking within Financial Structures have come and gone. Because the financial elite control those who govern, it takes systemic shocks like the stock market crash of 1929 and the global financial crisis of 2008 for them to even attempt to set regulations for the common good. But greed knows no boundaries.

Like the heads of most powerful entities, the financial elite take every opportunity to limit regulations that could impair their profit strategies. They push inflationary policies, implement strategies that ensnare governments in debt, and make running for political office so prohibitively expensive that candidates are forced to sell their souls to the elite who fund multi-million-dollar (and in some cases billion-dollar) election campaigns. Those who pretend to govern are now 'owned' by the elite.

Controlling politicians enables the elite to limit laws intended to protect society from practices known to generate obscene levels of profits (for example, payday lenders have been caught preying on the poor by charging upwards of 700 percent annual interest[132]). When governments are incapable of protecting the governed from predators, our systems of governance have failed us and need to be replaced with ones that protect and serve us all. Built on greed, dependent on growth, and operated for profit, we allow and enable the Financial Structure to control all others. Not convinced yet? Let's look deeper.

CASHLESS SOCIETY

To further their goals to own and control everything, the financial elite are pushing everyone, governments included, to eliminate cash and adopt digital money systems (think credit and debit cards - soon to be followed by digital currencies). Why? Because when that happens, they will for the first time in human history become necessary third parties in every financial transaction, meaning they will profit every time money changes hands. Use cash; bankers can't profit. Eliminate cash; bankers profit every time. Most people in developed nations already make regular use of credit cards which often charge annual interest rates exceeding 30 percent and place them in debt, guaranteeing profits to bankers who otherwise had nothing to do with the transaction. Yes, it's more convenient to use a credit card than cash, but it need not come at such a high cost.

PROFITS WITH EVERY TRANSACTION

Merchants pay processing fees on every credit card transaction and buyers become debtors obligated to pay billions in annual fees, interest, late charges, cash advances, and default interest penalties (often at usurious rates). Massive profits are generated through credit card charges and billions of Life Hours are wasted working to pay interest, fees, and penalties.

If that's not bad enough, those who suffer the most from these predatory systems are the people who can least afford to use them. They typically pay five to ten times the annual rates charged the wealthy. Aren't these rules backward from what they should be? Forced to pay high interest rates, millions are robbed of the ability to escape the shackles of poverty they are born into. These people can't send their children to school, put decent food on their tables, or live a dignified life. Many families suffer physically and mentally from debt stress.

Financial chains will drag you down just as assuredly as metal chains dragged slaves down for thousands of years.

Crippling the least capable by forcing them to pay the highest interest rates has severe repercussions that ripple throughout society for generations. When both parents must work to pay heavy debt obligations, their children are deprived of the most important role a parent has within society: caring for and providing their children with a healthy, happy, stress-free environment in which to grow and thrive. By dictating an agenda that denies a living wage and using financial systems based on digitally created debt money, the poor are ensnared within webs of debt from which escape rarely materializes. Multiple generations end up doomed to the lowest social echelons while the elite are ensured levels of profits impossible within monetary systems based solely on physical forms of money.

Governments borrow to provide police protection, water and sewer systems, fire protection, roads, bridges, airports, military, schools, postal services, health insurance, and social security. Some government borrowings are secured by taxes, others by hard assets like municipal water systems, schools, air traffic control systems, land, minerals, and buildings. When (not if) a governing entity can't collect enough taxes to repay debts plus interest owed, debt masters force the sale of public assets or extort punitive fees to restructure debt obligations.

Consider the sovereign debt crisis that Greece has endured in the aftermath of the 2007-09 Great Recession. Financial institutions packaged deals that almost overnight doubled Greece's national debt obligations. The result? The people of Greece have suffered through the longest recession of any advanced economy since the Great Depression. They have experienced lender induced austerity measures resulting in 25 percent unemployment rates, foreclosures and forfeitures of public property. They have lost businesses and jobs and have had wages slashed and taxes raised, leaving many in a prolonged state of crisis.[133]

Or consider a Wall Street loan sold to Detroit's Water Department that ended up being charged $547 Million *in penalties, to repay the loan early*, because it was too costly to maintain. Who suffers the consequences when 40 percent of Detroit residents' water payments go to pay that penalty? The residents of course, many of whom have had their water shut off because they couldn't pay the added costs.[134]

In another example, a Chicago Public School system was forced to pay $200 million to Wall Street firms *as penalties for early repayment of a loan sold to a school system already stripped to the bone.* The City of Oakland, California, was forced to pay similar early termination fees in another example of a bad deal sold by Wall Street.[135]

Debt masters' greed is nearly limitless. It won't be long before cash is a thing of the past. It may take decades for everyone to be brought into their new financial world order, but they are patient and willing to wait until systemic shocks present opportunities to pounce. When that happens, and it will, expect to start hearing about special drawing rights (SDRs), something imagined within the chambers of the International Monetary Fund (IMF), which will eventually be used to leverage reluctant nations into going cashless.[136] Not that going cashless is necessarily a bad thing. It's not, provided that the Financial Structure is operated to enable a robust humane society, rather than to control a heartless one.

ARE PUBLIC BANKING SYSTEMS THE SOLUTION?

In 1789, the founders of the United States adopted a Constitution which states in Article I, Section 8, that "The Congress shall have the power to coin Money [and] regulate the Value thereof..."

From its inception, a battle raged between Alexander Hamilton and Thomas Jefferson regarding whether or not the new government should coin and issue money as one of its fundamental functions. Hamilton won that battle. The right to create and control money went to private bankers and today the US Government owes its lenders in excess of $27 trillion. That figure does not include unfunded financial obligations or the debts racked up by state and municipal governing entities. Who ultimately bears the burden of paying all of the interest obligations? Who do you think?

The battle over the right to create money has been ongoing for centuries. In the 1860s Abraham Lincoln in agreement with Jefferson stated that:

> The government should create, issue, and circulate all the currency and credit needed to satisfy the spending power of the government and the buying power of consumers ... The privilege of creating and issuing money is not only the supreme prerogative of Government, but it is the Government's greatest creative opportunity ... *The taxpayers will be saved immense sums of interest*, discounts and exchanges. The financing of all public enterprises, the maintenance of stable government and ordered progress, and the conduct of the Treasury will become matters of practical administration. The people can and will be furnished with a currency as safe as their own government. *Money will cease to be the master and become the servant of humanity. Democracy will rise superior to the money power.*[137]
> (Emphasis added)

Lincoln was correct, but unfortunately his insight perished along with him, and the bankers kept rolling along until 1919 when the tiny state of North Dakota managed to establish the first and to date only public bank in the US. Of course, it faced extreme opposition by the banking cartel which hampered its viability because the cartel recognized a public banking system as an extreme threat to its own monopolistic practices. Although public banks currently operate successfully in a number of countries including Germany, China, Canada, India, and Switzerland, on a global basis they are the exceptions and are the subject of relentless attacks by the established banking cartels.[138]

Do you think that public ownership of financial systems should be the exception or the rule? If they can be designed to operate as

Lincoln envisioned, the answer should be clear. But, is it realistically possible to enable them to compete globally under systems of governance controlled by the financial elite? Here's some insight.

A proposal to reform the British banking system by making money creation a function of governance was recently considered in England where, as in the US, 97 percent of all money is created by banks in the form of debt. The proposal never gained traction and failed. Several attempts followed to elect officials dedicated to making this change; they also failed.[139]

Remember the one certainty within this universe is that everything must change. So, just because a structure or a system is one way today does not dictate that it must be that way tomorrow. Today's finance systems did not exist 400, or even 100 years ago. The Financial Structure will change again. The only question is when, how, and into what?

As governing entities have been denied funds to perform services their constituents need and deserve, those who govern are being introduced to the benefits of operating their own public banks. California recently legalized public banking systems for governing entities (excepting the state itself, sadly), and there is a growing movement in the US and elsewhere to establish more.

But, even if jurisdictions successfully adopt public banking systems, unless they establish their own separately operated and linked funds transfer systems, the best they can hope for is to operate side by side within a structure owned and controlled by the financial elite. Interest will still need to be charged and profits created. Strings will remain attached and the power of the financial elite to deny fundamental change will remain intact.

Public banking is a movement in the right direction. However, as currently envisioned, it will be incapable of igniting the level of change necessary to enable a new way of being. That level of progress requires fundamental change in the nature of all structures. Until that happens, humanity will remain in crisis and our problems will worsen.

HUMANITY IN CRISIS

Human crisis is defined by many things. Bad governance, corruption, irresponsible leadership, and the lust for power and greed are but a few of the things responsible for great suffering. But money is the determinative factor. It is the one thing that is cruelly defined by limitation, the one thing that if used differently could eliminate suffering, and the one thing entirely within our control.

[A]t the beginning of the year (2017) we are facing the largest humanitarian crisis since the creation of the United Nations [1945] ... Now more than 20 million people across four countries face starvation and famine ... people will simply starve to death [and] many more will suffer and die from disease ... children will be stunted from severe malnutrition ... livelihoods, futures and hope lost ... What I saw and heard during my visit to Somalia was distressing - women and children walk for weeks in search of food and water. They have lost their livestock, water sources have dried up and they have nothing left to survive on ... To be clear, we can avert a famine ... We're (the UN) ready despite incredible risk and danger ... but we need those huge funds now. Stephen O'Brien, UN Under-Secretary-General for Humanitarian Affairs in an address to the UN Security Council, March 2017.

What the UN needed in 2017 to save thousands of lives was a paltry $4.4 billion. Financial elites collect trillions of dollars in profits every year. These people could allocate a tiny fraction of those profits, or they could simply create new money, to avert the most extreme of humanitarian crises. But they choose not to.

Then there was the Ebola virus which as of July 2019 was once again raging out of control in Africa. Ebola is highly lethal. It causes blood vessels to burst and multiple organ failures. Uncontrollable vomiting, high fever, diarrhea, and bleeding from the nose and mouth are a few of the symptoms which often precede death.

> Less than five years ago, an [Ebola] epidemic in West
> Africa killed more than 11,000 people, shattering com-
> munities, destroying economies and leaving a generation
> of orphans behind. When it was over, world leaders took
> a solemn vow: Never again ... Yet ... epidemiologists and
> aid groups are dismayed by the many indications that the
> pledge has been forgotten. The World Health Organization
> spent months begging for the $98 million it says it needs
> to set up temporary health clinics and distribute vaccines
> that could stop the virus in its tracks.[140]

A mere $98 million was all that was necessary to save thousands of lives and prevent untold misery. Yet "key global powers are mostly watching from the sidelines"[141] meaning, they refused to send the money; so those without, suffered and died a horrible death as human crises metastasize.

In an age when money is manufactured out of thin air, to deny anyone any fundamental service because they lack money is beyond unconscionable; it is criminal. It elevates to a high crime, a crime against humanity, when people needlessly suffer and die because those who control money deny its use for humanitarian purposes. How easy it would be for the elite to save lives and prevent untold suffering. How cruel of them to not!

FEEL THEIR SUFFERING

Over 700 million people live in extreme poverty.[142] With little hope and less money, parents have no alternatives but to send their children out into the world each morning with hunger aflame in their bellies to comb barefooted through acres of trash and filth festering with disease and fraught with danger for food to eat or something of value to sell. For the millions of children living lives of destitution beyond imagination, there are but a few days each year when their eyes sparkle with joyful youth.

Now, try to imagine it is you who must send your children out as scavengers into this unimaginably cruel world. You fear for their lives but there is nothing you can do. You cannot afford to send them to school. You need each to scavenge for the next meal. Your husband can't help. He was crippled in an industrial accident and let go without compensation or medical insurance. He is a burden, another mouth to feed who will never be employed again. He lives in constant pain in your one-room shack on a dirt floor with a plastic film roof. Your mother recently moved in after your father died of cholera, an infectious bacterial disease that causes severe vomiting and diarrhea. Cholera is typically contracted from drinking infected water. Your clean water source dried up years ago. It is a half-day walk to the closest safe water source, but you no longer have the strength to make that walk and your children are too young and weak to make it either. So, your family drinks the only water they can, and it is filthy and disease-ridden.

Is it possible for you to imagine the despair, the horrors and the hardships you would face if this was your life? Try. Close your eyes and envision your own children in rags, savagely filthy, with bloated but empty bellies and listless eyes combing garbage dumps or back alleys for scraps of food. Make it real. Feel the despair. Make it yours. Try as you may, unless this is your life, you, will not succeed. Theirs are lives that few would wish on another. A life that, but for the luck of the draw, could have been yours or mine.

UNRELENTING POVERTY

According to the World Bank, as of mid-2018, nearly 3.4 billion souls struggle to meet their basic needs, surviving on less than $5.50 a day, with 10 percent of the population living in extreme poverty defined as less than $1.90 per day.[143] According to the United Nations, as of 2019, close to one billion people are without safe drinking water. Unclean water and poor sanitation are the leading cause of child mortality.

If you are reading this little missive, you are one of the lucky ones because there are over 775 million who can't read, including approximately 30 million Americans. In supposedly the most advanced nation on the planet how is that even possible? The answer springs from how we use money.

Unrelenting poverty triggers population growth. Birth control is often neither preached nor enabled in the poorest countries where sex is one of the few earthly pleasures. So, we add 83 million people every year, mostly from impoverished countries. At a moment in time when we can't properly feed and nourish over two billion people, when systems of governance are mired in conflict and systems of commerce are destroying Earth's life support systems, how can we possibly justify more growth, more people?

HUMAN POPULATION GROWTH (10,000 BCE TO 2019)

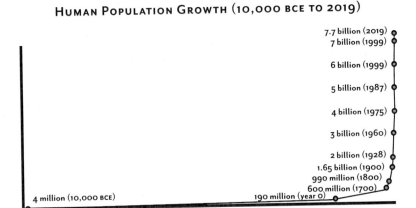

SOURCED FROM OURWORLDINDATA.ORG

One of the realities of poverty is that it feeds upon itself. The UN 2015 World Population Prospects Report, on page 3, states that:

> Population growth remains especially high in the group of 48 countries designated by the United Nations as the least developed countries (LDCs) ... Between 2015 and 2100, the populations of 33 countries, most of them LDCs, have a high probability of at least tripling. Among them, the populations of ... [10 countries] are projected to increase at least five-fold by 2100. The concentration of population growth in the poorest countries will make it harder for those governments to eradicate poverty and inequality, combat hunger and malnutrition, expand education enrolment and health systems, improve the provision of basic services and implement other elements of a sustainable development agenda to ensure that no one is left behind.

An impoverished population lacks the capacity to generate sufficient tax revenues rendering nations incapable of providing the basic services needed to help elevate people from poverty. And, people born into poverty tend to remain in poverty within structures that value money over people. One bad condition feeds the other. Millions of people die every year from malnourishment and starvation. Their plight goes mostly unreported. Theirs are the faces that should be plastered over news outlets, day after day, until starvation is a thing of past societies. Think about how many brilliant minds are robbed from inception of the possibility of ever achieving their potential because of malnutrition and disease. What a loss to society and a curse upon each suffering that plight.

Solutions to hunger are the low hanging fruit available right now to ease extreme suffering and make a better humanity. All that is required is a small fraction of the trillions paid every year to the financial elite or to the military-industrial complex to eliminate hunger, not in decades or centuries, but right now. The starving can't wait.

We have the ability to enable a civilization destined to experience incredible journeys of discovery. Those journeys begin after we have created new ways of being: ways within which we have learned to treat each other with respect, as equals, in exactly the same ways that almost every single one of us wants to be treated. That journey begins by changing how we do most things which we enable by simply choosing to use money differently, humanely. Read on.

HOW WE CONDUCT SOCIETY IS A MATTER OF CHOICE

From the United Nations Conference on Trade and Development, 2013, [ISSN 1810 - 5432] we learn that:

> Despite significant increases in agricultural productivity ... Around 1 billion people chronically suffer from starvation and another billion are malnourished. Some 70% of these people are themselves small farmers or agricultural laborers ... Enabling these people to become food self-sufficient or earn an appropriate income through agriculture to buy food needs to take center stage in future agricultural transformation.

The irony of hundreds of millions of small farmers suffering from starvation and malnutrition should not escape us, as profit-driven agricultural practices have stripped them of the ability to provide for themselves. By 2050, there will be another 2 billion mouths to feed. Food demand will increase by between 60 percent and 100 percent.[144] Yet, according to the above referenced 2013 UN report, unless we dramatically change *how* we produce our foods, we should expect:

> Much lower agricultural productivity growth in the future ... and a burgeoning environmental crisis of agri-

culture [which] are the seeds for mounting pressures on food security ... This is bound to increase the frequency and severity of riots, caused by food - price hikes, with concomitant political instability, and international tension, linked to resource conflicts and migratory movements of starving populations.

The UN recognized that:

The world needs a paradigm shift in agricultural development: from a 'green revolution' to an 'ecological intensification' approach. This implies a rapid and significant shift from conventional, monoculture-based ... industrial production towards ... sustainable, regenerative production systems that also considerably improve the productivity of small-scale farmers.

But:

The required transformation is much more profound than simply tweaking the existing industrial agricultural system.[145]

The changes needed for humanity to thrive are profound. The UN has stressed in report after report that humanity needs a paradigm shift in how we manage our affairs. We simply cannot fix just one system or another. All four of our structures and their associated systems are so interconnected that without an entirely new approach to how we do all the things we do; societal collapse is a near certainty.

Responsible systems of governance could mandate that in exchange for the monopolistic privileges granted the financial elite, they must create money for all projects necessary to eliminate grave suffering and deliver it without strings and without interest or security. But our systems of governance are fractured and subject to the will of the elite so, will they? Even though the solutions to so many of our problems are neither elusive nor complicated, you know the answer.

It is always the darkest before a new dawn. How we conduct society is truly a matter of choice, our choice. Be clear. No structure or system is set in stone. None have proven unworthy of change. For life to carry on, everything must change. Change requires moving along new pathways in new directions which reveal after new goals are set and actions initiated to achieve them. Change can be a beautiful thing if done the right way for the right reasons. For humans, the secret to evolutionary levels of change resides in how we choose to use money.

11

THE 4TH STRUCTURE

The 4th Structure came into existence to quell fear of the unknown. Its goal was to explain the unexplainable. This was accomplished by attributing natural phenomena to larger-than-life beings whose powers were vast and yet, also unexplainable. Those who claimed to possess an understanding of the phenomena were elevated to positions of power and prestige. They helped bring stability and cohesion to the community through the use of rituals intended to please or appease a god or gods.

As communities grew, Earth processes were accepted as part of the natural order of life. Rituals turned into practices which became institutions of religion used to both unite and control members within the community. Many systems of religion have developed over time, all different, yet all essentially the same.

Today, the major religions have one fundamental thing in common. They profess ways, practices, that if followed, offer access to an elevated life experience, whether in the here and now or afterward. Not all religions believe in a deity, although all claim the ability to connect their followers in some way to a greater reality, to something unseen and existing beyond the surface of the life that we each experience. What they profess is the ability to lead their followers to know what is presently unknowable, unexplainable.

Most religions attribute the unexplainable to a god, a universal spirit. Many have set coming to know their god as their ultimate goal.

But what does that really mean? Those who believe in God believe that God is all-knowing and the Creator of everything. "All-knowing" is an ethereal concept and "being the Creator" represents presence, a physical concept. Together, they pretty much define life within this universe. So, would it not be fair to say that if you believe there is a God and want to know that God in the deepest and most profound sense, one would have to come to know all there is to know and have to be all there is to be, as would be your God?

Coming to know God, would then equate to coming to know the truth about life, for God would be nothing if not Truth and Life. So, truth is what you would seek to know God. The search for truth will reveal the innermost workings of this universe, how life works. It may take us tens of thousands of years to discover everything there is to discover, and then to learn all there is to know which would theoretically enable us to be all there is to be. This would become a shared goal should we choose to understand in the broadest sense, the spiritual nature of life.

To know life means to know the true nature of all things. We aren't born with this knowledge; we have to acquire it. There is no writing from which we can learn all we need to know, yet that knowledge is everywhere, encompassing everything. Hidden in plain sight, it awaits discovery and reveals only to those who seek it out.

Learning is a multi-generational process of discovery dependent upon how well we pass along knowledge gained. The more effectively we educate ourselves, the more rapidly we will learn how to best use life's processes. Learning leads to knowing, which leads to that moment of ultimate understanding at which no barriers restrain us from being, pure being. Reach that point and no questions remain unanswered. That, would be the moment of ultimate realization, what some call the God Moment, when Nirvana, Heaven, Spiritual Enlightenment, the Freeing of the Soul, and Oneness are experienced. For these purposes, let's define that moment as Enlightenment.

And let's further define Enlightenment as that moment which occurs after ascending the evolutionary ladder by transcending the physical to become perfectly efficient beings capable of being any place and every place at any moment in time without limitation, without effort; pure being. That would be the moment of ultimate awareness when the true purpose of life reveals.

Enlightenment is instantaneous, yet eons in the making. To achieve it requires a process. Call it whatever you like. Seeking God. Seeking Life. Seeking Truth. They are all the same. We become seekers whose intention, whose stated life purpose is to understand how this universe works. This returns us to the original and most fundamental purpose of this structure, to explain the unexplainable, which is what those engaged in the scientific process look to achieve.

There are so many practical and philosophical questions to ask and answer. For instance, if we define "the beginning" as "The Origin," did anything exist anywhere before The Origin, or did everything just materialize to become what is? Was there a Creator and if so, did he, she, or it put everything in one location and then blow it all apart to set our universe in perpetual motion, or was this a random event? What structure held open the empty room that became our universe before it filled with galaxies, stars, planets, and space? Will its expansion be infinite, or will it come to an end, and if so, then what? Has this happened only once, or many times? When one universe is created, are others?

Within our universe, there is an entirely separate universe existing at the atomic level. Is it possible that sentient life forms are living on electrons that orbit their neutron just as we exist on an electron like planet orbiting a star? Could we be living on what appears to be an electron orbiting around an atomic level star when viewed (as we view the atomic universe) from the next larger dimension of existence?

What understandings of the nature of space will need to be gained to allow future travelers to safely navigate its realm? What secrets will have to be discovered to eventually allow us to traverse vast regions of space within nanoseconds?

Miles below ocean surfaces a few life forms thrive where all others perish. How is that possible? Some life forms survive thousands of years frozen in place; others sleep long winters in states of hibernation. What can we learn from them and how can we use that knowledge to help us successfully navigate pathways that await discovery?

We have just scratched the surface of the knowledge available about how our own bodies function, which raise questions such as how to: self-cure diseases, extend lifespans, prevent birth defects, hibernate to survive extended periods of zero gravity space travel, or teleport ourselves from one location to another. Hundreds of thousands of other questions about ourselves and what we are capable of await discovery.

From a broader, perhaps more spiritual perspective, can it be said that there is any true purpose to the human existence beyond that which we individually and collectively experience in our daily lives and if so, how can any of us come to truly know that purpose?

Is there any meaning to life beyond anything we are presently aware of, and if so, how will it be discovered and understood? What is the nature of reality? Where do we come from? What are we, and where are we going? What is consciousness? Is there a soul? What if anything happens after death?

Life is full of mystery. Do you believe that the answer to these and the millions of other profound questions about life will just be given to us by some omniscient being, or has reality taught that more than simple belief will be required of us? There are billions, perhaps trillions, of other questions about life to be asked and answered. Will we find the answers within storybooks written in ancient times, or will it take something else?

Who will be the ones to ask the hard questions about the ways of this universe and then dedicate their lives digging into the reality of what is, in search of the answers: the politicians, the warriors, the industrialists, the popes, priests, imams, rabbis, or other religious heads; or, will it be another profession which brings us closer to knowing all that is life? For an answer, consider the following from one who looked at life, and Life, as one and the same, but from an entirely different perspective than most:

In this materialistic age of ours the serious scientific workers are the only profoundly religious people.

- Albert Einstein, 1930

Perhaps Einstein should have used the word spiritual in place of religious, as there most certainly are millions of profoundly religious people. However, what Einstein was in effect saying is that in this era, the search to understand how our universe works, to explain what is presently unexplainable, is the modern equivalent to the studies of ancient texts by the pious.

He was saying that today, the search for the answers to the most profoundly spiritual questions about existence and the meaning of life is driven by the scientists, not by politicians, warriors, industrialists, or the pious. The scientists are the ones who dedicate their lives to deep study of life processes to gather knowledge and understanding to benefit humanity. Many of them are the people that you want standing at the forefront of society. These are forward-thinking individuals who dig deep and question all things.

On a mission of discovery in the search of what is, of universal truths, they follow the evidence wherever it may lead as they peel away life mysteries, layer by layer, until hopefully, all is revealed. Theirs is the only profession capable of finding ways of extricating ourselves from the mess we have created. They are the ones to look to if we are to create a future of limitless possibility. They can be our saviors.

If we are to survive and thrive, we need to rely on ourselves. We need to place our trust and faith with those of us who are focused on solving our problems. We must encourage and enable as many people as possible, as fast as possible, to become scientists. And we must free them of the burdens of daily existence to enable them to focus all their efforts on the study of life processes, both large and small.

The 4th Structure thus becomes the one within which those who seek knowledge and gather understanding reside. The other structures will exist to support and enable this one. Here is where we place our best and brightest, those truly devoted to the depths of discovery necessary to unravel the mysteries of this universe. From here our next prophets will emerge as universal emissaries. But, how will the rest of society respond to the wisdom they convey? If we can agree that it is in our collective best interest to create a higher purpose to the human existence than growth, consumption and profiteering, then perhaps they will agree that the purpose of our existence can be the gathering of an understanding of life.

THE STRUCTURE OF FAITH

The 4th Structure was created to explain the unexplainable. It has been the structure within which many have placed their faith. It can remain the structure of faith if society chooses to endow the scientists with the means to solve the vast array of problems we have created. This is the structure from which our salvation can flow as gateways of the imagination open to help chart a course for humanity into which the possible is only a discovery away.

We are curious creatures. Curiosity drives us to explore and with exploration comes discovery and the gathering of knowledge of the way things are. Knowledge gained awakens an awareness of life possibilities, further stimulating our imaginations and enabling us to be so much more. We have received a great gift: limitless imaginations and creative capacities that enable us to make real most anything imagined. Imagination is the ability to think, explore, and visualize beyond the outer limits of what has been experienced. To imagine is to see what can be.

Imagination is everything. It is the preview of life's coming attractions. It is more important than knowledge. For knowledge is limited to all we now know and understand, while imagination embraces the entire world, and all there ever will be to know and understand.

- Albert Einstein

What makes us unique is our ability to create what has been imagined. Creativity turns the imagined real, and, with every creative act we capture a glimpse of the greater beyond. So, imagine that humanity has evolved to become something far better than what we are this day. Imagine, our collective goals have changed. Imagine that we have chosen to travel pathways of discovery in search of universal truths, the discovery of which will help us explain the unexplainable and bring us closer to knowing the meaning of life. Place your faith with the scientists and the scientific process. Help them discover life's evolutionary keys. Use The 4th Structure and its associated funds (to be discussed) to enable evolutionary change.

BOOK V

TO CHANGE THE WORLD

12

Change Our Goals

Visualize Earth 80 years from now. What do you see? A world of plenty, fertile, lush, green and vibrant, or a world without forests, marred by acidic oceans, toxic air, and soils contaminated with industrial filth? Do you see gleaming mountain springs, bubbling with fresh water supplied to sparkling clean cities, or a world of waters unfit to drink, air unfit to breathe, and lands parched and incapable of producing food for eleven billion humans most of whom are living in misery? Has society evolved to provide equal opportunity to all members and become respectful of the sanctity of all life, or have we further devolved into a species of haves and have nots, constantly at war orchestrated by overlords sucking the lifeblood out of the masses for their own benefit and profit?

The facts are clear. We are in mortal danger. Earth's life support systems are being rapidly and systematically destroyed. In short order, they will be unable to support the type of society we all wish for our children's children. So, if we are to survive and hopefully thrive, we must change how we do most things. That means fundamentally changing how our structures and systems operate.

We have the capacity to change, to evolve new structures designed to support a vibrant society of beings living harmoniously with ourselves and nature, but we make no pretense of doing so. Why? Because humanity as a whole has embraced no goals beyond profit incentivized consumptive growth. It is time for that to change. It is time for us to grow up and change how we approach life by taking responsibility for *how* we do most things. This is not a big ask, but it is a big step.

To evolve, is a prime directive. It is the singular most important step a species can take. In a universe of change, failing to evolve, failing to change progressively, leads down well-trodden pathways of extinction. Evolutionary change is fundamental and all-encompassing. It is the type of change capable of transforming what once appeared impossible, into the mundane.

Is humanity capable of securing its future by making evolutionary-based decisions, or are we so chained to past ways that our ascendance is denied and the evolutionary opportunity lost? The answer will depend upon what you and the rest of us do, or fail to do, not some time in the future, but now, right now. Time is not on our side.

Change begins with our goals and an extremely well thought out plan to transition from old to new. All plans require objectives, goals. Ours are no different. They require us to unite in agreement to adopt lives of tolerance, compassion, hope, and certainty that a better future awaits the day we weave new structures and better ways of being into the web of humanity.

Change becomes real after we have incorporated a few really big goals into the fabric of a global society constituted to be: of the people, by the people, and for all people. It becomes real after we have directed everything that we do at accomplishing those few, really big goals.

To stay focused on reaching our biggest goals, we must continually ask ourselves if our smaller goals are directed at achieving the larger ones. If they are, we proceed. If they are not, we abandon them and redirect our efforts. This would include a process of questioning how we do most things. Even if we think we know the best way, most likely, we do not. Seeking clarity helps refine our travels through life, accelerate knowledge gained and enable progressive change, all of which lead to better ways of being.

If our goals are pure, simply stated, with clearly recognizable benefits, they will motivate change; and with change we can accomplish the seemingly impossible. Now, is our time to give the human life experience profoundly new meaning. Now, is our time of change.

CHANGE BEGINS WITH NEW GOALS

Our goals drive us into the future. They give us direction and if well chosen, they carry the potential for each of us to experience a purposeful and meaningful life. New goals pursued with passion and determination will propel us into a future well worth experiencing. Some goals are really big, some not so. Some are personal, some are societal. The best are a combination. They all have one thing in common, they guide us from here to there, provided enough of us act in concert to secure them.

Now is the first time in human history that we possess the ability and indeed, the opportunity, to design, craft, and secure our own future. But do we possess the will, determination, and courage to do so? No other being will do it for us. That is not the way of this universe. The future that we will experience will be of our own making. We possess the ultimate life freedom, that of self-determination. This is the freedom that will determine our future. What will we make of it?

To change, requires us to imagine and then create the future we desire. So, imagine there are billions of us who believe that there are better ways of being human, and that we can be better at being human. Imagine there are billions of us who are willing to do whatever it takes to move humanity from here to there, along new pathways of progressive change.

Imagine a society in which the family one is born into no longer determines one's fate; where each is born into a lifetime of opportunity, limited only by one's innate abilities; where your community's goal is to enable you to be the best you can possibly be and to support you becoming so in every possible way; and where the individual's goals support those of the community. In essence, imagine a society within which we are here to support each other in pursuit of the most fundamental of goals, the ones we hold in common.

A better humanity will exist when each of us is imbued with equal opportunities to prosper and achieve their potential. A better humanity will exist when new structures enable a society within which all have equal, unburdened access to healthy food, clean water, safe and comfortable living conditions, superior educational systems, plentiful employment opportunities, and the most advanced medical care. Within such structures, life is easier and more fulfilling.

Ours is the ability to imagine and then create the reality needed for us to thrive. We must dream it, design it, create it, and if we are sufficiently determined, make it so. Dare to dream a better future into reality; set one fundamentally powerful new goal for each structure to provide the direction needed to create that reality; and then commit to the process of attainment. As Governance is tasked with providing the rules and regulations within which society operates, let's begin there.

THE GOAL OF ONE GOVERNANCE

We are an amazing species. We possess unlimited potential. In less than 150 years we have made incredible technological advances, but the institutions upon which society is based have not advanced to keep pace. Ask just about anyone and they will tell you that their systems of governance are far from perfect. Many fail to meet even the most basic needs of the governed, which justifies changing them.

We have created a global economy, yet we fail at responsibly managing the affairs of a global society. Why? Because our structures lack morally rich, ethically-driven standards that ensure that those who govern at every level are held accountable for the decisions they make and harms they allow or ignite.

Without establishing one structure of uniform global oversight, humanity will remain just another organism consuming its host's resources until they both perish. Demanding profit-driven growth, rulers of all four structures oppose regulatory efforts to the detriment of everyone and everything. Operating competing, complex systems with little oversight, represents irresponsibility in the extreme; yet that is exactly how our global society plows ahead.

The result is that we live in a world with fractured, territorial semblances of governing systems that perpetuate endless wars, and endless competing claims to Earth's limited resources. Conflicts exist at every intersect, requiring a global perspective and a global management body to resolve. But there are none.

Rulers of nations espouse separatism which ignites competition, not cooperation. And, although governing is humanity's biggest business, we haven't come close to getting it right. Nations employ vast militaries. Some have harnessed the destructive force of the atom, others, more deadly bioweapons. Many rule with iron fists. Only a few act with the best interests of the governed in mind. All wield great social power. Yet most fail to accept the fact that with great power comes great responsibility.

True Leaders recognize that leadership carries with it the obligation to protect the best interests of their followers. Lead poorly, use force to drag the governed along, and social discord erupts, making governance difficult. Allow those with conflicts of interests to govern, and the people suffer from iron-fisted, highly extractive forms of governance that benefit a few and harm most everyone and everything else.

But lead responsibly, initiate actions intended to secure fundamental rights for everyone, and the burden of leadership is eased. Responsible leadership is forward-looking. It attempts to anticipate and reduce adverse impacts of activities in pursuit of socially beneficial goals. Unfortunately, responsible leadership is sorely lacking within most of our societies.

If we are to meet life's evolutionary challenge, we must change how we manage our activities, at all levels. Our structures and systems operate globally, so we must evolve one structure of governance capable of managing the needs of a global society. For this structure to stand a chance of success, it must present a far better form of governance than any ever established. That would be one that "is nothing less nor more than . . . leaders acting for the average citizen and pursuing the common good."[146]

Governance "of the people, by the people and for [all] people"[147] is the standard that best serves the average citizen in pursuit of the common good. It can be the standard of a new structure of global governance that most would enthusiastically embrace. Let's call that structure: "One Governance."

In 1776, the people of thirteen colonies declared independence from those who denied colonists fundamental rights deemed "unalienable." They formed a union, fought a war to free themselves from a system of governance that did not represent their interests. They created an entirely new system of governance which was broadly defined within a document that begins with three of the most powerful words ever penned: "We, the People."

The word "People" is capitalized, conveying truths so fundamentally profound as not to ever be dismissed. Within modern parlance, *We, the People* is all-inclusive. It means all people, irrespective of race, color, creed, or background. This was the most advanced form of governance ever created. It was supposed to change with time to meet its obligation to serve the People. Yet, as with all things human, it was far from perfect. Greed and lust for power usurped the founders' vision of governance in service of the People.

From the outset, the founders debated who should control a new monetary system, the government, or private enterprise. Hamilton and the bankers won out, opening the doors for the moneyed interests to control the actions of those who governed. Over time, the financially powerful chipped away at the American ideals. Now, nearly 250 years later, a unique system of governance by democracy has cracked. It no longer exists to serve the People (although given its roots in slavery, it really never has).

In 2010, the US Supreme Court in *Citizens United v. Federal Election Commission*[148] equated unlimited election spending by corporate entities to what had been considered a fundamental *human* right, free speech. That decision effectively legalized political bribery and turned the electoral process into never-ending financial orgies only attended by the ultra-rich and corporate elites. This decision solidified control of that system of governance in the hands of the wealthy, and confirmed that democracy in the US as originally intended, had failed. Look no further than the term of its 45th president, during which it became clear that this system of governance no longer stands as a beacon of hope, of justice, or as the model to which other systems of governance can aspire.

Beyond the failures of that one system of governance, it should also be clear that managing the impacts of a global society of over 7.8 billion via 196 different systems of governance, is simply impossible. And, we are not even trying.

The League of Nations was formed after World War I, and the United Nations was formed after World War II. Both were created by heads of nations who recognized the need for a cooperative form of global governance. But neither entity was sufficiently funded or endowed with powers of a global sovereign. One failed and the other is rendered incapable of meeting even its most basic goals of securing fundamental rights for all people because the governing elite refuse to empower it to secure those rights. As a result, billions suffer from extreme levels of deprivation and oppression, and billions more will soon expand their ranks.

No existing system of governance was designed to, or is capable of, responsibly and ethically managing the affairs of a global society of beings. None. All lack the ability to govern with foresight and immunity from the influence of the financially powerful. Beyond that, rulers show little interest in coalescing for the common good, even though they have been told time and again that not doing so dooms us all. So, what can we do?

To change the course of humanity, we have to unite and set new, foundational goals. If we are to have a shot at attaining them, we will need billions who of their own free will conclude that adopting new goals designed to support the common good is a worthy pursuit. For inspiration and insight into goals for a new form of global governance, consider some of the most profound words ever penned:

> **We hold these truths to be self-evident, that all [people] are created equal, that they are endowed by their Creator with certain unalienable rights, that among these are Life, Liberty and the pursuit of Happiness. That to secure these rights, Governments are instituted among [the people], deriving their just powers from the consent of the governed. That whenever any Form of Government becomes destructive to these ends, it is the Right of the People to alter or to abolish it, and to institute new government, laying its foundation on such principles and organizing its powers in such form, as to them shall seem most likely to effect their Safety and Happiness.**[149]

As so clearly stated, *the goals and the obligations* of those who were elected to govern were set "to secure" certain "unalienable rights" of the People to, among other things, "Life, Liberty, and the pursuit of Happiness." *Over 240 years ago, the founders of the United States recognized that when any system of governance failed to "secure" those rights, it was both the "Right" and the "duty" of "the People to alter or to abolish" the old systems and create new systems.*

Those who governed were directed to establish and maintain systems "most likely" to "effect" the "Safety and Happiness" of the People. Safety and Happiness. Pretty clearly defined foundational goals (and obligations) of a system of governance that was as good as it got for over two centuries. And, those same words stand today as beacons of indelible truths, as guides for those who govern to follow, just as surely today, as they did in 1776.

If all who govern do so with the singular purpose of ensuring the "Safety and Happiness" of "the governed," humanity would be tracking a far different and far better course than the one it travels this day. When they do not, it is both the right, and as stated later in the document, "the duty" of the governed to establish a "new government" to do so.

We, the People, stand at life's crossroads with one critical decision to make. Do we choose to follow evolutionary pathways by establishing new ways of doing most things, or do we continue doing the same things in pretty much the same ways we have for centuries as we continue our travels along pathways of extinction?

The answer will depend upon whether we continue using 196 competing forms of governance, at times trying to change each to be a little better than before, or whether we act boldly to break free of the old systems and create one new form of global governance "of the people, by the people, and, for all people"?

If we choose the latter, then we need to set one goal to rise above all others to serve as the guiding light at which all efforts of governance are directed. Perhaps the best way to select that goal is to use terminology that best defines what a successful form of governance is.

THE MEASURE OF SUCCESSFUL GOVERNANCE

In 1776, the founders declared that the purpose (the goal) of their new form of governance was to "secure" the "Safety and Happiness" of the People. That meant that the obligation of those chosen to govern was to create and enforce rules and regulations to secure the safety and happiness of the governed. As it is unlikely that most would be happy living in unsafe conditions, the fundamental goal of this new system of governance was simply to secure the happiness of the governed.

That goal would serve us today just as well as the fundamental goal of a new form of global governance, as it did for that new form of governance more than 240 years ago. In fact, experts now recognize that securing the happiness of the governed should serve as the focal point of modern governance, and a growing movement exists to make it so.

The global movement to put happiness at the center of governance reflects a mix of inspiring idealism and down-to-earth realism. Skeptics of the happiness movement believe that power, not happiness, is the (inevitable) business of government. Yet pursuing happiness is not only idealistic; it is the world's best and perhaps only hope to avoid global catastrophe.[150]

In 2011, the UN General Assembly established May 20 as the annual "International Day of Happiness," recognizing happiness as a human priority and deeming it to be a "Fundamental Human Goal" from which all things human can benefit. In furtherance of this recognition, the UN commissioned the annual *World Happiness Report*.

Happiness is a measure of an individual's state of mental well-being and the UN uses happiness as the best indicator of how well any system of governance is working, which only makes sense. If the governed are relatively happy, their system of governance is working relatively well. Conversely, if the governed are unhappy, their system of governance is working poorly.

Nations with the happiest people operate more harmoniously than others. Their systems of governance provide what the governed need and some of what they want. The *2019 World Happiness Report* focused on "happiness and the community," identifying the top ten happiest nations as Finland, Denmark, Norway, Iceland, Netherlands, Switzerland, Sweden, New Zealand, Canada, and Austria. "Income, healthy life expectancy, social support, freedom, trust, and generosity" are the things people living within the highest-rated nations place high values on.

At a time when nations are building walls to keep immigrants out, the *2018 World Happiness Report* added another analysis, that of migrant happiness in their host country. This report indicates that,

The most striking finding of the whole report is that a ranking of countries according to the happiness of their immigrant populations is almost exactly the same as for the rest of the population ...

Happiness can change, and does change, according to the quality of the society in which people live ... The countries with the happiest immigrants are not the richest countries, but instead the countries with a more balanced set of social and institutional supports for better lives.

Happiness has little to do with the rate of economic growth. In 2016, economic growth charts ranked Denmark and Switzerland at 158 and 174, respectively, yet both were ranked within the top ten happiest nations. What is apparent is that,

Almost all the countries in the top 10 have very low levels of inequality by world standards. They almost all have strong welfare systems and good healthcare. They have low levels of unemployment and high education levels. And they tend to have higher taxes.

Most critically, they almost all have short working hours. There is a very close correlation between the number of hours people work each year and the level of happiness. Happy people work less - and tend to live longer. Which all adds up to something quite interesting.

In a world where so many rich countries are pursuing economic policies that are focused on austerity or reducing the size of government or lowering taxes and boosting economic growth, is there a need for change? For the last thirty years, working hours have risen in many countries, education has become more expensive and healthcare harder to access. Might it be time for many political leaders to pause a little for reflection?

The policies being pursued in many parts of the world, and notably large parts of the rich world, are the exact opposite of what is needed to make people happy. Rather than pursuing growth, lowering taxes and shrinking government, politicians should reduce inequality . . . boost welfare. That's what makes people happy.[151]

The science of what makes people happy has been studied for over a hundred years. Below are a few excerpts from an article about happiness published November 2015 in collaboration with the University of California, Berkley, School of Public Health.[152]

Researchers think of happiness as having satisfaction and meaning in your life. It's the propensity to feel positive emotions, the capacity to recover from negative emotions quickly, and holding a sense of purpose. Happiness is not having a lot of privilege or money. It's not constant pleasure. It's a broader thing: Our ability to connect with others, to have meaningful relationships, to have a community. Time and again - across decades of research and across all studies - people who say they're happy have strong connections with community and with other people. That's sort of the recipe for happiness.

Does money matter? To a point yes, but beyond that point, no.

The assumption used to be, yes; more money will make people happier. But we actually have good data on that over the past 100 years. From the 1920s to the 1950s - an era of depression and world war - as household income rose there was an increase in people's self-reported happiness. But then the line just tapered off. Studies show that money increases happiness when it takes people from a place where there are real threats - poverty - to a place that is reliably safe. After that, money doesn't matter much. Research by the Nobel laureate psychologist and economist Daniel Kahneman showed that money increases happiness until about $75,000 annually, and after that our emotional well-being doesn't increase with income ...

MRI studies confirm that acts of giving, cooperating with, and lending support to others, gives us pleasure and hence make us happy. Our daily life experiences contribute significantly to our individual happiness. Being born into a world of poverty with little hope or opportunity of escape obviously makes each day's experience more difficult, less rewarding, and less likely to lead to a happy life experience. Living a life of fear in a war-torn area of the world will probably not lead one to happy people; their lives are too stressed ... If you are surrounded by happy people living in low stress, less competitive, more cooperative communities, you are more likely to lead a happy life. By living each day in gratitude for the life you lead, mindful of the potential consequences that your actions may have on others and practicing acts of kindness and forgiveness, you cultivate an environment of happiness that is contagious ...

Other studies reveal that: caring about other people releases something called the *"moral molecule"* which raise one's oxytocin levels making people happier; growing old brings with it a happiness factor; being healthy, exercising, having pets, volunteering to help others, doing more of what you are good at and less of what you are not so good at; being in life's flow by engaging in absorbing activities; gaining a sense of financial security and creating a life balance between work and play, all contribute to living a happy life.

Recent *World Happiness Report* findings reveal that happiness is the best indicator of human welfare and that people lead happier lives in societies that promote social equality. Unfortunately, statistics also reveal that inequality has increased significantly over the past decade "in most countries, in almost all global regions, and for the population of the world as a whole"[153] which is just one more confirmation that 196 different systems of governance are incapable of managing a global society of beings.

Interestingly, the systems of governance that have the happiest people tend to be defined by a term that has gotten a bad rap. Consider the following:

> The enlightened Danish woman defended her country's form of democracy with words Americans would do well learning and implementing sooner than later. The Danish woman told Oprah that happiness is considered a big success.

> Oprah pointed out that in fact, Denmark is a democratic country but that it had Socialist views. One of the guests acknowledged that without hesitation. The other woman gave it the necessary context.

> 'Well, you might think so,' the Danish woman said. 'We don't necessarily think of it as that. We all think of it as being civilized; that you take care of your old and your sick. And you make sure that people get well educated. So, we think of it more as being civilized.'

> And that is what separates ideologies. Some are humane while others are intrinsically selfish and thus evil. A civilized country is about having programs in one's nation that protect & invest in all of its citizens. Ayn Randian ideologies are about allowing the lowest savagery of our humanity to emerge.[154]

Self-interest versus humane acts for the collective good. Will we let a term like Socialism deter us from establishing a new system of governance designed to protect and invest in all its citizens, or will we stay the course and watch humanity devolve as Ayn Randian ideologies envelop the lands? The answer will depend upon whether enough of us care enough about the outcome of Earth's human experiment to form a new union, with new structures designed to enable a society within which the well-being of every citizen is paramount.

These new structures will succeed or fail based upon the goals of guidance chosen. To form a more perfect union and transform humanity The Goal of One Governance will need to be so fundamentally sound, and so profoundly positive, that if given the opportunity, most of us will enthusiastically embrace it as their own. Knowing that happiness is the best indicator of a well-functioning system of governance, and that with happiness comes a sense of well-being, let's agree that *The Goal of One Governance shall be to structure a society within which the "well-being of all people" is paramount.* Can you think of a better one? If so, please let us know so that we can improve upon this one. You'll find our contact information at the end of this work.

Well-being translates to everyone being born into a world of equal opportunity, with happiness an intended way of life. No argument will stand against actions to attain it, and no form of governance should aspire to less. But how do we define what we need from those who govern to secure our collective well-being, our happiness? The answer is simple. Ask.

Ask ten million of us from all walks of life and all corners of the globe what they need from those who govern to enable a sense of well-being, a sense of happiness among them. Prioritize their answers which then become interim goals chosen in pursuit of securing the larger structural goal. Repeat the process every year and then get to work creating a society that meets those needs. It can happen. But will it?

Naysayers will say, "Of course not. Such levels of change are simply impossible and even if they are not, there is no way that we can afford to make the kind of changes necessary to help so many people in so many ways." To which your response will be: "Can we afford not to?" We will turn to the issue of funding shortly.

For now, recognize that the actions necessary to fundamentally change how society conducts its affairs must be driven by the people of the world. We are the ones to establish and participate in a new form of global governance for everyone; one within which the other structures can most efficiently and humanely function to achieve our collective goals, knowing that enabling the well-being of all people is a necessary ingredient. *To structure a far better humanity, let securing the well-being of all people, stand as The Goal of One Governance.*

THE GOAL OF ONE COMMERCE

Systems of commerce operate at all levels of society, from one individual selling something to another, to mega-corporations producing products distributed and sold worldwide. Most operate within capitalistic systems which define success by growth incentivized with the lure of profits. We have discussed a few of the multitude of harmful impacts from operating businesses within these systems. Recognize that there is no universal mandate that businesses must be run this way. They are, because until now, we haven't: conceived of fundamentally better ways to manage our activities; implemented systems of governance to ensure best practices methodologies are used; and enabled systems of finance to fund new methodologies without stressing society in the process.

Business practices that came of age during the Industrial Revolution operated with little to no regulatory oversight. In many areas of the world that is still the case. In the beginning, our numbers were far fewer and our productive capacities limited, so the operational harms were less impactful and less apparent. Today, with 7.8 billion consumers, that is no longer the case.

Systems developed during the early years of the Industrial Revolution have changed little. Entities that practice self-regulation to effectively limit harms are almost unheard of, as within capitalistic systems such actions are correctly perceived as limiting competitive advantage. How so? Because not everybody is required to play by the same rules. If they did, things would be different, perhaps better, depending upon the rules. But because there are no uniform rules and regulations that all players within global systems of commerce must abide by, generally speaking, the company that brings the same product to market at the lowest price will dominate.

For example, how would your company compete on the global stage with a company producing similar products that pays employees one dollar an hour with no environmental quality safeguard requirements, when your company must pay a minimum wage of fifteen dollars an hour and deploy technologies designed to limit environmental degradation? It can't. Thus, the practices that dominate today's capitalistic systems of commerce, are the ones that pay the lowest wages and limit expenses associated with curtailing adverse environmental impacts; neither of which are good for society, or for Mother Earth.

This example should help clarify why most executives rebel against attempts to implement rules and regulations that are protective of society or of the environment, and why they fight regulatory measures that demand responsible management practices. The result is that irresponsibility rules within capitalistic systems, and we all suffer the consequences. So, what is to be? Are we stuck with a structure that abhors oversight, responsibility, and intervention by third parties for the greater good?

Directives that measure success by how large and how fast a business can be grown to produce the highest levels of profits without regard for the associated harms are certain recipes for disaster. They have delivered humanity to the brink of collapse.

What should be pretty obvious by now is the fact that operating businesses without regulations that dictate responsible oversight and practices, is a bad idea. Why? Because people running growth-based, profit-driven industries are disincentivized from self-regulation to prevent social and environmental harms. The structure within which these systems operate has clearly failed us. It is time to find another way, a better way.

Most of what we do happens within the structure of commerce. If we are to evolve from a pathogenic like organism aggressively attacking our host, we have to fundamentally change *how* we do most things. That means enabling systems of commerce to deliver the goods and services we all want and need in ways that are harmful neither to ourselves nor to the planet. To do so, to responsibly manage our affairs of commerce, requires a singular global structure within which a uniform set of rules and regulations are applicable to every person, every business venture, and every entity, no matter where it is located. Let's call that new structure, One Commerce.

One Commerce will need one fundamental goal at which everything done within that structure is guided by. It could be to do no harm. But arguments will be made that such a goal, if taken literally, will stop us in our tracks.

Instead, let's define *The Goal of One Commerce to be the production and delivery of all goods and services as efficiently as technologically possible at any given point in time.* The goal becomes one of practical efficiency. It translates into creating living systems of commerce designed to be constantly changing, constantly evolving new and better ways of doing the things we do. That sounds about right, doesn't it?

Of course, we will run into the argument that implementing such a goal is impossible, if for no other reason than we can't afford to be constantly upgrading our systems of commerce. We will discuss what evolving systems of commerce might look like shortly. For now, recognize the importance of incentivizing through systems of governance, and enabling through systems of finance, the development of ever more efficient systems of commerce, which brings us to the goal of the enabling structure.

THE GOAL OF ONE FINANCE

As we learned, of necessity, the goal of the existing Financial Structure is growth. Without growth, it will collapse and take down every other institution with it, which some think we can't let happen. That is why the largest financial institutions are believed to have become too big to fail. Having convinced those who pretend to govern that they truly are too big to fail, they now wield nearly limitless power over society.

And, because this structure must continue to grow, it must have outlets of growth, so our population must grow which means systems of governance and commerce must do so as well. But, change the nature and dictates of the Financial Structure, and the possibility of changing the others materializes.

The cold beauty of the existing Financial Structure is that although it must grow the money supply to survive, those who operate it have convinced the world that the supply of money is limited, that only they get to control it, and that if anyone wants access to their money, it has to be borrowed under agreements that often ensnare the borrower within inescapable webs of debt. As a result, most of us have unwittingly become modern-day slaves of the financial elite.

We have discussed the cruelty of systems that use money in limitation as a form of control of the populace. And we have discussed the fact that money is, and can be, anything we choose to make it. There is no universal dictate stating that money must be used sparingly. In fact, if the Universe were to comment on such practices, it would find them abhorrent.

So, let us right a wrong, the wrong being the wrong way to use money. Envision a new structure, One Finance, within which its most fundamental goal, *The Goal of One Finance, is to enable a civilized society, a humane humanity. We do so through mandates to create money, in abundance, to fund all of the things necessary to evolve a thriving, civilized society.*

We will shortly discuss how this iteration of the Financial Structure can work. Before we get there, we need to consider The Goal of The 4th Structure.

THE GOAL OF THE 4TH STRUCTURE

The 4th Structure is spiritual in nature. As such, its goals must enable a level of spiritual connectivity designed to inspire and guide humanity, as a collective whole, to achieve new and better ways of being. They must be all encompassing, and people must feel free to pursue their own spiritual connectivity. That means that The Goal of The 4th Structure must be sufficiently broad to encompass the ultimate expressions of the most fundamental aspects of the world's spiritual practices.

At the core of every spiritual philosophy is an ultimate but ethereal goal of attainment. For some it would be called Nirvana, for others: Heaven, Spiritual Enlightenment, Salvation, Freedom of the Soul, or perhaps Oneness. Each philosophy claims the unique ability to guide its followers in achieving its ultimate goal. All tie back to ways visualized by their prophets hundreds, if not thousands of years ago; ways crafted for small, relatively independent and less technologically capable societies.

But times have changed. We must now evolve better ways of doing almost everything we do if we are to both survive and thrive. To achieve that level of social change, our goals must reach across all structures and all systems, including the spiritual. And there should be no internal conflicts among them, meaning we must be united in their collective pursuit.

Uniting in action is the evolutionary step that we must take right now. Why is that? Because to exist as societies divided, prevents even the possibility of achieving fundamental social change, which by definition must be all encompassing. So, we begin by revisioning our societies to be cooperative in nature, in part by eliminating tension points, past ways that divide us, and in part by adopting new ways that unite us, which shared goals enable.

To help galvanize this level of change, The Goal of The 4th Structure must be both contemporary and inspirational. That does not mean that we should abandon the worthwhile goals of yesteryear. To the contrary, we simply revision worthy goals of the past to sync with new and better ways of being. Accordingly, The Goal of The 4th Structure should retain a level of spiritual connectivity linking modern practices to ancient quests to attain Nirvana, Heaven, Spiritual Enlightenment, Salvation, Freedom of the Soul, Oneness, and the like. The essence of these concepts is the same, so include them all within a broad definition of Enlightenment.

We also need to expand our approach to attainment and contemporize its definition. Because our capabilities of attainment have broadened, our philosophical and practical approaches to reaching this goal must expand as well. That occurs by modernizing our social and spiritual practices to sync with each other by focusing on the acquisition of knowledge and understanding to explain the unexplainable. As we expand our understanding of how the universe works, we should recognize the deeply spiritual nature of the process, as with each new discovery made, we come closer to experiencing the essence that is life. So, let's set *The Goal of The 4th Structure to be the attainment of Enlightenment.*

- 13 -

ELIMINATE THE LIE
EMBRACE ALL TRUTHS

We have monumental decisions to make at a time when the most powerful forcibly oppose progressive change. Will we continue with the status quo and allow thousands of years of reckless and destructive behavior to define our future, or will we free ourselves of the chains of past ways to enable the evolution of a society in search of truth and understanding? The answer will be determined by the goals *we* set, the decisions *we* make, and the actions *we* take together, as One. *We*, is the operative word. And *our* success will hinge upon *our* ability to eliminate the influence of those who practice the lie, and to support those who seek the truth.

Unfortunately, there are those among us who actively oppose progressive change, preferring to chain humanity to past ways. They will do and say whatever they feel necessary to remain in control by keeping things the same. Many of them embrace a phenomenon that has stymied humanity for thousands of years, *the lie*. These people practice *the lie*, believe in *the lie*, and value *the lie*. They are afraid of the truth and believe that deception empowers them, when in fact the inability or unwillingness to accept the truth and speak the truth is both self-destructive and counter evolutionary.

If we are to choose evolution over extinction, the importance of embracing the truth in all social aspects must be elevated, and *the lie* must be eliminated from accepted practice. So, let's briefly consider how institutions built upon foundations of lies hold us back and then envision how those built upon foundations of truth can propel us forward.

THE CULTURE OF THE LIE

A lie is "a false statement made with deliberate intent to deceive."[155] The lie requires two elements: intention and deception. Every lie is intended to distort or cover up some truth to lead or mislead another into thinking or doing, or not thinking or not doing, something. Lies have become a social norm, an accepted practice. Why is that when most people do not want to be lied to? Pretty much everyone wants to be told the truth. So why does anyone stand with those individuals who embrace the lie, especially now, when lying is massively destructive to the well-being of a species on the cusp of evolutionary change?

Lies appear at an early age. Learning that it is OK to lie in childhood has allowed the culture of the lie to metastasize throughout society. Adults lie fearing that a truth may reveal their mistakes, resulting in the truth being overlooked or covered up, which magnifies the harms from the mistake. How childishly backward to fear what is. Is it not far better to accept what is and go about fixing a mistake, than to live chained within the confines of the lie?

Yet, societies everywhere embrace lies with such regularity that most expect their leaders to lie, and lying leaders expect their subordinates to promote their lies. There is perhaps no better present example of how cruel, socially repressive, and environmentally destructive a society of liars can be than the one headed by the forty-fifth President of the US. People like him lie to gain advantage. They lie in fear of consequences that will rain down upon them for revealing the truth. And they lie to profit through activities sheltered by the lie. Lies retard social progress. They make us less humane.

Liars distort, bend, compromise, obscure, and otherwise make truths more difficult to gather. They jeopardize human existence by valuing profits over responsibility, war over peace, destruction over creativity, hate over empathy, greed over generosity, and the few over the many.

Lies kill and can be of such magnitude that they trigger a cascade of environmental degradation and social destruction. All lies are sins in the truest sense of the word as they keep us from Truth. Some lies elevate to crimes against humanity and/or against nature. To bring home this point, consider the following, which are just a few of the most damaging lies of the recent past.

LIES OF THE OIL AND GAS INDUSTRY

As we've discussed, oil industry rulers have taken the art of the lie to another level. In the process, they have doomed hundreds of millions to suffer, ensured financial calamity, and ignited systemic failures of planetary-level life support systems. They built their playbook of lies upon methods honed by an industry so adept at the art of deceit that notwithstanding that its product has killed far more people than any other, it remains one of the most widely used, ever.

LIES OF THE TOBACCO INDUSTRY

The tobacco industry has been dependent upon the dissemination of lies and misinformation for over 60 years. Although there is literally no socially redeeming value to the use of tobacco products, this industry exists with little to no regulation.

Tobacco "harms nearly every organ of the body." It causes nearly 20 percent of all US deaths and "is the leading preventable cause of death." Tobacco use causes cancer "almost anywhere in your body."

It increases the risk of heart disease and stroke by two to four times and lung cancer by 25 times.[156]

Tobacco products kill three million people every year, yet industry documents reveal what some have called "the most astonishing systematic corporate deceit of all time."[157] This product is as deadly as a bullet; it just takes longer for it to work. Yet, irresponsible leadership within systems of governance and commerce enable what amounts to a crime against humanity by allowing its use.

This industry has so successfully deceived regulators and the public into believing that smoking is not harmful, that even in light of overwhelming evidence to the contrary, most who govern allow rulers of Big Tobacco the freedom to wage global marketing campaigns targeting children, who become lifelong addicts.

Tobacco products are so highly addictive that even people dying from lung cancer cannot stop from taking the next drag. Watching loved ones suffering as they are dying from tobacco-induced emphysema and cancers is a gut-wrenching emotional experience. And addicts impose a heavy financial burden on society.

Unsurprisingly, tobacco products are so aggressively marketed to the world's poorest people that it evidences "an arrogance and fanaticism" almost beyond belief, helping ensure the poor remain poor by taking money to feed their addiction instead of their children. That same money could have been used to start a business, buy a computer, or educate the addict, but it isn't.

There really isn't much more that can be said about an industry that exists solely because its products are so highly addictive that it has had to rely on artfully crafted lies and political bribes, except perhaps to ask why hasn't society eliminated these products from its stream of commerce when to do so would save millions of lives, trillions of dollars in healthcare costs, and help the poorest escape poverty? There is only one answer to that question. Money.

This industry makes so much money that its owners can use a little to "persuade" officials to disregard their sworn duties to protect and serve the people. Many political campaigns in the US are funded with tobacco money, a practice that has legalized bribery by calling it something else. In other countries officials are more open about the process, simply expecting to receive bribes in exchange for allowing a harmful practice to continue, another stunning failure within existing systems of governance.

OTHER INDUSTRY LIES

Whether they are designed to cover up harms from products the manufacturer knows to be dangerous, like non-stick coatings on cookware that cause birth defects or herbicides known to cause cancer, or endocrine disruptors released within food packaging containers or industry practices known to be harmful to the environment like fracking or pesticide use, the list of lies within industries of commerce are nearly endless.

Perhaps the biggest and most pervasive lie throughout all industry is that "our employees are our most valuable asset." That statement is typical of disinformation campaigns waged throughout most industries to generate employee loyalty. So long as the cost of employee labor can be had cheaper than alternatives, the statement is true from the employer's perspective because they produce the most profits. But …

From the employee's perspective, if they were the most valuable asset, they would be the last to be sacrificed rather than the first during economic downturns. If that statement was true, theirs would be living rather than subsistence wages. If that statement was true, they would receive a fair percentage of the annual profits they are responsible for generating; but most employees don't, do they?

What is important to remember is that it is not an industry or a corporation that lies; it is the people who own and operate them that propagate the lie. People lie for any number of reasons, but ultimately, in business, the reasoning falls back to money and how it is used to shape society.

GOVERNANCE BY LIE

Like corporations, governments are not real; there is no 'thing' that is a government. It cannot exist without people. Conceptually, a government is nothing more than people working together to provide structure within which the rest of society operates by making and enforcing rules and regulations. They call their activities "governing." Don't make the concept bigger than it is.

Theoretically, governments exist to serve and protect the health, safety, and welfare of the governed. In a better world, that would in fact be true. But that is not how most forms of governance on this planet operate. A few are good. Some really bad. Many, in between. All are far from perfect and would function more effectively if lying and graft were not accepted practices. But the sad reality of governance is that, as Richard Nixon once said, "If you can't lie, you'll never go anywhere."

That is an astonishingly revealing admission coming from one of the world's most powerful rulers. It highlights expected practices for those seeking high social positions. Again, look no further than the forty-fifth President of the United States to see how far embracing the culture of the lie can take one, and how truly harmful doing so can be. Within so-called democratic systems, politicians lie to get votes and deceive to stay in power, doing whatever corporations and wealthy donors pay them to do in exchange for financing their political campaigns and / or being offered lucrative private-sector deals after leaving office.

Good people are turned bad and forced to lie, cheat, steal, torture, and kill because someone, somewhere, in a position of power will benefit. Those who attempt to govern in many democracies owe their allegiances to power-hungry demagogues, who bribe and coerce for personal or corporate gain, even though their salaries and perks of office are paid by the governed through the fruits of their labors turned into taxes. These are not hidden secrets. They are accepted practices that only we, the people, can change.

People instinctively know that using money or a favor to influence someone in a position of authority is morally and ethically wrong, yet they do it and we allow it everywhere. Once a bribe has been accepted, society suffers. Lucrative government contracts are awarded to build, for example, multimillion-dollar bridges to nowhere. In countries with large militaristic systems, the governed may suffer from the diversion of money from needed social services to the military when those who govern are effectively paid to lie. Think Iraq, 2003. The lie? The existence of "weapons of mass destruction." As a result of that lie, the military industrial complex received trillions of dollars and the people living in Iraq suffered extreme hardship, death, and destruction beyond our ability to comprehend.

Within all aspects of society, the culture of the lie builds upon itself until the lie is expected. At the heart of the cultural lie is money and the quest for power. If we are to create a better way of being human, we must change accepted practices. Instead of embracing the lie and obscuring the truth, a broad aspect of society must reward all who seek truths and penalize those who embrace the lie.

Is this level of change possible? Well, the answer rests with how we choose to use money. Use it to eliminate the need for bribery and coercion in governance; make it available without penalty to fund socially beneficial projects that meet the needs of many; create it to enable industry to produce ever more efficiently; use it to elevate the value of morality in society, and the answer is yes, we can eliminate the need for the lies that otherwise haunt us. But we are told that we can't afford to do any of those things because there simply is not enough money, which is the most inhumane lie of them all.

THE MOST INHUMANE LIE OF THEM ALL

The most inhumane of all deceptions ever perpetrated against humanity is taking place right here, right now. "There is no money … We can't afford it … There is not enough money to _____ (fill in the blank) … feed the starving … educate our children … pay for life-saving drugs ... clean up the environment ... and on and on and on." You name it, the lack of money is the granddaddy of all excuses used to justify why billions suffer extreme levels of deprivation.

The financial elite as *the* manufacturers of money have so artfully crafted a system of lies that is so grand, so intricate, and so secretive, that they have effectively obscured the simple truth of money, which is that it can be whatever we want it to be for use as abundantly as we choose it to be.

By limiting the use and availability of money in society, it is arguable that the financial elite have become the epicenter of the most inhumane levels of deprivation, social strife, war and suffering, there has ever been. As if that's not bad enough, by promulgating the false belief that money is a limited commodity and that we must pay them for the privilege of using it, these people are responsible for the deaths of millions and the destruction of the environment. Their ways imperil our very existence and should be viewed as both crimes against humanity and nature. What is clear is that the Financial Structure can be operated in far better ways, as will be discussed within Chapters 18-22.

As a species, our collective efforts should be aligned and focused on the search for truth. No one should be deprived of access to the truth. Just as the truth does not hide from the light, it can be obscured and hidden by those who lie or choose not to look. Philosophies may differ, but universal truths do not vary by perspective or belief; they are steadfast and await discovery. And the truth is that every person who embraces the lie, jeopardizes our very existence. It is time to eliminate the lie from accepted social practice.

Life's opportunities emanate from discoveries of universal truths. Truth is truth. There is no ambiguity about it; it is what is. We should not try to bend it one way or another to suit a particular perspective or belief. Accept what is. Try to understand it rather than bend or deny it. Whether you are a schoolteacher, a parent, elder, spiritual leader, an individual who sits at the pinnacle of society or one who resides elsewhere, whatever your role is, it is time to denounce the lie and embrace all truths, for as the saying goes: only the truth will set us free.

EMBRACE ALL TRUTHS

Ah, truth. The search for it is what life is ultimately all about. Those who dedicate their lives in search of a fundamental truth do so with a sense of purpose, knowing that their contributions, whatever they happen to be, are part of something grand, something uplifting, something spiritual. Truth is "the property of being in accord with fact or reality," "a transcendent fundamental," and "God."[158] Fundamental truths define broad properties of existence that are objective, verifiable. They are not subject to perspective or what you may want to believe they are. They are what is.

As knowledge of the nature of the problems we have created spreads, the enormity of the curative process may appear overwhelming. Some will simply give up thinking it's no use, we are what we are and nothing's going to change that. Give up and they will be proved correct. Others will attempt to change existing structures from within. They will meet formidable opposition and will fail in their attempts, if for no other reason than it took too long. A few will attempt to create fundamentally new and better ways of being as they travel along pathways differing from those of mainstream social endeavors. Their challenge will be one of focus and determination. Success for them dwells within the goals of the collective, in simplicity, and in their steadfast commitment to the process.

Most societies fail to elevate the importance of maintaining the sanctity of truths as foundational components within the systems they operate. The result is often the subjugation of truths to lies.

Lies are regressive acts. Seeking truths are progressive acts. If we want to be better humans, to progress as a species, we must imbed the values of seeking the truth, speaking the truth and accepting the truth of whatever it may be, throughout all levels of society. We do so by making the search for universal truths a fundamental social goal.

Goals designed to further the search for truth are progressive. They pull us forward in ways that transcend the past to enable new and better ways of being. Set the right goals, commit to achieving them, and there is little we cannot accomplish.

Facts are truths that define reality. Reality is the truth beyond the experience, its essence, what some call God, others Life. For most of human history, the truth of why things were as they are was beyond our ability to know, so we created systems of beliefs to explain the unknown. As societies grew, a few extraordinary people happened along. Finding wonder in the unknown and driven by curiosity, they observed, experimented, considered what revealed and then came to understand the truth behind their observations. They, were the first scientists.

Science is the study of reality in an attempt to understand truths behind the observed. Science is a process, a practice of coming to knowledge of what some thing is, how it works, and hopefully why. Some scientific revelations have shattered accepted beliefs so fundamental to society that public denial was tantamount to heresy. Volcanic eruptions, lightning, thunder, drought, and epidemics were all believed to be acts of unhappy gods requiring sacrifice in appeasement, until evidence developed through observation disproved the beliefs and changed destructive social practices.

For nearly 2,000 years, a large and powerful segment of the population believed that the Earth was flat, that it was the center of the universe, and that the sun revolved around it. These beliefs were maintained long after scientists had compiled sufficient factual data to prove them wrong. Why? Because it was believed that any such admission would weaken the position of those in power of the institutions promoting such beliefs. As a result, universal truths have long been subjugated to the lie. Time and again the social evolution of our species has been retarded by the lies of those in power.

Yet, when given the freedom to explore, we have made incredible discoveries of universal processes, life truths. From those discoveries we have gathered both knowledge and understanding of how some of those processes work, which we have creatively used for social benefit. The knowledge of how just a few aspects of this universe's workings operate has enabled our progression from cave dweller to lunar traveler.

Nine thousand years ago we discovered that plants grow from seeds which could be saved and used during the next growing season. That precious little truth gave rise to systems of agriculture capable of feeding billions.

Recognition that the wheel reduces resistance transformed our ability to travel from one place to another, making way for discoveries of ever more efficient ways of transport. The realization that interstellar bodies could be used to guide our travels lead to more sophisticated guiding methodologies like the compass and now, turn by turn voice guided global positioning system (GPS) applications available on your phone.

The discovery of microscopic life forms led to our understanding that they can cause disease which led to the discovery of life-saving antibiotics and antivirals. The recognition that eating certain parts of a plant could block physical pain lead to the discovery of anesthetics which now enables prolonged life-saving medical procedures.

We have been aware of a certain force of nature for hundreds of thousands of years, yet it took us nearly that long to figure out how to use it beneficially. Investigations into electricity enabled modern society and the technological revolution. The discovery that sound and light move in waves enabled us to communicate over vast distances, almost instantaneously.

The list of life-changing discoveries of universal truths is vast. The few that we have touched upon so far have transformed our lived experiences and propelled us forward, enabling us to become so much more than we were capable of envisioning not long ago.

Truths define life and give it meaning. They may not be what we want to believe in, but they define reality and should be accepted as such, not molded into something else. Yet, rulers of every structure and most systems abhor transparency, promulgate lies and punish those who divulge the truth about what they do. Punishing anyone who speaks the truth about another's actions (whether taken in the name of a government, corporation, financial or religious institution) is a regressive act, one detrimental to society and hence, a crime against humanity. With that understanding in mind, ask yourself how you should act when faced with a potential penalty for espousing a truth? For guidance, consider what Gandhi so wisely professed:

> Many people, especially ignorant people, want to punish you for speaking the truth, for being correct, for being you. Never apologize for being correct or being years ahead of your time. If you know you're right, speak your mind. Even if you are a minority of one, the truth is still the truth.

Truths must be revered, not feared. Recognize that a single truth is difficult enough to discover on its own. They become exponentially harder to discover when truths are feared or covered up. To be forced to live in fear of what is true, is to be forced to live in fear of life itself. That, some will declare, is a cardinal sin. So, as difficult as it may be, we must accept the truth of what we are, be willing to speak the truth to power, and choose to be different, to be better, to change our ways.

There are millions of examples of how truths benefit us and millions more of how lies do not. We all pretty much know that placing our faith in truths is good, and that doing the same with lies is bad, so we really don't need to spend more time on this subject other than to suggest that if you are to place your faith anywhere, believe in the intrinsic value of all truths. Use the scientific method to make new discoveries and then learn how to use what has been discovered for the benefit of all human kind. But recognize that technological advances alone will not save us from impending doom. That, will require fundamentally changing how we treat each other and those we share Earth with.

We possess the knowledge and the ability necessary to save the world and our kind. What we are now called upon to do is use that knowledge in fundamentally superior ways. That means eliminating the lie from accepted social practice and focusing on seeking the truth, speaking the truth, disseminating the truth, and embracing all truths. Do so, and we will have realized a better way of being.

14

A Better Way

To realize better ways of being we must look within our hearts, which feel what our minds fail to perceive. Instinctively, we know whether something is good or bad, right or wrong. That knowledge emanates from within. But few have learned to listen to their hearts and fewer still follow their heart's callings, which requires belief in the goodness that will result.

Following what the heart has to say requires a level of presence, practice, and focused dedication that society fails to encourage. If it did, when two opposed are enabled by social norms to open their hearts and their minds to hear, truly hear, what the other has to say, and when each has been prepared to let the past be just that, their conflicts will resolve because each has been freed to accept the essence of what the other seeks.

Is it not true that most of us would prefer to help, rather than harm another? Why is that? Because goodness permeates from deep within our souls, radiating as love, which opens pathways to better ways of being. As individuals, we gather great satisfaction from helping another. Every day brings hundreds of millions of examples of kind citizens acting to make a better world by helping another in some way. Whether it is protecting an endangered species, planting a tree, helping restore a sensitive habitat, or assisting an elder safely cross the street, lending an ear when there are no others who will listen, sharing a meal with someone without, providing shelter to a family in need, or holding the hand of one whose last breath is upon them, we humans have a great capacity for kindness, for love. And with each act of kindness, we make a better world.

Our challenge is to recognize that there exists a broader, more cohesive purpose behind every act of kindness. To realize that purpose requires us to connect everyone who wants to help us be better at being human within an umbrella of commonality. Doing so empowers a consciousness of change which enables a movement of fundamental change designed to secure better ways of being.

To find our way out of the mess we have created and into a future of promise and possibility requires acts of kindness and compassion directed at all our fellow Earth beings. Acts of kindness encourage reciprocal acts of kindness which compound to become transformative in nature. They allow us to shed old ways of being, which enables better ways of being, as we venture forth into the unknown in search of life truths. Truths discovered lead to knowledge from which comes understanding and ultimately wisdom, something our species is sorely in need of.

The search for truth entails journeys of action, of change. Such journeys are unbounded by the past, expressed in the moment, and alight with the possibility of a nearly limitless future. Every action changes the world. Destructive actions destroy it; constructive actions improve it. The more actions of one kind or another that take place, the greater the likelihood the result will reflect them. To enhance the likelihood of securing fundamentally better ways of being, our actions must begin at the local level, in part by elevating the importance of the educational process.

EDUCATION

Educate an individual to illuminate a life.
Educate a society to enlighten humanity.

To travel new pathways seeking to unravel life mysteries necessitates the gathering of knowledge of how things work and their interrelationships with all other things. This requires a robust educational process within which knowledge is built upon and passed from generation to generation. The stronger the educational process, the faster knowledge is gathered and new discoveries are made, bringing greater certainty to life and better ways of being. It is critically important to recognize that creating an educated society is a necessary prerequisite to evolving a civilized society, which is perhaps the only way to save ourselves from ourselves. Educating a society is a multi-pronged process. It entails educating both the heart, and the mind.

EDUCATION OF THE MIND

Once again, we have it backward. At a time when life-threatening planetary-scale problems must be solved for humanity to both survive and flourish, militarization is prioritized over education. Instead of putting the collective intelligence of an educated humanity to work solving our problems, we engage millions in militaristic activities while limiting access to a robust education to a few who typically serve Wall Street rather than Main Street.

In a world structured to foster inequality, access to higher education is conditioned. Financial resources are withheld from educators. Lack of money is used as the excuse for the inability to provide everyone with quality educational experiences. Funding cuts undermine a school's ability to stimulate a child's native intelligence and ignite her innate creativity, limiting the next generation to be workers relegated to performing relatively menial tasks, instead of elevating them to become entrepreneurs, technologists and intellectuals. We know that:

> The health of the nation's economy and our quality of life
> will depend crucially on the creativity and intellectual
> capacity of our people. If we neglect our schools, we dimin-

ish our future ... At a time when producing workers with high-level technical and analytical skills is increasingly important to a country's prosperity, large cuts in funding for basic education could cause lasting harm.[159]

How money is allocated within existing systems is a matter of choice. In 2016, the US Federal Government spent $1.3 trillion on military and related defense expenditures, which exceeded the combined military expenditures of the next ten largest militaries in the world.[160] That same year it spent less than $70 billion to educate its people.[161] That is not a wise use of resources.

Educating everyone as rapidly as possible is perhaps the single most effective step humanity can take to ensure its survival as "each year of education reduces the risk of conflict by around 20%."[162] Why is that? Probably because most educated people prefer not to put themselves in harm's way. So, doesn't it stand to reason that the way to eliminate war is to educate everyone as fast as we can and then provide employment opportunities suitable to their level of educational attainment. Sadly, at a time when the sheer burden of our numbers threatens all life on Earth, we limit access to a robust educational experience by limiting funding and setting a price tag which most can't afford, ensuring there will be many willing to fight, rather than many willing to unite.

Everyone knows the value of obtaining a solid education, so there is little reason to spend a lot of time with something we know to be true, other than to highlight a few of the most important reasons to highly educate everyone as rapidly as possible. For instance, studies confirm that an educated person is likely to elevate out of poverty, whereas an uneducated person is not. "As common sense suggests - and academic research confirms - money matters for educational outcomes. For instance, poor children who attend better-funded schools are more likely to complete high school and have higher earnings and lower poverty rates in adulthood."[163]

And most will agree that one of our collective goals should be the elimination of poverty. The best way to do that is to create an educated society that provides pathways to a better life and to a more successful society of beings.

Another of our goals should be to eliminate social inequality. Education is truly, 'the great equalizer.' But rulers don't want an equalized society, so they withhold funding even for the most basic levels of education which delays social progress, ensures the poor remain poor, and limits our ability to solve the vast array of problems we create.

Education provides the foundation from which knowledge springs. The more highly educated humanity becomes, the greater our capacities for discovery become. The more we discover, the more we can learn. The more we learn, the greater our chances of survival and the more attainable become our goals. The reasons to create a highly educated society are vast, not the least of which is the fact that the welfare of humanity depends crucially upon our collective intellectual capacity and creativity. The more people we highly educate, the more people are available to work on solving the planetary level problems we face, which of course enhances our chances of both surviving and thriving.

But educating the mind is insufficient to clear a major hurdle we face. That of the primal self, the selfish individual, the barbarian within. To step beyond ways that promote conflict and self-interest, and to enable the rise of a more harmonious, civilized society of beings, we must also educate the heart.

EDUCATION OF THE HEART

We educate to expand the foundations upon which to create higher functioning societies. We also educate to enable better ways of being which requires a different kind of educational process; it requires learning to be comfortable with each other. As so aptly stated by the Fourteenth Dalai Lama,

> My wish is that, one day, formal education will pay attention to the education of the heart, teaching love, compassion, justice, forgiveness, mindfulness, tolerance and peace.

The predominant actions of any society define it. Ones that act with great compassion and are just, forgiving, mindful, tolerant, peaceful, and loving, are civilized; ones that do not, are not. Even though many of us possess those fine attributes, the fact that we fail to express them in so many ways and in so many places means that as a species, we are not civilized. No society that allows billions to suffer or that acts with near total disregard of the adverse consequences from its actions on the environment and the beings it shares its planet with, is even close to being civilized.

Being, is a descriptive word, the manifestations of which define us. For humanity to be civilized, requires it to act civilized. To be civilized is to create environments within which we are more comfortable 'being' with each other. This allows us to be better at 'being' humane, a quality that manifests from the heart. Qualities that manifest from the heart require environments that enable them to blossom. Those environments are determined by how our structures operate. Structures designed to enable the evolution of a civilized society create environments within which teachings of the heart are incorporated into the daily activities of their members. They incentivize the practice of these teachings within the home, at school, and in all workplaces as a means of enabling humane societies.

Teachings of the heart are foundational prerequisites to evolving a civilized society. Why? Because knowledge without compassion is dangerous and subject to abuse by the beast within. It has brought arsenals of weapons of mass destruction to rulers who are neither just, compassionate, forgiving, tolerant, mindful, nor peaceful. They reign irresponsibly, often brutally. At some point a mistake will be made, weapons of mass destruction will be unleashed, and billions will die. Is that the fate you would choose for your offspring?

Education of the mind has not brought us peace. Rather, it has delivered more efficient ways of killing everything we encounter, fostering systems of industry that thrive on war and propagate aggression, ensuring that chaos reigns within the 196 societies competing for ownership of Earth's dwindling resources. Educating the mind is wasted without coupling the ways of the heart.

To live within a civilized society should be everyone's goal. Adopt it as the goal of our time and incorporate educating the heart along with the mind as intrinsic parts of the educational process to help make it so. When the collective acts of humanity follow our hearts' directions, all will be well.

So, seek truth. Embrace change. Educate everyone as rapidly as possible and behold our transformation into a society of civilized beings engaged in unraveling life mysteries. Favor education over ignorance, the intellectual over the ignorant. Do not wait. Remove all impediments to obtaining a robust educational life experience, for everyone. Create one system of global education, (One Global Education) within which everyone is enabled and encouraged to attain the highest levels of education they are capable of receiving, free of charge, and as rapidly as possible. We reveal how within Book VI.

When society has moved from one that cherishes the taking to one that cherishes the giving, it will have evolved. Give education freely and abundantly to enable transformational change and create a compassionate humanity.

TRANSFORMATIONAL CHANGE

Transformational change is fundamental. It is a caterpillar to butterfly kind of thing. The caterpillar and the butterfly have the same DNA. Each just expresses it differently. And the result yields a fundamentally different life experience. Earthbound and incapable of traveling far, the caterpillar consumes as much as it can as fast as it can before experiencing winged transformation, at which point it is released, freed to explore a far grander universe in a far grander way. One form consumes, the other soars and pollinates. So different, yet so essentially the same.

Humans have created structures and systems that work really well for a few, horribly for many, and not well for the rest. Like the caterpillar, we grow and consume just about everything within reach. Should we choose to be more butterfly-like, to be released to explore a far grander universe in far grander ways, we must transform ourselves by changing *how* our structures operate.

Transformational change is required when systems and structures are beyond fixing, as are ours. It replaces the old with the new, as must we. Per Industry Week,

> **Transformational change is not problem-solving. It is designing the whole system to meet the needs of customers and the future environment. It is an act of creating something, not fixing something ...**

> **Transformational change is about proactively creating the future organization and system. It asks, "Given the future environment, the technology, the market, and social changes, what do we need to be like in the future, and how do we create that future?"** [164] (Emphasis added)

"What do we need to be like in the future, and how do we create that future?" This work attempts to provide some guidance in answer to those very questions. And you, yes you, are encouraged to consider what we need to be like and then help make that change possible by connecting with others who know that if we do not, then there will be no future worth sending our loved ones into.

Humanity is ready for transformational change. People the world over are crying out for it. They have taken to the streets in protest of the way things are. But their actions are fragmented and directed at changing the particular system of governance they live within or at changing a particular system of commerce they experience negative impacts from. Unfortunately, those systems are too broken to be fixed; they need to be replaced, which is only possible after entirely new structures have been envisioned and created. That will necessitate billions uniting with other similarly-minded individuals in one coordinated global action to make it so.

Fortunately, we have the ability to "proactively create" the future "we" want. *We*, is the operative word. It is up to *us* to make it happen. *We*, have to lock onto the most meaningful things in life, the ways of being *we* collectively value most, and declare them as *our* goals. Those goals will provide a new direction for us, guiding us along new pathways upon which *we* create the society *we* want to be a part of. To achieve them *we* must envision a humanity that is grand and all-encompassing, and then *we* must act to make it so. But how will we know when we are ready for such fundamental changes to take place?

We will be ready when billions of us have said enough, *we* refuse to go along with the barbaric ways of those who rule.

We will be ready when billions stand together as one, committed to creating new ways of being that are held with such intensity that change becomes a foregone conclusion.

We will be ready when *we* have united as brothers and sisters in common cause, with goals that glisten with such clarity and purity of purpose that the advantage of adopting them is self-evident.

It is *our* time to leave the barbaric ways of the uncivilized behind and move toward the brilliance of a society united in search of the ways of the enlightened. It is *our* time to change from the ways of the consuming caterpillar to those of the butterfly in full flight soaring through this most wondrous universe. It is *our* time to experience transformational change. It begins within The Movement.

15

The Movement

We face immense challenges, great uncertainty, and tremendous human and environmental turmoil. We are growing, divided, and living within crumbling structures no longer capable of serving our kind. We are like a gigantic freight train continuously adding new cars overburdened with ever more occupants, speeding uncontrollably downhill toward a cliff at ever-accelerating rates with grave disregard for the consequences of our actions. Our sheer mass makes it impossible to stop and nearly impossible to make the directional changes necessary to avoid the extinction event that awaits beyond the cliff's edge.

Science advises that to change the direction of anything in motion will require a force powerful enough to move it in a new direction. The more massive the thing in motion, the more powerful the force of change must be. If humanity is to avoid extinction's cliff, we must move billions from the pathway currently traveled, onto a new one. This will require the greatest force of social change ever attempted. It will require billions of people who are guided by their hearts, enabled by their intellects, and inspired by the nature of all things, to unite in one movement of fundamental social change: The Movement.

A movement isn't called that for nothing. It has to *move* people. It needs lovers, and friends, and allies. It has to generate a cascade of feeling - moral

feeling. The movement's passion has to become a general passion. And that passion must be focused: the concern that people feel about some large condition "out there" has to find traction closer to home.[165]

(Emphasis added)

As so elegantly stated above, for The Movement to succeed, its goals must be so morally sound that they will create a cascade of positive feelings of such magnitude that billions will be moved to help accomplish them. If the foundational goal of The Movement is to move humanity from operating hundreds of fractured, barbaric societies, to operating one civilized society, and if it is supported by others designed to achieve it, do you think this goal will serve the purpose? We do.

So, let us state that *The Goal of The Movement is to create a humane global community; a civilized society.* This goal is big, simple, and clear. There can be no goal with greater traction at this moment in time.

Civilizations do not just materialize; they are creatures of intention, imagination, and creativity. Leaders must appear and chart a new course for humanity that is so clearly superior to the current one that a huge mass of humanity will move from here to there, creating one civilized society that encompasses us all. Achieving this goal will require an uncompromising force of will inspired by our collective commitments to elevate the purpose of the human existence by bringing the concepts of progress, of change, out from under the cloak of darkness that enshrouds them.

What you need to know is that this force of change already exists. It exists the world over, within the millions of communities and associations of people helping others by limiting our adverse impacts upon the environment and ourselves. People helping people. It is what we do when we are not pitted one against the other. When we are engaged in cooperative efforts to secure the common good, we can and will do the truly amazing.

Now is the first time in history that a global movement of a large percentage of the people is possible. Most of us can interconnect and communicate instantaneously. However, agreeing in concept but being unwilling to commit and participate to help bring about real social change is of little help. As Jane Goodall said,

What you do makes a difference,
and you have to decide
what kind of a difference you want to make.

Napoleon Bonaparte recognized that, "Ten people who speak make more noise than 10,000 that are silent." Billions of us can now 'speak' in unison, and when we do, the noise will be deafening and empowering. It is time for each of us to find our voices and not only speak, but act, to make a difference. Even though it takes tremendous courage to unite in action for the common good to enable the change humanity so desperately needs, we must muster that courage. And, we must be prepared to sacrifice a little today to build a movement of change that is so substantial that nothing can prevent it from realigning our trajectory.

Rulers will tell you not to speak in favor of The Movement or to waste time with it because its goals are unrealistic, or illegal, or heretical, or _____ (fill in the blank). If you listen to them and choose not to speak and act, you will prove them right. But should you decide to make a difference, to prove them wrong, then do not be deterred by whatever they say or do.

Today, there are millions of people and organizations working independently on important projects to make a better, more humane world. Each is valuable no matter how small its contributions, because a better world it does make. And we must keep at it, no matter the challenges, no matter the opposition. So, if you are not already a member of such a group, consider becoming one, as their actions speak for themselves.

Ultimately, the key to enabling transformational change is to create an inviolable linkage based upon commonality of purpose between every person and every organization desirous of creating a truly civilized society, a humane humanity. From this simple action comes immense power. Individually, each is limited in what they can accomplish. But collectively, by working together to secure our most fundamental goals, an indomitable force of change emerges. That force is magnified by The Movement, which is empowered when we share with it a small percentage of our resources, whether time volunteered, products donated, or funding provided. The process melds our collective goals. It unites us so that we speak with one voice determined to make a better world and transform the human life experience.

UNITED IN ACTION

To forge a just and forgiving civilization, *we stand* together as One.

To create a world where the well-being of all people is paramount and guaranteed as a fundamental human right, *we speak* as One.

To create a civilization free of hatred, war and violence, unrestrained by backward driven systems that take more than they give, *we act* as One.

Only together, united in action, will *we create* a civilized society.

The above, are self-evident truths. Because the nature of the change that we enable through these actions is evolutionary, it will neither appear to be fast nor easy. It is difficult to grasp just how encompassing this level of change must be to alter our direction and pull humanity forward by sheer force of will. Sacrifice and hardship will be thrust upon many, especially the few who elevate to lead the way. They carry the great burden of making transformational change happen. Protect them. Only together, united in action, can we move society out from the dark ages into civilization's light.

THE PROPHESY

As The Movement expands, rulers will lash out claiming we are a threat to humanity. Rulers of some governments pronouncing us terrorists will unleash their armies upon us. We take no action against them. We practice peace, not war, because, as Ben Ferencz said, "War can make murderers out of otherwise good people." And we are not murderers.

And we are not terrorists, although their actions will likely define them as such. They are the real threat to humanity. Not us. We force no one to practice our ways, whereas they force everyone they can to practice theirs.

Some religious rulers will preach that we are anarchists and threats to their religious orders. They lie to you when they do. We do not rebel against their practices. We practice tolerance in the face of their intolerance, hypocrisy, and lies. And we leave their followers free to choose whatever religious tenants they prefer. We are not anarchists, they are.

A few rulers of commerce will deny access to their goods and services under the mistaken belief that by so doing they will cause new system failures, bringing us back as their consumers. They will be wrong. Their acts will speed the development of superior systems incorporating best practice methodologies resulting in more efficient, environmentally sound systems of production and delivery of goods and services which will render their systems obsolete. This is their fear, not ours.

Existing financial systems are the most extractive of any ever created. They divide rather than unite. Their rulers will attack us for creating money to enable rather than enslave. They limit the use of money and use it as a weapon. We use money to elevate and empower all members of our civilized society rather than sublimate everyone to their barbaric one. Their acts stem from fear of power lost. Our acts stem from love of our brothers and sisters.

Theirs is the power to save lives and to heal and transform society, but they choose systems of death, destruction, and debt over ones that create prosperity and happiness. We choose to use money to prevent suffering, rather than cause it. Our structures will rapidly replace theirs as citizens of the world recognize the benefits from our ways and the extreme burdens from theirs.

Rulers will resist The Movement in every conceivable way, throwing obstacle after obstacle at us. When obstacles fail, unjustly labeling us traitors, terrorists, and anarchists, they will reign war and terror upon us, lashing out in savage fury to deny the peace and prosperity humanity so desperately needs. The horror of their actions will reveal them for what they are: barbarians.

When rulers order attacks, their followers will kill their brothers and sisters who cause them no harm. Blindly obeying orders ensures their followers remain slaves of the elite, whose actions threaten the very existence of humankind.

Everyone has a choice in how they will act. No one should act on morally reprehensible orders. In point of fact, it is your moral obligation to ignore any such order. Question authority. Question what you are told to do. Follow your heart. Follow only those who seek to bring what is true to the light of day, not those who distort it for profit and power.

Belief in the goodness of the human spirit is the way to enhance our collective life experiences as we come together to form a more perfect union. Acts of violence, destruction, hatred, and greed are crimes against humanity to be dealt with as each era dictates.

At first, it will appear they are winning as we do not resist old ways, choosing instead to focus all efforts on solidifying change by creating new, better ways of being. It may take time, but as awareness of a better way unfolds, an exodus of the people will flow to The Movement. They will become Members of Outposts. And they will be joined by leaders of nations and of systems who recognize the wisdom of The Movement. Soon thereafter, we will be One.

TO OBEY OR NOT TO OBEY?

The price of apathy towards public affairs is to be ruled by evil men.

Plato

Over two thousand years ago, Plato recognized that the price the governed pay for failing to act to protect the sanctity of better systems of governance, is that evil men will seize control and subvert those very systems to their own ambitions. They choose to rule, and they create laws to avoid being held accountable for their crimes. Laws are created to set boundaries and establish acceptable rules of social conduct. Some are good, some not. The Holocaust was legal within Nazi Germany. The genocide of indigenous peoples was also considered legal for colonizing powers. Slavery and segregation have been legal for thousands of years.

But just because a law is written does not make it right, and does not mean it should be obeyed. In a 1954 address to the Chicago Decalogue Society, Albert Einstein recognized: "One other human right, or the duty, of the individual is to abstain from cooperating in activities which he considers wrong" referencing "instances where individuals of unusual moral strength and integrity have . . . come into conflict with the organs of the state" by (for instance) "the refusal of military service." In referencing the Nuremberg Trial of German war criminals whose tacit defense to prosecution was that their acts were legal under German law, Einstein countered stating that "criminal actions cannot be excused if committed on government orders; conscience supersedes the authority of the law of the state." How profoundly true.

Dr. Martin Luther King, Jr. explained that there are "two types of laws: just and unjust." In a letter penned April 16, 1963, to "My Dear Fellow Clergymen," while confined in the Birmingham Alabama City Jail,[166] Dr. King stated that,

One has not only a legal but a moral responsibility to obey just laws. Conversely, one has a moral responsibility to disobey unjust laws. I would agree with St. Augustine that 'an unjust law is no law at all.'

Dr. King uses the word "disobey," which implies confrontation (albeit by his terms peaceful), which would be the appropriate action to take when there are no alternatives present. We, however, present alternatives that transform acts of civil disobedience to acts of abstinence. We simply ignore unjust laws by abstaining from following them, choosing instead to follow our own.

No law is so perfect that it cannot be improved upon. Laws that are contrary to the best interests of humanity are no laws at all and must cease to be, which happens when people stop obeying them. When faced with unjust laws, what will you do, obey, disobey, or ignore?

MILLIONS OF MOVEMENTS

**Public sentiment is everything. With it, nothing can fail.
Against it, nothing can succeed.**
Abraham Lincoln

There are millions of movements around the world with common goals. They all seek to create better ways of being. The fact that there are so many people engaged in so many acts to change the world for the better reveals what most of us already know, that public sentiment favors fundamental change. What slows the transformative process is the fact that the incredible energies of these so many people have yet to be harnessed in a focused way.

To succeed in creating a civilized society, we must focus the public sentiment by uniting movements of change in support of common goals to elevate the common good. Every movement of change begins with one person and proceeds to build consensus therefrom. On matters large, it can take decades, centuries even, to build public sentiment sufficient to fundamentally change some way; but it can happen.

For example, over the past several decades and notwithstanding fierce opposition from the powerfully entrenched, a few concerned individuals formed global organizations to, among other things, elevate an awareness of the dangers of global warming, and to stimulate a movement to change how we produce and deliver energy. As a result, multiple international agreements on climate change have been signed. But none had teeth.

So, just prior to the 2015 UN Climate Change Conference in Paris, leaders of Avaaz.org (a non-profit organization now with a network of over 65 million members in 194 nations promoting activism to help shape global decision-making) in conjunction with other similarly-minded individuals and organizations, coordinated 2,300 simultaneous events attended by 785,000 people in 175 countries that implored world leaders to unite to achieve one common goal: to create a "100% clean energy future to save everything we love." The largest climate mobilization event in human history received worldwide news coverage, prompting UN Secretary-General Ban Ki-moon to stress to world leaders that "The peoples of the world ... have taken to the streets, in cities and towns across the world, in a mass mobilization for change ... They expect each and every one of you to show leadership equal to the test. History is calling."

One hundred and fifty heads of states attended the commencement of the Paris Climate Change Conference, the largest single-day gathering of national leaders, ever. Upon reaching an accord (which culminated in a written agreement among 195 nations), French President Francois Hollande stated, "In Paris, there have been many revolutions over the centuries. Today it is the most beautiful and the most peaceful revolution that has just been accomplished - a revolution for climate change."

This event marked an attempt at a new beginning, a global effort to fundamentally change just one aspect of how humans do what they do. Although the accord set common goals, most were non-binding, which was necessary to obtain consensus. Why, in the face of so many global outcries were world leaders unable to impose binding and enforceable rules and regulations on just one aspect of global commerce? Why do you think?

To this date nations remain unwilling to empower the UN, so even committees like the UN Human Rights Council have only been allowed to declare, but not enforce and protect, the most basic of fundamental rights. And, even though 140 nations have incorporated "the right to a healthy environment" into their constitutions, most fail to abide by those obligations when enforcement would require actions against corporations.

Claims that multinational entities like Monsanto, Exxon, Dupont, and Phillip Morris are responsible for grave human and environmental damages abound. Monopolistic in nature, multinational entities have become so large and so powerful that they have effectively thwarted all attempts to create globally enforceable laws to protect the environment and the people against their abuses.

So, when citizens gathered their resources to bring light to these issues, the best that (for instance) a global network of food, farming, and environmental justice groups could do to right certain corporate wrongs, was to convene an International Citizens Tribunal to hear arguments (in this case) against Monsanto Corporation for committing crimes against human health and the environment. The year was 2017. The Tribunal, which consisted of an eminent panel of international judges, found numerous violations of fundamental rights. But, lacking enforcement power, all it could do was hear the case and issue *advisory* opinions, stating among other things that

> The Tribunal is of the view that the time is ripe to consider multinational enterprises as subjects of law that could be sued in the case of infringement of fundamental rights. The Tribunal clearly identifies and denounces a severe disparity between the rights of multinational corporations and their obligations.[167]

Corporate injustices plague humanity. For over a century the corporate elite have effectively thwarted international attempts to regulate their activities while strengthening laws that shield themselves from liability for violating even the most fundamental of rights. Their involvement in the drafting of international trade agreements between nations, notwithstanding clear conflicts of interest, has resulted in the creation of powers (if you can believe this) which enable corporations to prosecute nations for attempting to prohibit or limit activities that the host nation deems appropriate to protect their own if, for instance, a corporate ruler decides that the act of the host nation could impair its trade or profitability. Treaties like the little-known Energy Charter Treaty have empowered corporations to sue nations for billions of dollars after enacting laws banning such actions as the use of coal to produce electricity to comply with The Paris Climate Agreement.[168]

How bad will things have to get before we enable better ways of being? When large movements such as the Paris Climate Mobilization Movement fail to produce the necessary changes in a timely fashion, what can we do? The answer: Build a bigger, more powerful movement, one that encompasses the goals of the world's progressive movements. Consider that to be the task of The Movement. As the mother ship of all such movements, it exists to harness the collective power of millions of individual movements, interlinking each with each other through a platform designed to coordinate, enhance and empower individual movements of progressive change in ways never before contemplated. Only through one movement composed of millions of smaller movements engaged in progressive change can we secure a future for the collective good.

Much of what is discussed herein is formative. If you know within the deepest aspects of your innermost self that we must change, and if you possess a strong desire to dedicate some aspect of your life energies to support a global movement of fundamental change, become a progenitor of change, contact us at outpostsofchange.org and help us transform the world. Let us know how you can help. And be clear, we need all the help we can get.

The only thing stopping us from redefining how we interact with ourselves and our surroundings, is ourselves. Life on Earth is what we choose to make it. We have conquered natures' impediments to proliferation; now, we must conquer our own impediments to better ways of being by changing *how* we do most things.

To conquer the large, begin with the small.
Wu Hsin (Chinese philosopher)

We change the world, one person at a time. There are more than 7.8 billion of us, the large. We cannot change others, only ourselves, the small. So, begin with yourself and help make the changes within your own community that are the most impactful. Become one with The Movement so that together we build an indomitable force that changes the world by transforming our ways. Incorporate small acts to change the world for the better into your daily routine. Use social media to let others know of the things you are doing to help create better ways of being and hope they see the wisdom and have the courage to do the same.

Fundamental change begins with you and spreads to others, who of their own free will become the change we envision for a better humanity. To "become the change" means to act to make change happen. It means doing the things you can to make a better humanity and not doing things that are destructive to others or Mother Earth. The little things you do to make a better world add up.

When the small things each of us do to make a better humanity exceed the damaging things we do as a collective whole, the world will begin to heal and we will have begun the process of becom-. ing the change we envision. Unite in action with those who have the vision and the belief that transformational change is necessary, possible and evolutionary.

16

Take The Evolutionary Step

Life's gift is freedom of choice. With this gift comes great opportunity, and great responsibility. The time is upon us to decide how to march into the future. Do we continue to act as we have for thousands of years, moving forward in time with little foresight or intention, driven to grow, consume and profit by it, or do we fundamentally change how we conduct the business of humanity to experience evolutionary change? Make the right decisions and great opportunities await us. Make the wrong ones and grave suffering follows. The scope of these decisions is monumental and encompass the greatest level of responsibility to the future of humankind ever faced. Unfortunately, the world is governed by rulers operating within structures that render their ability to make the responsible decisions nearly impossible, so others must step up to lead us along new pathways.

Great leaders are needed, right now, to help us make the right decisions. Are you one? Will you step forward to help guide us onto evolutionary pathways? If yours is a calling to serve the greater good, then the answer is simple. Help one or help one million, the number matters not. It is the goal that matters. The one you help may help save one million. Help another and another will help you. Create environments that promote and incentivize the helping, and watch a civilized society begin to evolve.

Life's pathways beckon. You, who dedicate your lives to a higher calling, whatever that may be, can best serve by ushering all who will listen onto pathways of progressive change. Change in the very fabric of society is the necessary and defining action of this moment in time. Help us change the world by adopting better ways of being. Lead by example. Encourage your friends and loved ones to move from societies competing, to ones engaged in cooperative efforts for the greater good, the evolutionary step of this time.

RELEASE THE PAST

**Letting go gives us freedom
and freedom is the only condition for happiness.**
Thich Nhat Hanh

Opportunity lies ahead, not behind. Individuals who dwell in the past miss the opportunities of the present. To make the evolutionary leap requires humanity to have faith that a better future awaits all who just let go. Let the past be. To do so, embrace the present and make the most of each moment as it happens, for each is most certainly the only you will ever experience.

Every second is sacred. Each new moment brings opportunities of discovery of new ways of being and new ways of rectifying past errors. Learn from the past, but let it not shackle us, for to tie anyone to the past is to rob them of the present and deny them the future. Holding to past ways impedes our ability to change. So, it is incumbent upon each of us to release the past and move on.

FOCUS ON COMMONALITY

We are a destructive organism seemingly incapable of self-control. Promoting competition rather than cooperation, we kill almost everything we encounter. Competition blinds us to the results of our actions. Although we are faced with unprecedented challenges from operating competing but interwoven sets of social systems in near-total disregard of the impacts they ignite, tribal systems still rule in the twenty-first century. With 196 different forms of government along with untold numbers of corporate entities vying to control Earth's dwindling resources, and without uniform goals and uniform rules, it is easy to see how competition triggers death and destruction.

Nothing requires us to continue as we have been. We can change our ways. But the force of change must be strong and emanate from numerous sources before it takes hold. You, are a force of change. No matter your faith, ethnicity, or background, you can help others understand that cooperation, not competition, is the way to a better humanity. If the veracity of that statement is not crystal clear to you, read it again and then think about the difference in the life experienced when societies compete against each other versus when they cooperate with each other to achieve common goals. Stress points are removed and a sense of well-being develops when working with others for their mutual benefit. You know this to be true.

We are one species. It is time to start acting as one. But as the Fourteenth Dalai Lama so astutely recognized, "We are still focusing far too much on our differences instead of our commonalities." Focusing on our differences magnifies them and makes cooperative efforts much more difficult to achieve. Whatever our differences may appear to be, it is critical to accept that they are insignificant within the greater scheme of life. They are destructive to our collective well-being and detrimental to our survival.

What the Dalai Lama was saying, is that the way forward is to focus on the things we hold in common, which are the things we hold dearest in life; the love of a child, of family, of friends, and of our community. He was saying that the best way to end war, eliminate poverty, resolve our most prickly conflicts, eradicate inequality, create an abundance of opportunities, and to craft a sustainable pathway into the future, is to do so together, as One. One community acting in harmony with itself to resolve its most pressing issues. The way forward is to let go of past issues that have divided and focus on our commonalities which will enable us to concentrate on resolving the most pressing issues of this era

If there is to be a future worth entering, now is the time for our global communities to unite, to take responsibility for their actions, and to redefine our societies as ones at peace, existing harmoniously within the natural realm. If we are to effectively take control of our destiny, we need to promote the well-being of the commons and the happiness of the individual at every opportunity, for in the end, they most assuredly are one and the same.

ELIMINATE INEQUALITY

Inequality takes many forms. Rich versus poor, men versus women, black versus white, perhaps the three most glaringly apparent. Today, where one is born and who their parents are makes all the difference. But should it?

On December 10, 1948, "The Universal Declaration of Human Rights" (drafted by representatives from all regions of the world) was adopted by the United Nations General Assembly. This milestone document is the first formal proclamation of fundamental human rights equally applicable to "all members of the human family."[169] Read it.

Many books have been written about all forms of inequality. Most are self-evident and equally deserving of discussion; but because there simply are too many such issues to fairly address here, we will touch briefly upon just one, which when resolved, forms the basis for resolution of the others.

WOMEN

They comprise over 50 percent of the human population. They raise our young and care for our elderly. As a group, they are kinder, gentler, more nurturing, more empathetic, less likely to kill another, and as intelligent (if not more so) than men. Yet, because of these very same qualities, within most male-dominated societies and patriarchal religions, some are treated as property, some as slaves, and most as inferior beings with limited to no rights. It is time for these barbaric practices to end.

The United Nations Charter and the Universal Declaration of Human Rights (along with many other agreements) proclaim that all humans are born free and equal.[170] In 1979, in recognition that women everywhere have the least access to food, healthcare, education, training, and opportunities for gainful employment, the UN General Assembly adopted articles often described as "an international bill of rights for women" that obligate all Member States to protect the rights of all women to be free from all forms of discrimination, in all social aspects.[171]

Yet, over forty years later, women remain the single largest class subject to human rights violations. Why? Because the men who rule governments, corporations, financial and yes, religious institutions, refuse to release their domination over women. Although many world leaders have declared that every person is entitled to the protections of certain "fundamental human rights," many religious leaders fail to promote the same in a perverse twist of the tenants upon which their faiths were founded.

From a Nobel Peace Prize recipient, one of the most devout people of our time, a civil rights advocate, executive officer in the military, farmer, former US President, and a religious scholar, as excerpted from his writings of July 15, 2009 titled "Losing My Religion for Equality," Jimmy Carter provides this telling revelation:

Women and girls have been discriminated against for too long in a twisted interpretation of the word of God.

This discrimination, unjustifiably attributed to a Higher Authority, has provided a reason or excuse for the deprivation of women's equal rights across the world for centuries. At its most repugnant, the belief that women must be subjugated to the wishes of men excuses slavery, violence, forced prostitution, genital mutilation, and national laws that omit rape as a crime. But it also costs many millions of girls and women control over their own bodies and lives, and continues to deny them fair access to education, health, employment, and influence within their own communities ... The root of this prejudice lies deep in our histories, but its impact is felt every day. It is not women and girls alone who suffer. It damages all of us.

The truth is that male religious leaders have had - and still have - an option to interpret holy teachings either to exalt or subjugate women. They have, for their own selfish ends, overwhelmingly chosen the latter. Their continuing choice provides the foundation or justification for much of the pervasive persecution and abuse of women throughout the world. This is in clear violation not just of the Universal Declaration of Human Rights but also the teachings of Jesus Christ, the Apostle Paul, Moses, and the prophets, Muhammad, and founders of other great religions - all of whom have called for proper and equitable treatment of all the children of God. It is time we had the courage to challenge these views.

President Carter was not the first and will not be the last man to speak out against religious persecution of women. In ancient and in more evolved societies, during the bleakest of times the wisest of elders are called upon to serve as guiding lights to help direct necessary social change. They convey wisdom earned from lifelong experiences in time-honored traditions. President Carter is a member of just such a group, The Elders. The Elders are preeminent global leaders brought together by Nelson Mandela to support peacebuilding, help address major causes of human suffering, and promote the shared interests of humanity.

In an acknowledgment of perhaps the most massive, protracted, and profound violation of fundamental human rights to ever have taken place, The Elders recently called out religious leaders to eliminate "harmful teachings" and "emphasize the positive messages of dignity and equality that all the world's major faiths share," stating, "The justification of discrimination against women and girls on grounds of religion or tradition, as if it were prescribed by a Higher Authority, is unacceptable."

It is time to eliminate these most egregious inequalities. Change begins when True Leaders coalesce in action to free all women of subjugation, discrimination, and institutions of inequality. Equality begins within the home. To make that evolutionary leap from the individual mindset to that of the collective good, True Leaders help the rest of us recognize the critical importance of protecting and elevating our gentler half to stand as equals within the home and throughout all society.

But change is slow to take hold in our species. Although in many first world countries laws have been written to afford women and people of color more equal rights, they often do not go far enough, or are not enforced. And, in many areas of the world, "tradition" is used to justify the continual subjugation of women and children to the will of men. Because "it has always been this way" somehow justifies the ensuing commentary that "it will always be this way." That is so, until enough of us take a stand refusing to allow the past to dictate the present or define our future.

This is a time of great need and one of great potential. We have the potential to solve the multitude of problems we have created, but we need *everyone* to contribute by tapping into their innate intellectual capacities, right now.

This work presents a call to action. One that should not be disregarded or delayed as doing so impairs our collective chances of survival. That means we need to educate everyone as fast and as completely as possible because doing so elevates the intellectual capacity of the collective, which enhances our problem-solving abilities. Everyone, is the operative word to embrace in recognition that the systematic denial of women from equal access to the highest levels of education they are capable of attaining harms us all, as their potential contributions to science and humanity will certainly equal if not dwarf those of their male counterparts.

So, the women of the world must stand up for each other, speak out, and demand social equality for themselves, which equates to social equality for everyone. No race, no color, no creed exists without women. Create a society within which women are granted the same rights and privileges as men, and create a more balanced society. It is time for the women to unite and demand equality.

Equality is a cornerstone of a civilized society. It is also one of the cornerstones of The Movement, which broadly encompasses the movement of equality within which the kinder, gentler half of our species gather the strength, the will, the courage, and the determination to elevate their status as equals. Their responsibility is to use their own social networks in conjunction with those of The Movement, to join forces and act with one voice to help create a society within which every member enjoys equal social status.

Now, take a moment and visualize a society within which every person is born into a world of equal opportunity; within which hunger has been eliminated; grave disparity is nonexistent; each individual is enabled to achieve their potential; and everyone is encouraged to craft a life well worth living. This is not today's world, but it can be that of tomorrow should enough of us choose to make it so.

Women have been discriminated against for far too long and no other class of people being discriminated against comes close in size to the number of women being denied the same rights that men receive. To save ourselves from ourselves, women must unite. They will not stand alone. They will be joined by men and children the world over who refuse to partake within cultures that discriminate against our better half. When a representative percentage of the world's people stand arm in arm to ensure that women are treated as equals in the home, in the workplace, and within all institutions, we will have transformed society and set the stage for our own evolutionary change.

BECOME LESS TO BECOME MORE

The human organism is growing, rapidly. To support that growth, we are inefficiently consuming planetary resources at ever accelerating rates which has triggered the onset of the Anthropocene and the destruction of Earth's support systems. We have now reached a critical juncture in our existence. We can choose to stay the course and do little to reduce the harms we thrust upon Earth's ability to support life and watch the Anthropocene unfold, or we can take bold steps to dramatically reduce the impacts from our presence on Earth.

Should we choose to take bold action, the most effective and rapid step we can take is to reduce our population, which requires just one generation implementing the one child per family rule to shrink our presence by 50%. Follow that by a stabilizing two children per family rule and Earth will begin to heal, as shall we.

Yes, this may sound like a dramatic step. But if we cannot find our way to take the responsible steps necessary to save Earth from ourselves, we are in really big trouble. Sometimes we have to sacrifice today to ensure there will be a tomorrow worth participating in. This is one of those times. And in so many ways, having one child or two is the real blessing. So, focus on the benefits of being a parent who is able to provide your child with a life well worth living.

Now is the time for True Leaders to guide us, to show us the wisdom of embracing the small family, rather than promoting large ones. Now is the time to reduce our numbers, not by war, famine, or disease, but voluntarily, following a plan that keeps families intact and protects their health and well-being. Now is the time to nimbly and responsibly move our societies to change by eliminating growth as our goal, reducing our numbers, and creating new structures and systems to serve a higher purpose, to save ourselves from ourselves. That is what is required of us at this moment.

So, do we choose evolution over extinction? One requires the actions of many to fundamentally change how we do most things which opens pathways of evolutionary opportunity; the other assumes we do nothing so bold as we stumble along pathways of extinction. If we choose to travel evolutionary pathways, then we must act to responsibly secure our future by proactively managing our affairs. Do so and eliminate great human suffering, starvation, conflict, and all the other things we do which harm ourselves and the environments that we are dependent upon. To enable transformative change, replace goals of growth in numbers, with goals of growth in knowledge and understanding. We must become less, so that we can become more.

17

The Moment For
Transformative Change Is Now

It always seems impossible until it is done.
Nelson Mandela

Technological advances enable a global community capable of simultaneously communicating and coordinating a global Movement of Change. You will be told that the goals of such a movement are impossible to achieve, and so it will seem, "until it is done."

This is *the* moment to develop a sense of evolutionary consciousness. It is *the* moment of change, *our* moment of transformative change. Embrace it. Let a consciousness of change meld into your very being and know that transformative change is what we need.

Transformative change is fundamental change at the very core of society. It affects everything we do. To achieve it requires the shared contributions of billions and a level of intention and coordinated commitment unprecedented in human history. Although the burdens of accomplishment are substantial, the rewards more than justify the process.

Transformative change requires cooperative efforts to achieve common goals. Today there are millions of movements directed at improving the human plight. Some are small, others large. Most are defensive in nature, attempting to right existing wrongs and reduce harmful impacts from bad practices, which limits the effectiveness of their efforts in the face of powerful opposition. Movements of resistance bring injustices to light, but results are typically slow to materialize, which is problematic in a rapidly deteriorating environment where great harms metastasize daily. So, a different approach to bringing about fundamental social change is necessary.

That approach exists within The Movement, which is designed to operate outside the confines of existing structures even though it develops from within, a seeming contradiction. Those of The Movement travel pathways differing from the conventional. They establish their own inviolable communications systems inter-linking every individual, every Outpost and every progressive movement, a seeming impossibility, until it is done.

To build The Movement from within existing structures requires members of existing movements to unite their movements with The Movement. Simple linkage is insufficient. It requires contributing some percentage of each movement's resources to The Movement to secure the benefits of transformative change for all.

Leaders must recognize that the ultimate goal of every progressive movement is held in common: to create a civilized global community living in harmony with itself and nature. They must recognize that the larger a unified movement of change becomes, the more likely it is to succeed. They must offer some of their own resources and join with others who do the same to enable one large, powerful movement of change.

But be warned, if leaders of existing movements are unwilling to contribute to benefit humanity on a larger scale, then The Movement will fail and the outlook for humanity will remain bleak. Conversely, the sooner and faster individual movements meld with The Movement, the greater the likelihood of its success. After millions of movements have linked within The Movement, transformative change locks in.

Movements of change inevitably require some level of perceived sacrifice. Everyone must find a way to give a little today such that tomorrow we all reap the benefits. So, if you are a member of an organization working in ways large or small to create a better humanity, your responsibility is to ensure that a small percentage of that organization's resources is allocated to secure the greater good.

Leaders of existing organizations will find the best ways of contributing to The Movement. Some will easily step beyond the fear of control lost or asset reduction upon recognition of the wisdom of joining forces with others whose core values and objectives are held in common: to create a global community founded upon principals designed to secure the greater good. Those who do and who convey that same wisdom to their followers, are True Leaders. True Leaders convey a sense of hope, of determination, and of gratitude for the efforts of others. And they convey a sense of humility for the privilege of partaking in a rarefied and glorious event, the evolutionary transformation of a species.

LEADERSHIP

A movement of change will not succeed if governed by rulers. Movements require visionaries who accept the burdens and great responsibilities that accompany actions to free themselves, their communities, and organizations from conventional practices and ways of thinking. These individuals elevate to become True Leaders in part by introducing others to the benefits of The Movement, knowing this as perhaps the only the way to achieve transformative change. In so doing, they partake in something far grander than anything ever attempted.

The process of breaking free will neither be easy nor painless. It requires true dedication by those who choose to be led, rather than ruled. Leaders at all levels of society will guide their communities to meld with The Movement, in recognition that the joining strengthens our collective abilities to do what is right, rather than what is expedient.

Elevating to a position of leadership is a great honor, yet it carries with it the great responsibility of shepherding the evolution of a global society. To galvanize transformative change requires planning, guidelines, organization, commitment, and True Leaders who display only the highest levels of moral, ethical, and intellectual traits. They serve as our guides.

But beware. Leaders lead. Rulers rule. There is a huge difference and those chosen to lead must be guides, not rulers. Why? Because rulers shun personal responsibility for the actions they initiate. They blame others for their own faults and misdeeds, and they insulate themselves from liability for harms they direct. To obtain and retain power, they become indebted to enablers who in exchange are allowed to do as they please. Rulers turn a blind eye on the needs of the many. They lead the fray in taking everything they can from as many as they can, sacrificing their morality in the process.

True Leaders, however, are indebted to none. They selflessly serve the many who ask nothing but their best efforts. They find ways to provide for all, freeing society of the bondage of past ways in search of a better future. Driven by the highest moral and ethical dictates, they care for the well-being of others, and find ways to build bridges, welcoming their fellow beings with open arms. True Leaders embrace the responsibility that comes with high positions, often sacrificing themselves to help others. And they know the truth living within the saying "together we stand, divided we fall," recognizing that "*we*" is the operative word for humanity.

Rulers have dragged humanity to the brink of extinction, reigning hardship, pain, and despair on billions. They divide us using intimidation, fear and ignorance to secure their positions. Conversely, True Leaders find ways to ease the pain and provide hope and opportunity where there has been none. Their followers do so freely, knowing their leaders act for their benefit.

True Leaders lead by example. If we seek to evolve a civilized society from one that is anything but, our leaders must exemplify the standards by which the rest of society is judged. Rather than insulating themselves from responsibility for the actions they direct, True Leaders stand responsible for them. They direct actions intending to do no harm and enable systems that operate with foresight through the use of forward-looking funds that promote research into the benefits and burdens that could result from actions contemplated.

Be vigilant about who you allow to elevate to leadership positions, as rulers will take advantage of others and the positions occupied. They will foment anger and hatred that lead to war and social unrest, repressing even the best-intentioned efforts of others to create better societies. The time of rulers has come to an end.

Now is the time of True Leaders. Their actions are morally driven, ethically based, transparent and beyond reproach, leaving little room for discord. Without discord, happiness may follow. It is up to us to decide who leads and we choose to allow only those qualified as True Leaders into high positions.

THE SOLUTION

The solution to ending human suffering and creating a society of civilized beings is available to us right here, right now. Its success depends upon the will of the people to incorporate into society fundamentally new goals. Changing how we use money is intrinsic to the process. Money is a tool. That is all it is. It is a creature of our imagination available for use in any way enough of us agree upon. We can use it to save lives, prevent starvation, eliminate the need for war, revitalize Earth's life support systems, build state-of-the-art communities powered by clean energy systems, establish global health care systems, eliminate wasteful business practices, replace old technologies with new ones, and establish state of the art education systems equally accessible by everyone. The list of the benefits to humanity by changing how we use money is endless. Use it to enable new goals and new ways of being, and the evolution of the society most of us want and deserve becomes a very real possibility.

Our potential is to travel pathways of discovery that lead to places of profound wonder and profoundly wonderful ways of being. To realize that potential requires us to change. Our challenge is to overcome self-imposed limitations and fears of change. In so doing, we create the freedom necessary for transformative change to take hold. Now ...

IMAGINE

Imagine - The Movement is in full stride. Billions have united in peace, working together to create new ways of being based upon common goals for the common good. Imagine - billions of us have agreed that:

The Goal of The Movement is to Create a Humane Global Community, a Civilized Society.

The Goal of One Governance is to Ensure the Well-Being of all People.

The Goal of One Commerce is Efficiency.

The Goal of One Finance is to Enable a Humane Humanity.

The Goal of Leadership is to Serve All People.

And The Goal of The 4th Structure is Enlightenment.

Life opportunities are everywhere. Ours is the opportunity to evolve new ways of being, to transform competitive social institutions into cooperative ones designed to enable the emergence of a truly civilized global community with common goals for the common good, in other words, a humane humanity. Adopt near-term goals to guide that level of transformative change and long-term goals to place us upon pathways of discovery seeking truth and gathering knowledge and understanding of the ways of this most incredible universe.

BOOK VI

A BLUEPRINT
FOR CHANGE

All works of humankind are imperfect. As we travel through time, it is our collective obligation to refine the social structures and systems that can be refined, and abandon and replace the ones that cannot. Our existing structures and many of their systems have failed us. They must be replaced. To evolve a civilized society, we begin by envisioning and then adopting new goals and new ways of being. We have discussed what those goals might be. Achieving them requires little that we don't already know as we possess the intellectual and technological capacity to rapidly and substantially transform our societies by improving *how* we do almost everything.

Remember that every structure and every system is a creature of our collective imaginations. They exist for one thing and one thing only: to serve us, all of us. If we want them to serve us better, reimagine them and act to give the reimagined life.

What follows, is an overview setting out the foundations upon which an evolved civilized society may spring. It is a gateway of sorts, one through which we must pass to enable us to travel pathways of endless possibility. It is not intended to define particulars. Rather, it sets out mechanisms that are available to us right now, which if adopted will effectively and positively change the course of human history. Think of the concepts that follow as tools capable of igniting transformative change. They are not intended to be dispositive or all-encompassing. Rather, they stand as examples, as suggestions, of some of the many possible ways of implementing systemic changes to better serve us all. Use them liberally, and creatively.

It is up to us to define the best ways to accomplish our shared goals. So, stretch your imaginations. Explore alternatives. Do not let details stand in the way. They are the small stuff, the things that if allowed will distract from the important stuff. Instead, agree upon the most fundamentally important goals. Keep them at the forefront of your thoughts. Use them as guides to help us experience the wonders of transformative change.

18

ONE FINANCE

Money is a tool. That is all it is. It was imagined thousands of years ago to enable commerce, the transfer of goods and services among us. Today, those who are allowed to create it limit its availability and charge for its use. Using money this way burdens and divides us just as assuredly as it concentrates control of the many into the hands of a few, who get obscenely rich by it. Most importantly, using money this way imperils our future. The role of the Financial Structure in a moral society should be one of servant, not master. So, if you prefer to live within a moral society, help redefine the Financial Structure to serve us equally.

TO ENABLE A HUMANE HUMANITY

The Financial Structure controls all others. Fundamentally changing how it operates to enable a morally rich, ethically driven society provides the key to unlocking evolutionary pathways. Change this structure and hope and inspiration will blossom, as what was once deemed impossible becomes reality. Use this structure differently to enable endless opportunity, eliminate poverty, bring a higher purpose to our collective lives, ensure social justice across all aspects of society, and create peace where there is none. Contrary to what the financial elite will tell you, the supply of money can be both unlimited, and controlled to eliminate misuse and prevent it from accumulating in any pot beyond the real value to society of the actual services rendered by the recipient.

Enabling a just and humane humanity can and should be the sole function of this structure. To do so, The Financial Structure must be founded in reason, developed in equality, and designed to promote the best of humanity by incorporating goals of well-being and the search for knowledge and understanding.

There are billions of people across the planet whose daily existence is threatened in one way or another. Theirs are lives of desperation and deprivation. Born into conditions that doom them from the outset because they lack access to food, clean water, modern sanitary systems, medical care, safe and secure communities, and decent employment opportunities that require a solid educational background, they live compromised lives. This is the first time within human history that not a single person's life needs to be so compromised. The only thing preventing us from adopting new ways of serving each other so that human deprivation becomes a thing of the past is ourselves. To change ourselves in this way is a matter of choice and, a matter of will.

Do we want, really want, to eliminate starvation and war, create endless employment opportunities, incentivize efficiency and the utilization of best practices methodologies while building a global debt-free network of state-of-the-art healthcare, education, and clean energy systems to serve everyone? If so, we must commit to repurposing how we use money. Within a repurposed financial structure, money creation becomes a function of separate systems designed to enable specific projects.

But the financial elite and those they control will warn that new monetary systems are not possible if, for no other reason than that human greed will corrupt its intended purposes. They should know. And they will be right if you stand with them and refuse to partake. However, they will be proved wrong as billions commit to a morally just, ethically administered way of being, in recognition that by so doing, we enable a future within which a robust and civil society may flourish.

ETHICALLY ADMINISTERED

Nearly 2,500 years ago in ancient Greece, Socrates conceived the importance of living ethically and passing that wisdom to future generations. He believed that virtue was found in human relationships, love and friendship, and that happiness is gained not through material acquisition but by doing what is right. His teachings ring just as true today as they did back then.

Happiness is a sense of well-being, of feeling good. It is a way of being that most would love to enjoy. It doesn't take much for people to be happy. Give us a chance to live within a just, ethically administered, morally rich society and happiness becomes a foregone conclusion. The time is upon us to stop playing games and start doing what is right, by adopting standards that mandate responsibly based, ethically applied and morally directed decisions in all of the things we do.

How each of us live our lives truly matters. What we do today defines our children's world of tomorrow. Most want them to be happy. So, shouldn't our efforts be directed at creating a society capable of enabling their happiness? We can. How? By uniting instead of dividing, by providing everyone with tools that help them reach their innate potential, by placing responsibility for the things we do where it belongs, and by mandating action through foresight.

Opportunity is a necessary ingredient to making a better humanity. Give a person a chance and most will find a way to make a better life. Give the people a chance and most will promote the common good. Give us stability and we will make peace. Give us a worthy goal and we will reach it. Give us hope and we will survive. Give us encouragement, and we will thrive. Give us opportunity, and there is little we cannot accomplish.

Our destiny is ours to define. The things we are doing right now dictate what our future will be like. We have the opportunity and the ability to change how we do most things for the better; establishing a morally based, ethically driven, responsibly managed civilized society in the process. Do so and create a society which most would proudly and lovingly gift to their children. To begin, elevate Socrates's teachings to stand as principles at the fountainhead of society. Then, establish One Finance to enable, without limitation, a society of individuals working cooperatively to achieve its goals.

WITHOUT LIMITATIONS

Envision One Finance as the mother fund within which separate funds exist to create, without limitation, all money necessary for humanity to thrive. The primary funds within One Finance are the One Finance Fund, One Governance Fund, One Commerce Fund, and The 4th Structure Fund. Within the purview of each primary fund reside sub-funds designed to enable the systems within each structure.

Those chosen as Funders must evidence the highest moral and ethical standards. Those elevated to leadership positions within each fund must be exemplary. Neither moral shortcomings nor ethical violations can be tolerated.

Funders must be highly educated, scientifically trained, forward-looking individuals familiar with cutting edge technologies to qualify for and carry out their roles. Each sub-fund will be managed by individuals with expertise in the particular type of system being funded.

Funders provide an additional level of oversight into the management and use of funds. Their responsibility is to ensure adequate funding on a continuing basis sufficient to enable best practices methodologies to empower each system or sub-system to accomplish its mandated goals. They act in capacities similar to those of venture capitalists and boards of directors by engaging in major decision-making processes.

Money is their tool of choice. Used wisely, it will catalyze evolutionary change. To those ends, Funders make no loans. They simply create money (just like bankers, the various federal reserve banks and crypto currency creators do today) for socially beneficial projects. No interest is ever charged, and no repayment is ever made. Money is born, distributed throughout systems of governance, commerce, finance, and The 4th Structure, and then eliminated after it has done all it was programmed to do.

Sophisticated computer programs link all funding actions from the point of money creation through its expiration. This enables Funders to anticipate production and delivery expenses, oversee product prices, determine the amount of digital money necessary to be created, and manage the flow of money throughout society. By design, money is prevented from building in excess in any pot, eliminating the possibility of extreme financial inequality and undue financial influence. Managing the flow of money this way may sound like an impossibility, and it is within existing social systems. But it is not within newly imagined systems using blockchain technologies.

Of course, checks and balances at the highest levels technologically possible will be built into each Funding System. All Funding Accounts will be monitored, expenditures preapproved, traced, and accounted for, ensuring funds flow only to enable specific projects as carried out by specified individuals. Rules and regulations on the use and extinguishment of money will be implemented to prevent even the temptation of transgression.

There is nothing complicated about it. One Finance, as a structure, shall remain simple, transparent, progressive, and designed to enable a humane humanity. This means access shall be equally available to every person with a supportable project, idea, need, or goal to improve the human life experience.

The following are but a few examples of the nature and operation of the funds of One Finance.

19

THE FUNDS OF ONE GOVERNANCE

I am not an advocate for frequent changes in laws
and constitutions, but laws and institutions must go
hand in hand with the progress of the human mind.
As that becomes more developed, more enlightened,
as new discoveries are made, new truths discovered
and manners and opinions change, with the change
of circumstances, institutions must advance also to
keep pace with the times. We might as well require
a man to wear still the coat which fitted him when
a boy as civilized society to remain ever under the
regimen of their barbarous ancestors.

Thomas Jefferson, 1816

No form of governance is perfect, or even close. Existing structures
are old, and their systems of governance are barbarous. They were not
designed to serve billions. They prevent evolutionary levels of change,
enable inequality, and promote social injustice resulting in extreme
suffering and environmental destruction. Structures and systems
that cause harm are wrong. And frankly, as Jefferson also stated: "It
is more honorable to repair a wrong than to persist in it." He was
correct. But, when repair is not an option, the structures and systems
of the era must be replaced. That is what happened in 1776 when thirteen British Colonies declared their independence from the Crown.

It took a Revolutionary War in 1776 to set things right, which the
founders did by instituting "new Government, laying its foundation

on such principles ... as to them shall seem most likely to effect their Safety and Happiness."[172] In so doing, they established the best form of governance to date, one that provided great opportunity for those willing to risk everything to join. Read this paragraph from the US Declaration of Independence once again:

> We hold these truths to be self-evident, that all [people] are created equal, that they are endowed by their Creator with certain unalienable Rights, that among these are Life, Liberty and the pursuit of Happiness. That to secure these rights, Governments are instituted among [the people], deriving their just powers from the consent of the governed. That whenever any Form of Government becomes destructive to these ends, it is the Right of the People to alter or to abolish it, and to institute new Government, laying its foundation on such principles and organizing its powers in such form, as to them shall seem most likely to effect their Safety and Happiness.

Those are some of the most profound and prescient words ever written. They are as applicable today as when they were penned nearly 250 years ago. They spell out what should be the singular purpose of all forms of governance: to secure the "Safety and Happiness" of the governed. So simple. So clear. So profound. And, if we embrace the truths that exist within them, so powerful.

The founders recognized the absolute right (we would say "the absolute obligation") of the People to institute new forms of governance when "any form of government becomes destructive" to the "unalienable rights" of the People to "Life, Liberty and the pursuit of Happiness." Read the entire document. It enumerates and validates the same reasons for breaking bonds with 1776 governing institutions as exist today with most nations.

There can be no higher purpose of any governing body than to secure the happiness and well-being of the governed. Unfortunately, there are very few governments that operate to secure the happiness of their people, and fewer still that can peacefully change their ways to set things right.

The largest business on the planet is by far, governance. It takes a lot of effort to set and enforce the rules and regulations of 196 different nations, along with whatever additional services each system provides. Most systems are different and because there are so many different sets of rules and regulations, conflicts abound. Additionally, within any one system of governance there may be many different levels of governance, from local to regional to national, each charged with rendering different services to the governed.

Hundreds of millions of people are employed in one way or another by national systems of governance and affiliates. Each is hampered by monetary systems that operate in limitation. From Third World nations unable to provide safe drinking water systems to First World nations unable to provide the same, they all struggle because they can't afford to provide something of significance to the governed. Yet, that need not be the case. We can envision one system of global governance capable of ensuring that the needs of everyone are more than met.

You will be told that it will be impossible to get 196 different nations to agree on a common set of rules and regulations, and they will be right. Why? Not because it is impossible to develop a singular, superior system of governance. The problem lies with those who rule. They fear the loss of power that comes with their rule, so they will do whatever they can and say whatever they must to create barriers to change. So, we, the People, must unite to make a union more perfect than any there has ever been. It can happen.

This is our time, our opportunity, and it is our obligation to create the change humanity so desperately needs. We do so by envisioning a new form of governance that is more just, more equitable, and more capable than any previously devised. Within it, there are no nations and no boundaries separating one from another. Within it, life is simpler, easier, more secure, and more fulfilling than ever. True Leaders will guide the formation of One Governance to facilitate the well-being of all people. We enable those virtues through The Governance Fund.

THE GOVERNANCE FUND

The Governance Fund (TGF) is established to create money to enable the development and operation of one system of global governance designed to provide state-of-the-art administration of local, regional, and global governing entities to enable a civilized society. By creating money to fund all systems of governance, we provide for true governance, one that will galvanize a fairer, more just, and more equal society for all people.

GOVERNANCE WITHOUT TAXATION

People have complained about unfair systems of taxation forever. They have been forced to sacrifice to pay taxes to a sovereign who has imprisoned them, taken their lives and possessions, conscripted them into servitude, and worse, all because of an inability to pay taxes to run some unjust system of governance. Many systems of taxation are rigged to favor the wealthy which promotes inequality. That will no longer be the case. People will no longer suffer the burden of taxation or the indignation of servitude and inequality.

Those burdens vaporize and the chains of taxation are lifted because we create money to fund, without limitation, all systems of governance. No longer will anyone be forced to toil in service of rulers. Most systems of governance have it backwards. Individuals who govern are there to serve the people, not the other way around. And governance without taxation frees those who govern to serve everyone equally, eliminating conflicts of interest, bribery, systems of inequality, and countless Life Hours wasted on tax-related issues. Governance without taxation frees us to pursue higher interests, which accelerates evolutionary trajectories.

FOR ALL PEOPLE

Governance is simply a structure that establishes acceptable parameters within which society operates. Outmoded systems benefit those who rule. At its core, the systems of One Governance will exist to serve all people. They stand on the principle that all people are endowed with unalienable rights to Life, Liberty, and the pursuit of Happiness, which translates to equal rights, equal protections, equal opportunities, and equal access to the best of everything that humanity is capable of rendering.

FREE OF UNDUE INFLUENCE

To ensure these principles are met, those who govern must be free to make morally based, ethically correct, and environmentally sound decisions. They must not be subject to corruption or undue influence in any form.

Creating money to fund governance destroys the chains of influence exercisable by those of wealth and power, eliminating the need for governance by force, intimidation, or exclusion - all fundamental flaws of existing systems. It also frees individuals to aspire to a higher calling, service of the many.

Just as history reveals there can be no true freedom under profit-based systems where greed trumps morality, The Governance Fund energizes systems within which we are free to pursue careers of choice, not necessity. Freedom blooms within structures that serve the greater good, the true calling of The Governance Fund.

HOW ONE GOVERNANCE AND ITS FUNDS MAY WORK

All funds exist to enable some function within society. Each incorporates a uniform system of checks and balances tying their systems to the parent system. Funders analyze and, where appropriate, grant-funding requests. Their responsibility adds an additional layer of supervision, albeit broad, to the administration of the project or system funded.

One Governance is charged with the oversight of all operations of governance from local to global. To enable globally interdependent systems of governance designed to interconnect at all levels, we establish The Governance Fund.

TGF is one fund composed of many parts. It enables the global structure of One Governance. Its leaders are the most experienced and capable of all Governance Funders. Having risen from the ranks based upon the assessments of their contemporaries and recognition of outstanding character traits, these individuals accept the great responsibility of ensuring that all aspects of One Governance are adequately funded and devoid of abuse.

Governing systems may exist purely as oversight and enforcement entities, or they may exist to perform any number of other functions, as initially set by the Founders. Whatever their functions, they are enabled by a particular sub-fund which is dependent upon TGF for operational funding and oversight.

Only one of the four structures must consolidate to bring peace and prosperity to humanity, governance. Our well-being is secured when threats of war have been vanquished and competition between nations eliminated. This is best accomplished under the umbrella of one form of global governance.

Conflicts retard human progress whereas cooperation enhances it. Societies designed and operated to promote cooperation are clearly the evolutionarily superior forms of self-management. One Governance shall be designed to promote cooperation, eliminating conflicts inevitable within structures that promote competition. Implement it as soon as its constitution has been agreed upon by the Founders. Billions are not necessary to give it life. Just a few who agree to partake in an experimental system of governance designed to enhance and enable our collective well-being. So, envision it, design it, implement it. The People will follow.

Discussions begin among those few individuals who have evidenced the highest leadership qualities. They are individuals whose morality and ethicality stand unquestioned, individuals who have consistently placed the well-being of others ahead of their own. They join with constitutional and historical scholars, elders, and others knowledgeable of the pros and cons of existing systems of governance, to create the broad framework of a new form of governance designed to be superior to any previously created. This becomes possible because we have changed the role of money in society. The Founders are now free to imagine new systems of governance knowing that TGF will enable the Goals of One Governance, as directed by the governed. One form of global governance for all people will provide superior life experiences for everyone.

It does not take much to satisfy our needs. People need safe and secure environments within which to raise their families and they must be presented with plentiful opportunities to engage in meaningful professions from which living wages are earned. TGF enables the same and more. Peace and security reign supreme within structures designed to change with the times and operated to exceed our needs.

As the transformation from brute force to reason progresses, the need for militaristic force diminishes. Nations morph into regions within a larger union eliminating border tensions. As areas of conflict evaporate, a new-found sense of well-being emerges within the broader scope of society and with it, the reality of world peace through One Governance enabled by The Governance Fund takes shape.

We are one species. It's time to start acting as One.

What follows are some suggestions from which discussions may proceed about foundational principles of One Governance. This is a beginning. Our website opens the discussion to all who wish to contribute to the foundational process.

FOUNDATIONAL PRINCIPLES OF ONE GOVERNANCE

The business of governing how and what we do dwarfs all other endeavors. Every human activity needs structure, rules and regulations that establish what is acceptable behavior and what is not. With 196 nations and 196 would be rulers who prefer their own rules over those of others, is it any wonder that conflict enshrouds our species?

Systems that operate well are structured well. The more efficient the system, the better it runs. Governance is no exception. While it is beyond the scope of this work to define the particulars of a working body of One Governance, the following foundational principles may be of assistance:

1. Govern uniformly without boundaries and without nations. We are one people existing on one planet. Act as One.

2. All people are created equal. Live by that maxim. Treat everyone the same. Provide everyone with equal access to social services and backstops designed to enable our collective well-being. Structure all systems to provide services that help make life easier, and unsurprisingly, the governing process will be easier.

3. Adopt laws that impose consequences. People will continue to do bad things, illegal things, destructive things that harm others, society, and the environment if there are no real consequences to them for the harms they cause. Correlate the consequences to the level of harms caused by their actions and ensure the consequences are applied uniformly.

4. Impose higher standards of conduct as the potential consequences of a decision increase. Live by the

maxim that "with great power comes great responsibility." Although these standards must be equally applicable throughout all levels and aspects of society, those within governing systems are theoretically the most powerful and thus must be held to the highest moral and ethical standards. Theirs, are the powers to corrupt and be corrupted. More importantly, theirs are the powers to prevent the same. Limit their powers to corrupt; disincentivize their willingness to be corrupted; enable their powers to serve; and create just rewards for the highest levels of service.

5. Enforce laws uniformly, without exceptions. Laws reflect the morals of society. Before society can move forward, equality must reign supreme; every citizen must receive parity under the law. Societies that treat the powerful differently, that allow them to corrupt with impunity, are societies unfit for modern times. Laws must contain no exceptions allowing any individual who commits a harmful act within the administration of any system or structure to be treated any less severely than another committing the same act outside that envelope.

6. Treat governing as a business. Only those trained to govern, get to govern. At this moment, governing is perhaps the most important business of humanity. Conduct it as such. Human progress is dependent upon cooperative systems. Most entering any new system of governance should have a scientific background from which to assess the benefits vs the burdens of a requested action. As with all other systems, only the most highly qualified as judged by their peers may elevate through our systems of governance.

7. Those who govern hold the public trust; accordingly, they shall be held to the highest moral, ethical, and societal standards. The higher one elevates, the greater the social responsibility owed. No matter the position occupied, there shall be no immunity from prosecution for violation of the public trust.

   a. Outlaw lobbying. No direct or indirect lobbying of any decision-maker shall be allowed. All interested party contacts should be through junior staff, in writing, setting forth actions requested and regulatory concerns. Transparency in all levels of society, and governance in particular, is paramount.

   b. Enact and enforce laws that make bribery or the use of undue influence over any decisionmaker or public servant, a crime. Strictly enforce these laws.

   c. There exists a moral imperative upon which every structure and every system shall be founded. Safeguards must be implemented to ensure that every person is taught from their earliest years the critical importance of maintaining a society that operates only with the highest moral and ethical standards.

   d. Forbid nepotism. Every position occupied in society must be based solely upon ability, merit, qualification, and experience.

8. The Goal of One Governance, to secure the well-being of all people, stands as the prime directive of One Gov-

ernance. Elevate that goal into a mandate stating what One Governance is charged with accomplishing. All other goals of governance should be singularly focused on enabling governance to meet its obligations as set out in the prime directive.

9. Establish fundamental goals designed and prioritized to efficiently, ethically, and humanely provide the means within which all structures and systems operate and importantly, ensure transparency in all human activities.

10. Call on the most experienced scholars, the Elders, and True Leaders from a broad range of disciplines and societies to help design and implement One Governance. They shall take their guidance from the governed, the People.

   a. A survey (the People's Wisdom Survey) of at least ten million people from around the world shall be conducted and the results published and prioritized by region, to determine the most immediate things needed from governance to meet their needs and enable their happiness and well-being. The survey results shall guide the formation, foundational principles, guidelines, and operation of governance at all levels.

      i. Additional goals of governance based upon survey results shall codify the people's needs and wants at the local and regional levels. They shall establish the immediate objective actions of local and regional governance.

      ii. Annual updates of the survey shall be

conducted, made public, and used to both confirm that governance is operating to fulfill its obligations and where it is not, to provide notice to those at higher levels of governance to allocate more resources to the areas not meeting current goals. This survey shall also help set new goals as times change and society evolves.

b. Meld the wisdom of indigenous peoples with scientific data to establish ever-evolving best practice methodologies that limit adverse impacts on Earth's life support systems and then use the results to guide the operation of all social systems.

c. Design each new system with forethought, utilizing forward-directed planning to serve a global society.

d. Give deference to the wisdom of locals when considering activities that may impact their communities.

e. Politicians, rulers, dictators, lobbyists, and any person with a substantial interest in any existing system or enterprise shall be prohibited from partaking at any level in the development or operation of new structures or systems. Exceptions may be granted to anyone (known by their actions) to be dedicated to enabling a progressive humanity.

11. No taxes. The Governance Fund replaces obsolete tax-based systems of governance.

12. Implement new funds to support and enhance all socially progressive programs.

13. Forgive all debt, by law. Debt jubilees have been common practice throughout the ages, beginning in ancient Babylon and continuing to modern times. They have played a key role in easing the pain of every major period of financial crisis.

Under Jewish Mosaic law, creditors canceled the debts of fellow Israelites every seventh year. Every forty-ninth year was called the Year of the Jubilee "when freedom from debt and servitude was proclaimed throughout the land."[173] Debts were canceled because loans were seen as a means to help one's fellow man, rather than as a means to make money or enslave another. Cancellation events were considered "occasions of great festivity." No wonder.

In modern times, during the 1930s, "Most of Europe's governments had a significant portion of their liabilities written-off for good." A 1953 agreement abolished "all of Germany's external debt,"[174] which elevates recent objections of the German Government to cancellation of Greek debt to the height of hypocrisy.

In 2015, Croatia wiped out the financial obligations of some 60,000 people who according to Milanka Opacic, Deputy Prime Minister "will be given a chance for a new start without a burden of debt." Although the Croatian debt cancellation was limited to the poorest of the poor, it was well-intended and follows a practice of debt cancellation which is long and deeply ingrained within humanity.

Global financial systems will soon experience unprecedented levels of disruption. They teeter on top of mountainous debts. Worldwide debt exceeds $260 trillion. Wall Street derivative obligations add an estimated $300 trillion, possibly more. Unfunded retirement, social security, Medicare, and other social service obligations of governance and commerce add trillions more.

Debt obligations overburden society, including most governing entities. These burdens can be eliminated with a Global Debt Jubilee when existing financial systems next collapse. At least 98 percent of the population will joyously celebrate the day the world is given a fresh start, at which point a new Financial Structure, perhaps similar to that envisioned herein, could replace the obsolete ones that have heartlessly ruled for so long. In fact, why wait? Plan and put in place new systems to operate within a new Financial Structure designed to eliminate the burdens that debts place on humanity. You will know when the time is right to implement it.

14. Recognize that fundamental structural change will take centuries to complete. Administrative positions within governance will best be satisfied by individuals who remain focused on meeting the prime directive of One Governance. As long as each individual continually asks themselves "will the action I am asked to direct help meet The Goal of One Governance; is it the best course to follow to get there; and if so, how do I help implement it?" they will meet their obligations to the governed.

   But beware, some answers may not come easy. Use little goals to help alleviate transitional stresses. Build one small goal on top of the next to reach the fundamental goal of each structure. And, be sure that those most in need are the first to receive the benefits. Finally, be patient, yet persistent.

15. Start locally. Provide services following principles targeted at delivering the things that people in your com-

munity need most. Expand from there and happiness will follow. Others will join, helping ease transitional burdens, as many hands make light work.

16. Visionary governance creates more jobs than there will be people available to fill them.

   a. Opportunity and planning necessitate social mobility.

   b. Areas deemed least habitable should be responsibly abandoned. People will need to relocate. It is the great social responsibility of all systems of governance to ensure an orderly transition of population centers. Historically significant developments should be preserved, perhaps becoming centers of education and tourism.

   c. New urban centers utilizing state of the art planning and construction techniques will be built at locals best suited for habitation, taking into consideration climate change and the capacity of local Earth systems to support a thriving community.

17. Govern efficiently, yet responsibly.

   a. The concepts of politicians and lobbyists are stricken from the vocabulary of governance.

   b. Governance is a profession. It is to be conducted as such, and subject to the highest moral, ethical, and practical standards.

18. By law, all profit-based systems are banned and declared illegal. There are better ways.

19. From Scientist to Leader. Scientists, not politicians, not corporate or financial elites, and not people of religion, are the only people who study our impacts on Earth and on ourselves. Those among them proven to be forward thinkers are the ones to elevate to lead society. They are the ones capable of envisioning and implementing new systems designed to operate harmoniously with nature to avoid taking too much, too fast, of Earth's bounty. They are the ones who have called out to the elites to change their ways, but few have or will, so a different kind of leader is necessary.

New leaders should be trained to look ahead, anticipate the likely outcomes of mass human actions, and then direct the implementation of only the most efficient, least harmful ones. New leaders must heed the advice of experts to enable responsible systems of management designed to usher us through perilous times. The age of change is upon us. Embrace it. Elevate scientists to lead us into a future of prosperity and wonder. Set high goals. Evolve One Governance to secure our evolution.

One Governance exists to ensure that society operates to carry out our goals. TGF exists to enable One Governance to do just that. Use it wisely and look to the Elders for guidance.

THE COUNCIL OF ELDERS

No existing system of governance has proved fully capable of managing its own affairs, much less those of a global society, so a new one must be envisioned and deployed. We have discussed a few salient features to consider incorporating into new systems designed to better serve humanity. What we haven't discussed is a way to provide some level of assurance that new systems will remain true to their foundational purposes.

To accomplish those ends, consider establishing an independent oversight panel to function something like a board of directors. Call it the "Council of Elders." Its obligation is to ensure that all structures and associated funds remain focused on accomplishing their goals. It is the highest of honors to serve on the Council of Elders, which exists to serve humanity in the broadest sense. The Elders function as our guides. They are the guardians of our future. They are selected to steer humanity along pathways of discovery. They quite literally chart the course upon which humanity will travel.

Their decisions stand as directives to be carried out by True Leaders. How they are ultimately selected is up to you, the people, the Founders, and the generations who follow. To qualify, these individuals must have from their earliest days recognized the sanctity of life, all life. They must be big picture thinkers who have throughout their careers in service of humanity consistently placed the best interests of the community above their own. These are individuals who have displayed a great capacity to guide through the most turbulent of times with an unrivaled sense of equanimity and clarity of purpose. They envision pathways upon which humanity will travel with a true sense of purpose, having gained wisdom through lifetimes of experience.

These are the wisest, most compassionate and ethical of individuals; the ones who embody the epitome of morality and foresight. Their obligations are to ensure that the individuals operating at the highest levels of governance, commerce, finance, and science, act to carry out our collective goals. Choose them wisely and recognize that one does not necessarily need to have reached a certain age to serve on this council. Every now and then a rare individual will appear displaying a level of wisdom far beyond his or her years. Should one happen along, feel comfortable including them on the council. Whether these are lifetime appointments or for a set term is for you to decide.

We now highlight a few examples of more specific funds that may tie to systems of governance.

DISASTER RELIEF FUND

Famine, starvation, drought, earthquakes, floods, storms, and the like all create intolerable conditions for hundreds of millions of people. The purpose of the Disaster Relief Fund (DRF) is in the name. The DRF is empowered to create and disburse all money necessary and appropriate to alleviate human suffering by broadly providing for the well-being of everyone affected by natural and human-induced disasters.

Humanitarian entities such as the various United Nations divisions and NGOs that exist to ease pain and suffering from such events will no longer be hampered by the lack of funds to help people in need. Less than five billion dollars was all that was required by the UN in 2017 to avert mass starvation. Bankers could easily have created that money and disbursed it to the UN to prevent untold agony. But they did not, and millions suffered needlessly. So, instead of having to beg for money or supplies which are often not received, humanitarian aid entities will be fully enabled to carry out their missions by tapping into the DRF.

People caring for people is what a civilized society is about. People love helping others and right now we need all the help we can get. When a new way presents that is so clearly preferable to all others, most will jump at the opportunity to be included, choosing a better life for themselves and their families. Bring forth that knowledge to all in need as the DRF will create untold numbers of well-paid employment opportunities. Show them kindness and offer them the opportunity to elevate their condition by helping create a better world, but make no demands and set no conditions to receipt of our goodwill.

THE GLOBAL RELOCATION FUND

We create money for humanitarian purposes, not for profit. We choose to elevate the purpose of humanity from growth to discovery. We act to support this purpose by creating new ways of conducting the business of humanity.

There are tens of millions (soon to be hundreds of millions) of people who because of war, famine, global warming, or lack of opportunity, have been or will be forced to flee their homes and find new homes, new jobs, and establish new communities within which they can survive and hopefully thrive. Existing systems of governance, commerce, and finance do not support these absolute needs; in fact, a large percentage of nations reject refugees, forcing them to relocate to places of little opportunity and barely tolerable living conditions.

The year was 2018. The place: The United States of America. It was a time when nations were building bigger border walls and enacting policies to keep even those most in need out. Rulers there implemented policies not seen since the darkest of human times, the Holocaust era, evidencing the very worst of human nature. Lacking all sense of decency, no, morality, authoritarian rulers directed minions to rip nursing infants from their asylum-seeking mothers' arms. Some told parents that their children were being taken to bathe or play when in fact they were separated from their parents and incarcerated in warehouses at locations undisclosed to the parents. The sole purpose of such actions? To dissuade others from coming.[175] Talk about barbaric!

Try to imagine the horror experienced if your child was ripped from your tear-streaked arms, screaming in terror as she was taken to an undisclosed location, perhaps never to be seen again? Now try to imagine yourself as that child. At that moment in time, over 11,000 children were forced into federal detention facilities often run by for-profit corporations and held caged like criminals under zero-tolerance policies. In many cases, records from which children could be reunited with their parents were not kept. In other cases, parents were deported without their children, who remained in detention centers. Neither child nor parent knew where the other was. Now, try to imagine the irreparable psychological damage suffered by both parent and child as a result of 21st Century barbaric practices. Try as you may, unless you have suffered this plight, you cannot.[176]

In many other parts of the world, as you are reading these words, people are being forced into refugee camps, having fled their homelands out of fear for their lives, with little other than the clothes they were wearing. It's winter. Tens of thousands are crammed into tiny tents and forced to endure freezing temperatures because they have no money to pay for warm clothing, heaters, or fuel. Job opportunities are few, so they suffer, living wholly dependent upon the UN or NGOs for food, water, medical care, and other necessities that may never arrive.

As nationalistic and corporate dominance attitudes have intensified, well-meaning efforts to stem that tide often prove futile. Existing structures have failed us. The only alternatives are the same that have proven time and again to be the best. We, the people, must create new structures and new systems within which a humane society may unfold.

We do so in part by establishing the Global Relocation Fund to create money, without limitation or repayment obligation, to fund all relocation expenses and provide all associated services and necessities for those without. All who are rejected by existing societies or forced by circumstances beyond their control to require our assistance will find a home, a job, and a community with us, as enabled by the funds we create.

CLEAN WATER FUND

We live in a time of grave humanitarian crisis. Contaminated waters plague the world's environments, killing millions every year and causing untold numbers of hospitalizations that could be instantly eliminated by providing purification systems wherever needed. The technologies already exist to purify contaminated water, save millions of lives, and prevent massive levels of suffering. So why aren't they being deployed right now? The answer resides within the concept of money and how we have allowed it to be used.

Humans have been around for approximately 200,000 years. For all but perhaps a hundred of those years, water, a life necessity, was considered a natural resource freely available to everyone. But today, billions are deprived of free access to clean water simply because of how society has chosen to use money.

We choose to change that dynamic by declaring free access to pure water a fundamental human right. We establish the Clean Water Fund (CWF) to protect that right by creating money to manufacture, deliver, and operate water purification systems wherever needed. Just as bankers create and distribute money throughout society, so must we. But we do it differently; our funds burden no one with debt. No community will ever be denied delivery of any system designed to provide a life necessity, save lives or prevent human misery because they can't afford it. Nor will they ever be asked to pay for it.

It costs nothing to create money. Its use without limitation is our gift to enable a civilized society, without condition, empowering us to deliver compassion and hope to those without. Along the way we create millions of employment opportunities in the production, delivery, installation, and operation of clean water and associated clean energy systems to power them. Know that with each new system put into operation, we make a better world.

SANITARY SYSTEMS FUND

We create money for just causes. Billions of people live in squalor, lacking modern sanitary systems. We choose to alleviate a fundamentally cruel condition that people are born into by establishing the Sanitary Systems Fund to create money to bring state-of-the-art sewage treatment facilities and associated infrastructure to all in need, without cost, debt, or repayment obligations. Millions of jobs are created to develop, deploy and operate these new systems, and extreme suffering is eliminated as burdens on Earth's support systems diminish. Step by step, we make the world a better place and build momentum within The Movement.

WORLD HEALTHCARE FUND

A healthy population is a necessary ingredient of a civilized society. To help create this society, everyone must be guaranteed unlimited free access to the best of healthcare services, as the health and well-being of every individual is truly sacrosanct. In recognition thereof, we elevate receipt of state-of-the-art healthcare to a fundamental human right guaranteed to every member of our society.

Building a global healthcare system will take time and the concerted efforts of millions. The process starts with you and builds within your community as individuals and organizations engage to help make the world a better place; first, by ensuring that all fundamental rights are met and adhered to in their community, then by supporting nearby communities in their efforts to perfect the same. When communities of the world have linked in support of each other's needs, by the sheer mass in number of individuals acting in pursuit of commonly held goals, we will have changed the course of humanity.

So, we establish the World Healthcare Fund (WHF) on the guiding principle that every person is guaranteed, as a fundamental human right, the best of modern healthcare services. The WHF shall create all money necessary to provide state-of-the-art healthcare and wellness services, free of cost, to everyone.

As with all funds, money for this project will not come from any government, or out of any individual's pocket, or from any existing banking entity. No excuse exists for anyone to be deprived access to this most precious and humane of services. Funding is provided to build and operate new hospitals, clinics, and wellness centers creating tens of millions of jobs in construction, infrastructure, commerce, science, technology, medicine, pharmaceutical, and associated industries to support this system as its benefits spread throughout society. Arguments that hospitals and clinics are underfunded, understaffed, and unable to provide quality healthcare services or that drugs and other treatments are too expensive, cease.

Communities most in need will be the first served, following a logical progression until all communities are well-served. Of course, what must also be envisioned is a global system of commerce within which most of our activities take place. That means there must be enough of us committed to The Movement to ensure global supply chains becoming operational. The Funds of One Commerce will help enable just that.

- 20 -

THE FUNDS OF ONE COMMERCE

Growth and profits. What more could anyone want? How about a society within which the business of humanity is the search for and acquisition of knowledge of how every aspect of this glorious universe works and why? How about a society within which necessities are provided as a foregone conclusion and cooperation, not competition and conflict, reign supreme?

In a world where captains of industry are hard at work maximizing profits by minimizing expenditures, it is nearly impossible to incentivize forward-looking, socially responsible management practices, so we approach the solution from a different direction by introducing a new structure with new goals enabled by a new form of finance.

Here, goals of growth driven by the lure of profits have been jettisoned, replaced by goals of ever-increasing efficiencies that reduce resistance in life. Here, travelers are propelled into a future of limitless possibility and endless technological innovation. Their destiny takes them to the stars.

The old and the new represent two completely different visions of society and approaches to life. Each utilizes the same structural concepts within which society operates. Each structure performs the same functions. The only difference between the two visions resides within their goals, which direct how their respective systems operate.

Fundamentally different goals about *how* to do what we do result in fundamentally different outcomes.

The goal of the existing structure of commerce is to produce ever-increasing levels of profits as fast as possible, untethered by regulation, with little regard for the adverse consequences of their actions, whether upon humans or the environment. Their systems typically delay operational changes to prolong profit extractions instead of infusing profits to innovate rapid change and eliminate harms from their practices. The goals of this structure are destructive to nature and ourselves. They were developed for a bygone era and are obsolete.

Contrast those goals with the Goal of One Commerce, which is to operate all systems of commerce as efficiently as technologically feasible at every given point in time. To achieve this goal, the Funds of One Commerce create money to enable change as rapidly as we are capable of innovating it. Their funds expedite the transition to systems that minimize and ultimately eliminate harms to the environment and ourselves from *how* we do most things. What makes this structure unique is that its funds enable and incentivize its systems to be constantly evolving.

Just as One Governance is a new form of governance that evolves separately and distinctly from existing structures, so too is the structure of One Commerce, which operates independently from existing structures. Adopting new structures within which the boundaries of new ways of being materialize will have a profound impact on our collective life experiences.

Imagine a world where profit margins no longer dictate how and when we do what we do. Imagine a world where all systems of commerce incorporate best practices methodologies that are incentivized and enabled to evolve more efficient pathways as new technologies present. Instead of designing products to become obsolete within a few years of production, forcing ever-increasing levels of consumption and waste, imagine a world where our products and systems are designed to evolve systemically, helping to minimize collateral damage from production and deployment practices.

Research into the development and implementation of pretty much everything we do takes on new meaning and ever-increasing levels of significance. Fear of jobs lost and distrust of the technological revolution evaporate as innumerable employment opportunities are created and environmental harms are diminished.

Whereas rulers succeed in resisting change in part by spreading fear of jobs lost to technological innovation, we incentivize change and eliminate fear of it by providing funding to train everyone interested in developing new skills applicable to new-age careers.

Think about building entirely new, highly evolved, living cities that extract atmospheric carbon for use as structural components which helps to reverse global warming impacts from our presence. It is possible. With technological innovation, subsistence jobs are eliminated and replaced by positions employing highly trained, well-paid workers and technicians. No longer will anyone be forced to toil deep within a coal mine or left unemployed when oil and gas drilling operations are shuttered as alternative clean energy systems are brought online. Life opportunities expand with change, not the reverse, as fear-mongers would have you believe.

Instead of being abandoned, everyone seeking gainful and meaningful employment can be retrained to serve society in better, more efficient, more meaningful, and more rewarding ways. Funding for retraining and lifestyle enhancement is provided without burdening the recipient with debt or other mechanisms of servitude. To incentivize the acquisition of higher-level skills, living wage incomes are provided during retraining processes.

The Funds of One Commerce exist to provide the things we need to improve the human life experience. They galvanize change to enable a better humanity. Although no one will be left behind as money is created to ensure a basic level of existence for those in need, everyone will be encouraged to contribute.

Systems can be designed to incentivize participation and disincentivize the freeloader if that is a concern, but (as we know) most people when you really get down to it gather a sense of purpose and self-worth when contributing in some meaningful way. Most people simply prefer to be busy. Make it easy and rewarding to contribute, and most will. Allow people the luxury of self-discovery, to figure out where their strengths reside, and watch them blossom once they have. Encourage and enable people to find some passion in life and most will joyously contribute to the greater good. We do so by establishing the Funds of One Commerce.

THE COMMERCE FUND

The Commerce Fund (TCF) is the parent fund within which all system funds reside. It exists to enable the goals of One Commerce. It is comprised of many parts, each of which exists to provide funding for some worthy aspect of society, whether providing basic infrastructure for necessities or the operation of businesses to produce and supply goods and services.

Have an idea for a new business or a new, more efficient way of producing or delivering something to enrich the human life experience? Need funding? Pitch the idea to a committee of TCF and just like pitching that idea to a banker or venture capitalist, if they deem it a worthy enterprise money will be created to develop a product, run a business, or provide some service with oversight and guidance from experienced personnel.

Replacing profit-driven systems with efficiency-based ones helps eliminate poverty, inequality, pain, suffering, environmental contamination, and other adverse impacts that human populations exert on Earth's support systems. It also creates limitless employment opportunities and the very real possibility of a humanity finding better ways of being.

The following are but a few examples of possible funding entities and the things we can accomplish when money is used as a tool to enable a civilized society. It is for you to decide where a particular fund resides. Whether within the structure of governance or commerce really shouldn't matter.

COMMUNITY DEVELOPMENT FUND

To assist with the transition from one set of social systems to another requires that we reimagine all communities. So, we establish the Community Development Fund to create money to build temporary communities for millions in need and then to fund, without limitation, the planning and construction of new, state-of-the-art communities to best serve everyone.

This is a massive project that will create nearly limitless employment opportunities throughout all levels of society. It will require great patience, persistence, and generations to bring to fruition. And, it will be perhaps the first of many grand projects within which our creativity is enabled to truly serve us all.

This fund provides for the development and operation of optimally sized, strategically located, state-of-the-art communities - living communities - designed to evolve. Efficiency in design, location, and delivery of all services through all sectors is key. Temporary communities are built as a first priority to house refugees, those most in need, and others to be engaged in the development process.

Best practices methodologies set standard design criteria typically requiring intense planning and impact analysis to deliver the highest quality living environments designed in harmony with nature. Projects are neither rushed nor delayed. Do it right or not at all is the standard.

Only well-qualified individuals fill positions. However, we will train and engage everyone who desires to partake in building the communities they will call home. And, we rob no one of their dignity by forcing them to work for slave's wages. Instead, we provide living wages and incorporate principles of equality in everything we do.

Equal pay for equal service (no matter where on Earth they are performed) sets the standard of standards. This way we eliminate capitalistic practices that drive down wages by shopping for workers willing to exist on subsistence pay because there are no alternatives. Our practices enable greater efficiencies in production by incentivizing local and regional production of products best suited to the area.

We do not take from bankers and capitalists, who extract profits from every financial transaction forcing wages so low and prices so high that borrowing is a necessity. Their choice is to enslave the masses, ours is to empower humanity. We cast aside all attempts to use money to enslave, control and profit. Rather, we use it to enable the transfer of goods and services within society, as originally intended.

AGRICULTURAL PRODUCTION FUND

In 1950 there were 2.5 billion people. Today there are 7.8 billion and in 80 years there will be over 11 billion.[177] Existing agricultural production and delivery systems are incapable of responsibly serving our current population. They promote environmentally destructive practices, supply us with nutritionally deficient foods laced with cancer-causing chemicals, and force billions to suffer from malnourishment and starvation. The harms they ignite metastasize with each passing moment and we all suffer.

Contrast the old to new agricultural production systems driven by best practices methodologies that are bioregenerative in nature. These systems optimize productivity and deliver nutritionally rich foods in ways capable of reversing the adverse effects of current industrial practices. They reduce the impacts from our presence by, among other things, capturing carbon in the soil (helping reverse global warming), and eliminating the use of pesticides and herbicides that kill pollinators and beneficial microorganisms (helping restore the health of Earth's reproductive and digestive systems).

We know how to produce the foods every parent wants for their children; all we need to do is enable it. So, we establish the Agricultural Production Fund to protect our future by enabling the delivery of nutritionally rich foods produced in environmentally sensitive ways utilizing state-of-the-art best practices methodologies.

This fund, like most, is tied to a division of One Governance, which in this case sets and enforces rules and regulations for the efficient operation of responsibly managed food production and delivery systems. It is also tied to the Science and Technology Fund to enable scientists to work with food production planners, farmers, and indigenous peoples to identify the regions best suited for food production, and then develop and implement best practices methodologies for each locale to meet the goal of producing and delivering the highest quality foods in the most environmentally compatible ways.

It is our collective responsibility to ensure that our systems operate to restore and enhance the health and well-being of all citizens, as well as that of our mother - Earth. As we enable new structures and new systems to support each other, we evolve a unified society operating harmoniously within a vibrant set of life support systems.

RAINFOREST RESTORATION FUND

"[T]he inner dynamics of a tropical rainforest is an intricate and fragile system. Everything is so interdependent that upsetting one part can lead to unknown damage or even destruction of the whole. Sadly, it has taken only a century of human intervention to destroy what nature designed to last forever."[178]

The advent of agriculture set the stage for accelerated population growth, which together are primarily responsible for the destruction of the Earth's forests. In 1950, rainforests covered more than 14 percent of Earth's land surface. Today, they cover 6 percent. Approximately 200,000 acres of rainforest are burned every day (1.5 acres/second) to log timber and then farm or ranch the barren land.[179] Population growth fuels deforestation as do inefficient, unregulated food production practices. Experts estimate that all rainforests will have been consumed within a century.[180]

Forests play a fundamental role in Earth's Respiratory System. They pull carbon dioxide from the atmosphere and release tremendous amounts of oxygen in exchange. As we continue to rip apart Earth's Oxygen Production Systems, the implications should be obvious. Human activities have caused an irreversible decline of atmospheric O_2.[181] And, of course, rainforests make rain. They produce a huge percentage of the world's freshwater, playing an intrinsic role within Earth's Circulatory and Thermoregulatory Systems. Destroy the rainforests and lose freshwater production resources, heat the planet and accelerate desertification.

Beyond those concerns, recognize that we have little knowledge of the significant life support functions performed by the more than 50 percent of the world's terrestrial plant, animal, and insect species which live within rainforests. As we devour Earth's rainforests, we are wiping out planetary-levels of biodiversity, vaporizing hidden secrets that could cure disease, provide natural insecticides, enable longevity and even interstellar travel. This truth was aptly conveyed over four decades ago by Harvard's Pulitzer Prize-winning biologist Edward O. Wilson when he stated that:

The worst thing that can happen during the 1980s is not energy depletion, economic collapses, limited nuclear war, or conquest by a totalitarian government. As terrible as these catastrophes would be for us, they can be repaired within a few generations. The one process ongoing in the 1980s [which continues unabated] that will take millions of years to correct is the loss of genetic and species diversity by the destruction of natural habitats. This is the folly that our descendants are least likely to forgive us for.

Ours is a great opportunity to right past wrongs. The introduction of the Rainforest Restoration Fund enables us to provide the resources necessary to rescue one of Earth's truly great and necessary wonders. From the acquisition of vast tracts of lands suitable for restoration to the development of Outposts within which restoration projects are managed, come lifelong career opportunities to engage in truly meaningful and rewarding life experiences for scientists, local and indigenous peoples, technicians, and all others who choose to help accomplish this noble task.

Ancient societies lived with, respected, and revered nature. Contemporary societies have removed us from her. But, as our perspectives expand to encompass the broader aspects of the marvels of this incredible universe, we come to understand the wisdom and the importance of time well spent within all that is of nature. We have the opportunity and the capacity to rejuvenate the world that has been gifted to us, and we can find great joy in so doing. Whether from the benefits received through the Rainforest Restoration Fund or through the Whole Earth Fund, we can restore Earth's life support systems and enable a far better humanity.

THE WHOLE EARTH FUND

Imagine a world radiating purity, in balance, and bursting with life. This is a world where her waters are safe to drink, her air healthy to breathe, her lands rich in biodiversity, and her oceans brimming with life. It was the world we inherited. It was the world that gave birth to our kind. It was the world of yesteryear, green with splendor, sparkling with blue, and plentiful with life.

Although this is not our world today, it could be again. If you had the power to heal your mother, would you? Well, you do. The opportunity to heal our mother is entirely within our control. We have the ability to set new goals, to take responsibility for the things we do by managing our numbers and regulating our business practices. But doing so requires the participation and dedication of many. Will you unite with others who of their own free will choose to help secure our future by doing what they know is right and true?

To help enable us to do just that, we establish the Whole Earth Fund to revitalize Earth systems and solve the vast array of environmental problems we have created. With unlimited funding to work on solving these problems, new technologies will reveal and new under-standings will awaken, allowing us to stimulate the healing properties of Earth's life support systems. This process will expand our under-standing of how life works and create millions of worthwhile, fulfill-ing career opportunities throughout all levels of society.

It is our great opportunity to restore to good health the planet which gave us life. As we embark upon this journey of discovery, of change, recognize that the process of change requires nothing exter-nal, no force of nature other than our own. It is one of discovery which begins with ourselves. It reveals what we are and leads to an under-standing of what we can be, one people of collective mind who enable their own transformation. Embrace the process of change and dis-cover far better ways of being.

THE OTHER FUNDS OF ONE COMMERCE

We haven't touched upon the bulk of the things we do that the funds of One Commerce will enable. We don't need to.

As The Goal of One Commerce is to operate its systems as effi-ciently as technologies allow at any given point in time, the salient point is that all systems of One Commerce should be designed with foresight to incorporate anticipated technological innovations. Just as old cells are regularly replaced within our own bodies to enable its internal systems to function longer and more efficiently, the funds of One Commerce enable the systems of One Commerce to revitalize as new technologies come available.

We have provided a few examples of how these funds might work. What is important is that you recognize that how we choose to use money will determine our destiny. Use it wisely and there is little beyond our reach. The funds of One Commerce can quite literally be as limitless as our imaginations allow. Use them responsibly to help enable the evolution of a civilization destined to explore the universe, which brings us to the scientists and the funds that enable them to do their thing.

21

The Funds Of The 4th Structure

The 4th Structure exists to provide the platform from which the search for life's most profound and elusive secrets takes place. This is where the scientists reside and where evolutionary pathways are discovered and traversed. Here, the imagined becomes real, which we enable through The Funds of The 4th Structure.

THE EDUCATION FUND

The acquisition of knowledge is truly sacred. It is what life is about. As knowledge is accumulated, the impossible becomes anything but. It sustains us during times of extreme stress as it provides access to doors previously unseen. Knowledge is one of the cornerstones of civilization. It is something acquired, and it builds upon itself through the educational process. The educational process is one by which knowledge acquired is passed along generationally. One of the most important things to recognize about education is that it truly is 'the great equalizer.' It removes social barriers, eliminates conflict, and creates boundless opportunities. And, it is a fundamentally necessary ingredient to evolving a civilized society.

Accordingly, it is incumbent upon us to create systems within which temples of knowledge and wisdom are plentiful and available to all who seek shelter within. Access shall be granted without condition or burden, financial or otherwise, to all willing to embark on journeys of learning upon which many new pathways will unfold. Some pathways lead to knowledge of how things infinitesimally small can be so powerful. Others, to knowledge of how things infinitely large can be traversed instantaneously. All, make possible the accumulation of wisdom through heightened life experiences.

We gain knowledge most rapidly when we enable the broadest spectrum of people to access state-of-the-art, well-orchestrated educational systems within which the accumulated knowledge of humanity is made freely available to help galvanize change. Within existing systems, education is deployed in limitation. The best is reserved for the elite few who can afford it and sometimes for the exceptional few who stand above. Elsewhere, the lack of money is used as the excuse for the limitations endemic within our species, especially within most educational systems which were neither designed to stimulate the imagination nor foster creativity; the two things in combination that make humans unique, and the two things necessary to optimize if we are to save us from ourselves.

We exist at a time within which planetary-level changes that we have triggered metastasize into massive problems requiring planetary-level solutions now, not later. Yet, our knowledge of how planetary-level systems function is extremely limited. Meanwhile, the resources allocated to recognize and then solve the problems we have created are even more limited. Without the rapid acquisition of vast amounts of knowledge from which creative solutions may come, we are in big trouble. Einstein said, "We cannot solve our problems with the same thinking we used when we created them." He is correct.

We need an abundance of innovative, creative thinkers to generate solutions to the social and environmental minefields left by earlier societies. Yet, as of 2016, 93 percent of the world's population had no college degree.[182] At a time when knowledge acquisition is so critical to our survival, less than 1.2 percent of the world's adult population hold doctorate degrees.[183] If we are to not just survive but to thrive, we have no choice but to elevate the educational process from one of a lowly sub-system into perhaps the greatest institution ever devised.

Know with certainty that an uneducated society is one incapable of navigating pathways of evolutionary change. And know with equal certainty that an educated society is a prerequisite to evolving a civilized society. Like food and water, a highly educated humanity is now a life necessity.

A FUNDAMENTAL RIGHT

To address what is most certainly the social imperative of this era, we declare unlimited access to the best educational systems we are capable of delivering, a fundamental human right, one that guarantees everyone a seat within our temples of knowledge and wisdom without condition, without burden, financial or otherwise. We encourage everyone to become as highly educated as their abilities and interests allow. But, declaring a fundamental right is one thing, securing it is another, one that will require deploying state of the art educational systems globally.

Today, most education systems encourage rote learning. They are obsolete. Within more advanced systems, educators are trained to encourage out of the box thinking to spark the imaginative creativity and ingenuity of their students. As the imaginative spark that solves a previously insolvable problem may strike at any age, we deprive humanity of our most unique feature whenever we deprive anyone of the most robust educational experience they are capable of receiving, no matter their age.

Knowledge is power. It is through the educational process that we acquire more knowledge. So, we bring power to the people by establishing The Education Fund (TEF) to provide unlimited funding for the creation and operation, in perpetuity, of a global education system designed to nurture the spirit and tickle the imaginations of everyone, from preschoolers to centenarians. TEF enables everyone to receive free and unlimited access to the highest levels of education they are capable of attaining. Arguments that any school system lacks funds to deliver state of the art educational experiences instantly vaporize. Arguments that one education system is better than another vanish, as a uniform system is established to replace millions of existing systems operating at vastly different levels because of vastly different resources.

The Education Fund enables entirely new ways of efficiently and effectively building and passing knowledge from one generation to the next. The best teachers and professors, as recognized by their students and peers, elevate to master instructors to convey the most effective teaching methods. And, just like other professions, attending advanced training programs and obtaining renewal certificates is mandatory. Within this system though, funding continuing education is automatic and covers all costs so that every teacher can attend without concern of lost wages or employment security.

We recognize that it is not sufficient to educate just the mind if we are to free humanity from the destructive ways of intolerant, aggressive, territorial, and self-directed individuals. They lack true compassion and are hostile to those who act selflessly for the betterment of all. Our challenge is to craft a caring society from a cruel one. The solution resides outside the confines of the obsolete structures that bind us to past ways. It requires us to travel new pathways upon which we have chosen to do things differently, better.

Remember that our actions define us and the nature of our societies. If you want to live within a civilized society as opposed to a barbaric one, you must act civilly, not just one day a week, but every day. Within civilized societies, kindness is a way of being. It doesn't take much to act with a degree of kindness. In fact, as someone once said, "We don't have to agree on anything to be kind to one another." How true. Acts of kindness open pathways of communication and cooperation which are fundamentally necessary to travel if we are to evolve a civilized society. What differentiates a civil society from a barbaric one is that civil societies focus on commonalities, not differences, which illuminates the necessity of emphasizing acts of kindness in the things we do, not just some days, but all days.

Acts of kindness are behavioral traits best learned within the home and at school. This enables them to carry forward into adulthood. So, we incorporate acts of kindness into our daily routines to enable kindness to emerge as a dominant social trait. Think of doing so in life experience terms. Ask yourself if your life experience would be better at a place where most people act kindly toward you, or where most treat you harshly? The answer should be pretty clear. And recognize that the structural concepts, system practices, and social ways of being discussed within this section, are representative of life within Outposts, as highlighted within Book VII.

It is one thing to speak with moral conviction, it is quite another to consistently act with the same. That requires practice and repetition. So, we embrace teachings throughout all levels of society that encompass education of the heart, along with the mind. In the process we emphasize the importance of acting morally, ethically, and compassionately, by reinforcing these traits through teachings of tolerance, forgiveness, and mindfulness of the impacts each of us creates as we move through life. To create a civilized society, we must elevate morality and ethicality from the philosophical to the practiced, which we do by incorporating teachings of the heart in our daily routines.

For humanity to become better, each of us must learn to be better, so that collectively, we are better. The Education Fund enables a profession whose importance has been neglected for far too long. From this point forward all teachers will be highly compensated for their contributions. Importantly, TEF frees teachers to inspire creativity, a sense of morality, acts of kindness and cooperative efforts by eliminating cost concerns. And of course, the faster and more efficiently knowledge is spread, the faster and more efficiently knowledge can be acquired.

Today, the bulk of human knowledge is already made freely available by the Wikimedia Foundation which exists "to build the most accessible and comprehensive source of free knowledge in the world."

The founders of Wikipedia believed "that knowledge is a fundamental human right." They acted upon that belief and created an online resource that now delivers "free knowledge" to nearly half a billion people every month, in hundreds of languages around the world. Knowledge is input, edited, and refined into the Wikipedia system by a diverse community of volunteers. Everyone is a potential contributor. This is a system of the community, funded by the community, and existing for the community. It is made easy to access and is a shining example of the best of humanity, a beacon of hope, and a portal into how to do things in the future.

To create a society that values knowledge over ignorance and to lift the veil of poverty from the impoverished, we remove artificial barriers limiting access to the best educational systems by establishing The Education Fund. Doing so allows us to build a society founded upon ever-evolving educational systems designed to stimulate the mind, illuminate the soul, and empower our innate creativity enabling us to begin unraveling life mysteries, layer by layer. As we do, our life purpose clarifies and the human potential emerges.

THE SCIENCE AND TECHNOLOGY FUND

*Most everything the human mind can
conceive, and believe, it can achieve.*

The Science and Technology Fund (TSTF) is created to enable the broad pursuit of knowledge and understanding without the imposition of monetary limitation. As with all other funds, Funders will serve in oversight capacities, helping to ensure the efficient use of resources, exploratory and otherwise.

The fact that we may be generations away from learning how to make use of some universal resource should not prevent investigations into how to acquire the imagined. Investigations must begin somewhere. Often, unanticipated discoveries emerge during the exploratory process, so funding should be made available to pursue projects far beyond our present technological capabilities. These are projects of the imagination, ones requiring out of the box thinking in pursuit of vastly different ways of accomplishing some goal, like removing 'forever' toxins from Earth environments, or enabling intergalactic travel, or finding cures for the vast array of maladies that afflict both the many and the few. Not long-ago, thoughts of manned lunar landings were considered fanciful, yet within ten years of setting that as a realistic goal of pursuit, it was achieved. Goals pursued with focused efforts and adequate funding are pretty much all we need to accomplish the truly remarkable.

The Science and Technology Fund exists to enable the truly remarkable. It exists as the parent fund which may crossover with other funds. Whether it is some form of medical research, an investigation into how to clean up the environment, or an inquiry into the most efficient modes of terrestrial or interstellar transport, TSTF will be the starting point for funding requests. If a request is granted, a sub-fund will be established to create funds and oversee the endeavor. The following are just a few of the many sub-funds that could fall within the purview of TSTF.

THE ENERGY PRODUCTION FUND

Energy. It is the most fundamental of universal stuff. All life forms require it; they take energy from one thing and convert it into another. Energy, it is said, can neither be created nor destroyed, only changed in form, which brings us full circle as this work is all about change.

Our sun's energy warms Earth and powers her support systems, which in turn enable our existence. We are dependent upon energy from many different sources. We pull it from the foods we eat and extract it from the wind, the sea, the earth, the sun, and from atomic particles. We use it to grow and cook our foods, warm and cool our homes, power modes of transportation and all forms of commerce. We use it and need it to power society.

The conversion of energy from one form to another is an efficiency thing. Do it well, efficiently, and a lot of energy can be extracted from a speck of resource with little waste generated. Do it poorly, inefficiently, and you create a lot of waste and use up a lot of the resource. The process of liberating energy by changing it from one form to another creates waste. That is basic physics. The more efficient the systems of liberation, the less waste we create. The converse is also true.

With nearly eight billion people on the planet, we use a tremendous amount of energy. Millions burn animal dung, sticks, and branches to cook their meals and warm their homes while billions of others receive energy from burning coal, oil and gas products. Generating energy this way is inefficient. We know this. Their waste products contaminate everything and are responsible for triggering the global warming crisis as well as causing cancers and a vast array of other problems with broad implications that we are slowly becoming aware of.

How we produce energy is a matter of choice. We know how to do it more efficiently, but existing systems prevent decision-makers from rapidly adopting better alternatives, so the obligation of changing these systems is ours. We must pioneer pathways of change in our energy production and delivery systems, which we do through The Energy Production Fund (TEPF).

The Energy Production Fund is established to enable the rapid deployment of state-of-the-art energy production systems the world over. Clean technologies exist. We choose to deploy them now, beginning locally with those most in need and expanding to transform global energy production systems. No longer will anyone have to toil deep within the Earth in coal mines, or in oil and gas production facilities that expose them and their neighbors to toxic chemicals. No longer will they have to work for people whose primary concern is the production of profits, even when they only come at the expense of their workers and neighboring communities.

New energy production systems are necessary everywhere. The deployment of them will create vast numbers of career opportunities that participants may be proud of engaging in as they help provide a necessary resource in fundamentally better ways. And our new systems are designed to eliminate inequality. Equal pay for equal services no matter where performed is a foundational principle. And all employment opportunities are well paid. Systems of subsistence become a thing of the past.

Our future is dependent upon reducing human impacts on Earth's life support systems. The Energy Production Fund frees humanity from the chains of fossil fuel dependence. It opens new pathways to secure Earth's well-being, and our well-being, enabling us the ability to access more life opportunities. Initially, TEPF will be used to enable the rapid transformation of all outmoded energy production systems into state-of-the-art means. Eventually, it will be used to fund research and development of new technologies to power highly efficient systems of travel.

Burning fuels to power transportation is archaic. Whether using the sun, the wind, the oceans or the Earth to create electricity to power maglev trains, hyperloop transportation systems, vehicles that seemingly levitate or to create hydrogen to store and generate electricity for use overnight when wind or solar are unavailable, there are far more efficient methodologies of getting us from here to there and powering society.

Space beckons those who choose to master travel. Imagine utilizing cosmic energy sources to transport humans across vast regions of space within a relative blink of the eye. It is possible. Now imagine doing it yourself, without a machine, thinking yourself from here to there. Impossible? Only if you believe it is. All things become possible as we discover new, more efficient ways of doing the things we do.

TEPF will enable us to revitalize the environment, protect our health and welfare, provide stimulating new careers, and solve some of life's great mysteries. It makes possible the creation of energy production systems capable of powering a civilization of universal explorers. Use its funds wisely. Build living energy production systems that evolve to empower the evolutionary process.

THE EVOLUTION FUND

To evolve. To create a civilization. To become better beings. To use our life force energies more efficiently and more compassionately. These are a few of the opportunities of this era. They are realizable, provided we act with unwavering focus and courage to achieve the intended results.

Evolutionary change moves a species from a less efficient state of being to a more efficient one. It is rare. And it is fleeting. The potential to experience evolutionary levels of change exists within all life forms. It occurs either by chance or intention.

Evolution by chance is just that. Evolution by intention requires just that. It presents as one of life's great opportunities which must be acted upon and realized when it appears, or the opportunity will be lost. Evolution by intention is the evolutionary step required of us right now. No matter how difficult, no matter the resistance, we must recognize, embrace, and immediately act upon the opportunity to secure our potential to evolve to a higher, more efficient state of being.

Doing so enables us to live longer and feel better because we encounter less resistance in life. As resistance subsides, life pathways become easier to travel, which enhances our ability to acquire knowledge and understanding. To help secure that potential we establish The Evolution Fund to create money to catalyze evolutionary change. This fund is broadly managed by The Elders, who enable our greatest thinkers in conjunction with those most wise to do what they are best at. Whatever they need to ensure the evolution of our species is provided.

How do we piece together the numerous components fundamentally necessary to creating the society envisioned without losing the vision in the details? How do we educate ourselves sufficiently to embrace this vision as our own? How can we possibly ensure the continuity and viability of a message of change that is so disruptive to existing ways? There are thousands of how questions. Only the most directive need to be answered now.

What is critically important is beginning. The process begins when a few great thinkers, a number of visionaries, some Elders, True Leaders and others committed to securing evolutionary change, unite to make it so. We know that we must change and that the nature of the changes necessary are ones that must emanate from within the very core of our beings. To enable a society in search of knowledge, understanding and the ways of this universe, we establish The Evolution Fund.

THE TRUTH THAT SETS US FREE

Money is a tool, a creature of our imagination. It can be used as an unlimited resource to catalyze human evolution, or as a tool to prevent it. Choose wisely.

Just because money has been used one way for thousands of years does not dictate that it cannot be used another way to better serve us all. It is time to enable money to be used as an abundant resource, available not for personal enrichment, but for social enhancement. In conjunction therewith, we adopt systems designed with foresight and craft structures to incentivize and enable the evolution of a humane humanity. We choose community over profits, and cooperation over competition. In the end, we choose to use money without debt, obligation, or limitation to catalyze the evolution of a civilization destined to explore life's greatest wonders.

22

THE TAKEAWAY FROM BOOKS I-VI

Earth is a living, breathing organism comprised of sophisticated interdependent systems, the basic components of which are living things. They are responsible for creating the Eden we call Earth, and we are responsible for destroying it. If we are to save ourselves from ourselves and survive the Anthropocene, we have to create better ways of doing most things, not sometime in the future, but right now. That means fundamentally changing how we manage our affairs and operate our systems of commerce, which we enable by changing how we use money.

Fundamental social change requires a vision of how we want to be. Do *we* want to forever be at war with ourselves, or do *we* choose to be at peace, living harmoniously with all who share this beautiful planet? These are the most basic decisions for us to agree upon and only *we* can make them. Most of us, if given the choice and critically, the opportunity, will choose the latter.

How we get from here to there is guided by our goals. We need a higher purpose to provide more meaning to our collective life experiences. Consider The Goal of The 4th Structure as the one capable of providing that purpose. Then consider how the new goals suggested for the other three structures may guide us onto new pathways upon which new and better ways of being materialize. The social and environmental benefits to be derived from implementing those goals has been highlighted.

We possess the freedom to determine our own destiny. No individual, no ruler, no divine being will see us through to that point from which everything emanates: the point of pure being. That obligation falls squarely upon us. It is a together process, a *we* thing. *We* must unite as a global community with unified goals designed to enable us to change how we do most things, or *we* will suffer the consequences.

It is not as if we can't recognize the harms we thrust upon Earth, or for that matter on ourselves. We have evolved that ability. Most of us know deep down and with absolute certainty that we must change how our societies operate. Until recently, we haven't had the ability or the insight into how to do so. The internet and associated technological advances provide the ability. Perhaps this work will assist in some small way with the insight.

We know that solutions must be globally based and all-encompassing. We know that comprehensive planning and coordinated efforts across all systems and structures are necessary to ignite fundamental social change. And we know that to have any chance of success, these plans must be so clearly beneficial that most people will want to adopt them as their own.

This is the first time in human history that this level of change has become both necessary and possible. Nothing of Earth or of this universe other than ourselves prevents us from achieving this level of change. In fact, if we were to really pay attention, we would recognize that the universe calls out for us to change.

Remember, it is not what we think about ourselves, or believe about some greater being that will determine whether or not we survive and thrive as a species. It is, in point of fact, *what we do that will be determinative*. And right now, the collective weight of our actions is moving us in the wrong direction. We are doing most things the wrong way for the wrong reasons. That must change.

The pace at which new scientific discoveries are being made will help buy time to transition societies from old to new. We have developed the technological capacity to live more efficiently and more harmoniously on this spectacularly beautiful planet. Yet, it is neither a matter of intellectual capacity nor technical ability that is necessary to secure our future. It is a matter of will. A matter of choice.

Your choice is to live within existing structures, try to modify them, or free yourself and adopt new ways of being designed to better serve us all. The easiest thing to do is to do nothing and let the chips fall as they may. We have discussed the likely outcome.

The next easiest course of action is to recognize that current pathways are leading in the wrong direction and then try to make corrective adjustments here and there with a few acts of resistance thrown into the mix. We have discussed the likely results as well.

The final choice is the most difficult, but the most rewarding. This one requires us to travel new pathways. To leave the old ones behind and step upon new ones. It requires the coordinated actions of billions who possess an intense desire, coupled with supreme courage and unending persistence, to create a far better way of being than any humans have experienced.

Freedom of choice is the most basic of freedoms. Let no one bind you to their choice. Neither your parents, your teachers, the politicians, the media, rulers of commerce or finance, nor those who preach to you, have the right to dictate your life's path. You get to decide. Open your mind. Explore the possibilities. Think for yourself. Open your heart. Choose pathways that ring true and follow them.

Life has bestowed upon humanity a great gift, freedom of choice. We, the collective that make up humanity, are granted the opportunity and the freedom to determine our own destiny. We evolved the ability to recognize the consequences of our actions and are now given the ultimate freedom, to ignore the consequences, or to stand together as one people determined to save ourselves from ourselves by responsibly and ethically managing our affairs.

Life's greatest freedom, that of choosing our own destiny, has presented. What will we make of it? To help answer that question, consider the following as a primer to what may be, should we choose to follow pathways designed to enable evolutionary levels of change in the ways of being human.

BOOK VII

OUTPOSTS OF CHANGE

Humanity stands at evolution's doorstep. This is that singular moment in time when driven by necessity, life gives us a nudge as the evolutionary opportunity presents. To realize that opportunity we must recognize the absolute need for transformative change and be willing to risk everything to make it happen. Opportunity through self-determination is the ultimate freedom.

We are an amazing and at times wonderful species with a great capacity for goodness. Every day there are millions of altruistic actions, people helping people, that compose an intrinsic part of the whole of humanity. New associations are constantly being woven to solve problems that affect the common good, right recognizable wrongs, preserve land and wild habitats, craft strategies for a more sustainable future, bring clean water to those without, seek cures for the seemingly incurable, protect children from abuse and ensure women are treated equally with men, provide food and medical care to those in need, bring sight to the sightless, clean up toxic pollution, feed and house the homeless and refugees of war, argue for protections against corporate acts of irresponsibility, seek justice where there is none, bring education to those without, and to create opportunity where none was thought to be had.

We know how to be better at life. And, given the opportunity, we will accomplish great good. We have the ability to secure that opportunity. It takes agreement, courage, and the coordinated actions of many.

Tribal societies with imaginary boundaries drawn on some map are antiquated concepts of a bygone era. We are One. One species, distinct from all others; individually unique, but globally One. We live, or we die, by the decisions we make as a collective whole. The power of change lives within each of us and emerges when we choose to act as One, for the benefit of all.

Now is our time, a time that calls for the best of our selves to unite as a community of one mind, of one spirit, with one immediate goal: to create a civilized society that thrives on the acquisition of knowledge in search of the ultimate answers to the most fundamental of questions. This is our Time of Change. We do so by establishing Outposts of Change.

Outposts of Change are places where well-being is the goal of governance, efficiency the goal of commerce, enabling a humane civilized society the goal of finance, and pursuit of universal truths the goal of science. When all four goals are in place and being actively pursued, humanity may indeed find its way onto evolutionary pathways.

Outposts enable The Movement whose goal is to create a civilized society. Chance will not make it happen. Rulers will not allow it to happen. It happens when you and those who care enough about humanity unite to form a vast, interconnected community within which goals to enhance the human life experience materialize reality.

Outposts are places of the heart, where new ways of being enable a new form of society within which every Member lives with the intention of helping each other in furtherance of our understanding of life. Within Outposts, the spirit is nurtured and every soul well cared for.

Outposts are evolutionary centers, places of possibility that shape reality. They form platforms upon which change solidifies, thrusting humanity forward into a future of promise and well-being.

Places of well-being do not just happen; they must be created, intended. They will appear one here and one there, eventually everywhere, each unique yet common by design. They are places of a cooperative society within which happiness is a treasured value and wellness of utmost importance.

Outposts are real places. They emerge in full splendor when our collective actions have become so strong and so present that even those who initially opposed evolutionary levels of change have come to realize it as the better way of being. The process begins right here and right now, with you.

23

BIRTHPLACES OF AN EVOLVING SOCIETY

New Outposts take time, great effort, and careful planning to fully develop. They require the best minds to create structural foundations upon which new societies, defined by equality of being with opportunity a shared commodity, spring into existence, operating both efficiently and harmoniously as an intrinsic part of the surrounding whole. They are birthplaces of an evolving society of universal beings.

COMMUNITIES OF FELLOWSHIP

Outposts of Change begin with a few courageous individuals who embrace their communities with such feelings of fellowship, goodwill, and intention to make the world a better place that others readily join, creating a movement, The Movement, to ensure there is a future well worth sending our children's children's children into.

WITH GOALS HELD IN COMMON

Outposts develop within your community and communities alike the world over by adopting uniform structures of governance, commerce, and finance which enable The 4th Structure. They are designed to achieve goals that benefit us all. Goals that most of us hold in common.

EXISTING FOR EACH OTHER

Outposts exist within everyone who wants to help us be better at life. There are millions of people around the world who sacrifice the only thing that they truly possess, the time they are granted to live a life, to help their fellow beings. Many live unheralded, often impoverished lives helping others. They do so with compassion and with love, knowing they make a difference. To enhance another's life experience is ultimately what we are all about. There is little beyond a life lived in true service of humanity. It is for now, the only thing that truly matters. Within Outposts, we exist for each other.

COMMUNITIES IN ACTION

The actions of a single person cannot fundamentally change the course of humanity; it takes communities in action to do that. But what you do with your life does matter. Do one thing to make the world a better place regardless of how insignificant it may seem, and you have. Make it a habit. Do one thing every day to make a better world, and you will have completed 365 such actions in one year. That makes a very real difference. Now visualize a time when two billion people have adopted the same habit. Two billion actions every day equals 730 billion actions every year making a better world. Over a 10-year span, 7,300,000,000,000 of such actions will fundamentally transform us.

We are social creatures. We like talking about what we and others are doing, so start the conversation. Talk about the actual things you have done or plan to do to make a better world. Ask others what they are doing. Connect with those who are engaged in the process. This is important. There is great joy to be had at the end of each day when reflecting upon the good things we have done. These are contagious actions that build their own momentum. When they become topics of general conversation, a Consciousness of Change will envelop society. Many such actions translate into significant change and slowly but surely, a better society will emerge as more and more of us live consciously, act courageously, give compassionately, and treat everyone the way they would like to be treated.

Create an Outpost. It begins with you and others like you. Or join an Outpost and become part of a community in action. Remember, everything you do impacts the world around you. You either change the world for the better, or for the worse. For humans, there is no middle ground. Your obligation is to become aware of the consequences of the things you do and then decide how you want to live your life. Sitting in a church, temple, mosque, or other place of worship listening to a sermon doesn't necessarily help, no matter how profound the sermon may be unless it prompts you into taking action to help make life better for others. What is important is that you act. You must do something, anything, to help build a community that exists to secure the well-being of each member. Within Outposts, you will find that community.

WITH UNWAVERING DETERMINATION

Outposts are places within which the community acts to make a better humanity, in part by enabling the happiness and securing the well-being of its Members. Happiness is contagious. Smile at others and others will smile back. Help a stranger and a stranger will help you. It doesn't matter what the act is so long as it is intended to help make the world a better place, because it does. Now, imagine that every day there are billions of people engaged in making ours a better world. How long will it be before our society is a vastly superior, happier place to be? That world will be our world when there are enough of us acting with unwavering determination to make it so.

CHANGE GATHERS MOMENTUM

Outposts are places of action that build upon themselves, generating hope as meaningful change becomes apparent. The more actions directed at making a better humanity, the greater the likelihood of meaningful change. So, act with others and build your Outpost of Change. The faster you spread the word, the sooner change comes, gathering momentum as your community of friends, family, and acquaintances builds in support of each other. It begins with one and soon becomes many.

BELIEF ENABLES CHANGE

Outposts become a force when enough people believing in the possibility of change agree to use money to enable rather than limit humanity. That is all it takes. A little understanding of how to better use money, followed by your belief that its use within evolved structures will enable fundamental change in the ways of being human. Belief enables change. Believe in the power of Outposts.

FAITH PAVES THE WAY

Outdated financial systems work only because people have faith that they will. Our new systems require nothing more. Assume they will work and they shall. As people better understand the function of money in old versus new societies, they will abandon the old and transition entire economies into the new. Recognize that we are doing the same things within new structures as we always have, just more humanely and more efficiently. Have faith that new structures will work better than the old. Commit to them. Faith paves the way.

FOUNDING MEMBERS

There will be wealthy individuals and influential governors who, recognizing this to be the singular moment within which the pathways we travel determine the outcome of Earth's human experiment, choose to dedicate their lives and accumulated resources to being Founding Members. They will join with visionaries, elders and other individuals dedicated to the process of enabling transformative change to form a "think tank" of sorts within which The Movement will be orchestrated and new structures defined and established. Land will be acquired and gifted for new Outposts. Goods and services will be supplied in exchange for our money, restoring the original function of money and enabling the transition from old to new. You, may choose to become a Founding Member.

ELDERS

Ancient societies valued the Wisdom of Elders. Three generations, sometimes four, lived under one roof. Parents toiled daily while elders looked after their young, teaching and imparting wisdom accumulated over lifetimes. We revive that age-old tradition within Outposts, in recognition of the great value elders bring to society. No longer will they be viewed as financial or life burdens to their children. Their needs are met within the community, enabled by The Elders Fund, freeing them to rekindle their ancient and revered roles within the family and their communities. Everyone benefits as new meaning and purpose flow to young and old alike.

COUNCILS OF ELDERS

We also establish The Council of Elders, consisting of those members of society who have over the years displayed the highest levels of ethics, morality, compassion, and wisdom as determined by their respective peer groups. These individuals tend to be visionaries who hail from all walks of life. They are engaged to guide society safely into the future and as such, are the final arbiters of our actions. It is the highest of honors to serve on The Council of Elders. Their decisions determine the broadest scope of actions taken. Those serving at the pinnacle of each new structure report directly to The Council of Elders.

Lesser Councils of Elders are established to broadly oversee the operation of each new system. Those who serve in this capacity must evidence the same personality traits as those required of members of The Council of Elders. These individuals are charged with the great responsibility of ensuring that new systems follow pathways designated by The Council of Elders.

We also establish Local and Regional Councils of Elders to broadly oversee individual and regionally based Outposts, ensuring that our collective goals, values, and ways are both maintained and allowed to evolve over time. Local Councils report to Regional Councils who report to The Council of Elders.

COMMUNITIES OF FAMILY AND FELLOWSHIP

Within Outposts, we recognize the importance of caring not just for every Member of individual communities, but for every Member of every community, for we are all One. In truth, the well-being of humanity is dependent upon the well-being of each member; so, we revitalize both the community spirit and its purpose within Outposts, which exist as communities of fellowship.

Outposts are places of family within which the community provides support and opportunity for parenting to elevate to an art form. New parents are given generous leave from their respective professions to care for their newborns without any concern of job security or financial need. Leave to Care carries forward long enough to establish the child as the center of each parent's life and solidify each parent at the center of their child's life. And every Outpost is empowered to allocate great resources in making each child's first 25 years the most nurturing and enabling of their lives. Here, elders are granted the great privilege of imparting life-lessons learned and the wisdom that often follows the experience, upon the most precious of resources, our children.

PLACES OF EQUALITY AND COMMONALITY

Outposts are places of sublime equality. All men and all women are endowed with equal rights, including the right to equal pay for equal service, no matter where they live. Neither has the right to domineer over the other. Neither has the right to dictate which social practices the other must partake in. No matter the ancestry one may be born into, all individuals are treated equally, provided the same opportunities, and given the same freedoms of choice in life.

Fundamental Rights of Being reign supreme within Outposts which are enabled by a common Constitution, the sharing of uniform principles, ideals, and goals, no matter the location and no matter the cultural background of the community. Outposts develop over time, at first within existing communities, then as new ones. And, with each new Outpost, the invisible threads that constitute the essence that links us all strengthen, empowering each Outpost and each Member to be more connected and more complete.

With the accumulation of knowledge, understanding, and efficiency of being as fundamental goals, Outposts are designed to change, to improve, and to evolve as knowledge is acquired. Outposts exist to enable inclusive communities designed to enhance the human potential and create opportunities for living more fulfilling and enjoyable lives.

TOGETHER, WE SIMPLY ARE BETTER

Never before have we had the opportunities that stand before us. And yet, never before have we had the challenges and responsibilities that stand before us. As we strive to be better, we redefine our systems to be better, in every way. To be operationally more efficient, we design systems to yield more from less, using best practices methodologies. To optimize each individual's life experience, we provide opportunities for each to be the very best they can be. And, in recognition that the health and well-being of the whole is dependent upon the health and well-being of each individual, we provide access to the best of everything society has to offer, equally, to every Member.

We are nothing without each other. We are better, more complete, more satisfied, more fulfilled, and happier when we join forces to achieve common goals for the common good. It is that simple. It is that fundamental. Together, we simply are better.

Life's challenge for humans is for us to figure out how to thrive, not just individually, but as a collective whole. That requires us to evolve, to fundamentally change how we do most things. Our ability to do so is enhanced when working together as a whole, engaged in pursuit of common goals for the common good.

Conversely, our evolutionary potential is diminished within societies competing against each other as fractured nations and corporate entities vie for dominion and control of the last vestiges of Earth's limited resources. Continue along existing pathways and we will have failed life's test, with extinction not far off.

So, recognize that Outposts provide the opportunity and the capacity for us to responsibly manage our affairs on a global basis as one organism trying to make a go of it on this most wondrous of worlds. Technological advances over the past fifty years have been exponential. With better structures in place, knowledge gained will enhance everyone's life experience, affording us the ability to move from fractured societies where most are engaged in some form of physical labor, to one within which most contribute intellectually. Within such societies, suffering becomes a thing of the past as each of us is presented with nearly unlimited opportunities to experience a life well-lived.

FREEDOM IS ELEMENTAL WITHIN OUTPOSTS

Ours is a together process. It requires a cooperative spirit. It requires the efforts of many working together to gather and refine knowledge into understanding, which is ultimately what we seek. To gain knowledge, we must dig deep within the inner resources of our minds to discover the workings of the universe. Unraveling universal mysteries may be an involved process, but as they reveal, they present in the most fundamentally beautiful and understandable of ways; $E=MC^2$ is a prime example.

Outposts develop and thrive through cooperative efforts. As we learn to live more fulfilling lives, and live to learn all that we can, the wonders of our universe will reveal in glorious splendor. Outposts may be complicated structures with many intricate details technologically tied together to form an operating whole, but that whole affords each of us the opportunity to live simpler, more efficient, more focused, and more fulfilling lives.

The ability to experience every glorious life moment, is a gift. Within Outposts, everyone is encouraged to fully and joyously experience all that life has to offer. Humanity benefits from our collective experiences. Together, we celebrate the joy of discovery in appreciation of something gained and something released. Within Outposts, we embrace a way of being within which every spirit is encouraged to soar to the highest of heights by experiencing every moment in its fullest.

No longer will anyone have to scour the land for food or water, expending life energies on matters of subsistence. No longer will you or your children live in fear of the ravages of an impoverished life or be forced to live burdened by debt owed to those who lay claim to your life's productivity for their profit. Freedom from debt releases the soul to soar to the highest of heights, gathering strength, knowledge, and understanding along the way. Freedom, is elemental within Outposts.

INEXORABLY LINKED

Our communities grow in strength through the power of the collective. That power must be nurtured and protected. We do so by inexorably linking each Outpost with each other, making our bonds so secure and so directed at attaining our goals that no opposition to evolutionary change can succeed.

FOUNDED ON A HIGHER SENSE OF PURPOSE

Outposts are born in support of a higher purpose for humanity. They are designed as efficient, organic structures to house communities operating in harmony with life's rhythms. People willingly risk all to build communities where the possible becomes reality, in selfless expressions of faith, complete with the understanding that if they do not, then who will? Their work is founded on a higher sense of purpose that elevates the commons in support of the individual.

BUILT UPON FOUNDATIONS OF INDELIBLE TRUTHS

Outposts thrive off each other. They become stronger, more resilient, more present, and more likely to succeed with each new addition. They are beacons of light and of hope aglow with universal truths. They replace greed with community, unburdening each Member's soul by promoting the morality of the commons. And, they are built upon foundations of indelible truths, enabling humanity to travel pathways of discovery. Seek Truth. Act as One. Become One; one society of beings traveling universal pathways in search of knowledge and understanding.

SUCCESS IS NOT A FOREGONE CONCLUSION

Success is not final. Failure is not fatal.
It is the courage to continue that counts.
Sir Winston Churchill

Recognize that fundamental change will not happen overnight and a world full of gleaming new Outposts will not come into being within a few years. It will take time before they become the way of our species. And, be not mistaken in thinking that their success is a foregone conclusion. It is not.

Great fortitude and determination of purpose are necessary for Outposts to survive. Be very clear. With each act committed against us in opposition to our new ways of being, we become stronger and more determined to reach our goals. Acts of opposition solidify our understanding that fundamental change is absolutely necessary to secure our survival.

And understand that suffering often precedes change; in many cases it is what motivates change. As to fundamental change, expect massive resistance by rulers of existing but obsolete systems. They already act mercilessly to maintain power and profit from the toils of their subjects, so we should expect no less from them in the future. Some are brutally abusive; others refuse to interfere to prevent violations of even the most basic of human rights. Their systems promote division by limiting power and opportunity to the few. They kill or imprison those who speak in opposition of their oppressive regimes and they allow the financial elite to enslave most in debt so pervasive that all systems and most people can be controlled by just a few.

Obsolete structures ensure great disparity while sucking joy from life. They force the many to cower under the weight of oppressive regimes and debt-induced slavery. The elite gain from our blood, our sweat, and our tears. They gain what we lose. They gain power from unending wars to support militarized economies, and we lose the blood of our young and of innocent bystanders whose lives are needlessly lost to perpetuate their wars. They gain from systems of inequality designed to extract profits from the labors of many while we toil and sweat for subsistence wages. And they gain by operating systems so oppressive that billions shed tears while suffering lives of great deprivation.

ANTICIPATE AND PREPARE

However, this need not be the way of this world. Human suffering ends as Outposts proliferate. But proliferation requires us to act with the utmost courage, determination, and commitment to the establishment, defense, and permanence of Outposts before they will take root. Only by ensuring that all Outposts, their structures, systems, and Members are inextricably interconnected, do we enable their survival.

Outposts thrive by our commitments to each other. Rulers will attempt to disrupt our systems and dismantle our structures by severing communications between Outposts and preventing new Outposts from coming to be. Do not succumb to their tactics. Anticipate their actions. Prepare and initiate alternative strategies.

As The Movement builds, the best and brightest will gravitate to Outposts in unprecedented numbers. They join because they envision the possible and embrace the opportunity presented through participation in a movement to create fundamentally better ways of being human. By abandoning greed-based systems in recognition of humanity's need for fundamental social change, they exchange today's profits for tomorrow's promises.

The first entirely new Outposts may appear as experiments of something new, something different. And they are. They are born through efforts of many and led by a few who seek a better way for all. Leaders of change know there are always better ways to be, and they help plan societies of change in recognition that without change, there is no life. They know change is the substance of life, so they make way for change, to make way for life.

OF THE PEOPLE, BY THE PEOPLE, AND FOR ALL PEOPLE

Founding Members will donate vast tracts of land and provide a broad array of other resources from which the seeds of change sprout small cities to house the first of many new Outposts. With the help of philanthropists, visionary leaders from within existing systems, and of millions like yourself, come Outposts of Change which are ever-evolving communities of The People, by The People, and for All People.

SEVEN GENERATIONS WALKING TOGETHER THROUGH TIME

While we speak of shedding ancient practices that hold society back, we embrace wisdom gathered from life's lessons learned. Many ancient and indigenous people were careful observers of the natural world, of life, perhaps the first true scientists. Their survival depended upon nature's rhythms, her bounty, and the precise knowledge of which plants could heal and which could kill, which conditions could support life and which could not. Most lived in harmony with nature, conducting their affairs with intention and forethought. Those who did not, perished.

Theirs were generational societies, often four generations living together under one roof. They passed accumulated wisdom from generation to generation in story and song for thousands of years. Seven Generations Walking Together Through Time cared for each other and the world around them. Each generation was taught to consider the impacts from the things they did by asking: Do our decisions honor those who came before us, and do they make way and prepare a hospitable world for the seven generations who will walk these lands in the years to come?

Their questions become ours. If the answers are yes, we proceed; if no, we do not.

Wisdom gathered to promote our collective health and well-being may be instructive, directive, and profound. Above all else, it is worthy of passage through time. So, as we travel along pathways etched in time, if we are wise, we will incorporate the Wisdom of the Ancients into society by regulating our actions with foresight, utilizing knowledge gathered to analyze and balance the benefits of proposed acts against potential adverse consequences, as viewed from the Seven Generations Walking Together Through Time perspective.

In recognition thereof, Outposts incorporate best practices methodologies into every phase of operation to create and maintain living environments in harmony with nature's processes. Human creations are imperfect, so we design Outposts as living systems, intended to evolve as more efficient technologies and better operating strategies reveal.

COMMUNITIES OF HOPE, POSSIBILITY, AND FULFILLMENT

Outposts are communities of hope, of possibility, and of fulfillment. They are designed to seamlessly interconnect the individual with the community and to usher in an age of possibility where every parent's hope for their child to experience a life full of opportunity is a shared goal. Whether through meditation, study, or association with others of similar interests, room is made for each person to live fulfilling lives within a socially active community whose goals embrace better ways of being for everyone.

EXISTING TO STIMULATE BETTER WAYS OF BEING

Outposts are designed to stimulate creativity and better ways of being. They provide gracious forums for the humanities with centers of art, theatre, sports, and culture harmoniously interwoven within natural settings. They enable and encourage their Members, throughout all phases of their lives, to intimately connect with nature, the beauty of which frees both mind and spirit to explore the essence of their own existence, stimulating realms of creative thought not to be experienced otherwise.

Outposts thrive because they encourage everyone to be inquisitive, to consider what is possible, and if interested, to help make it so, creating boundless opportunities along the way. They embody systems of higher learning woven into the very fabric of society. Within Outposts, we live to learn and as we do, we learn to live more purposeful, more fulfilling lives.

Life, at its most fundamental level, is exquisitely simple. Profoundly simple. Simplicity may be difficult to perceive, yet it is the object of our quest for understanding. Our deepest thinkers peer into the depths of reality to know and define small parts of its essence, which they beautifully express within the most simplistic of terms.

Yet, pathways to such expressions tend to be neither simple, nor short. To know the whole, each of its parts must be dissected and understood. To turn complexity to simplicity is the most stimulating of life challenges. It often takes unique, keenly persistent individuals capable of focusing on the elusive before the profoundly mysterious reveals in all its magnificence, and in ultimate simplicity. Such, is life.

Outposts exist to provide each Member with opportunities to live fulfilling, meaningful lives. To be fulfilled is to know peace. The Imperative of the Commons is that each person is to be recognized as an intrinsic part of the whole and to be provided with opportunities for self-fulfillment, as the health and well-being of all humanity is encapsulated within the health and well-being of each Member. Humanity is nothing if not the sum total of all our parts. It is thus incumbent upon humanity as a whole to care for the well-being of each member because in so doing, we make the whole of humanity better, stronger, and more fit to meet the challenges ahead.

You may be invited to join an Outpost, perhaps as a technician, carpenter, teacher, scientist, doctor, engineer, or simply as a worker to assist others in the process. Whatever your profession, know that when you enter our community, your responsibilities expand to encompass the good of the whole. But know also that the responsibilities of the whole expand to encompass the good of each Member.

Within Outposts, you will be presented with opportunities not available within obsolete societies. Opportunities are directed at making the world, our world, a better place for all. You may enter as a worker with few skills, yet your child will be afforded every opportunity to grow to be a world-class scientist or a leader in whatever field he or she may be drawn to.

And, while your child is engaged in life studies, you will be encouraged and enabled to become the best, most knowledgeable person that you can be. Outposts are designed to stimulate better ways of being by enabling everyone the opportunity to develop the skills and interests from which a purposeful, happy life, a life to be treasured, is a shared commodity.

ENTER THE AGE OF UNDERSTANDING

Pathways of discovery run through the elements of this universe. To be enlightened is to know, to understand, and to be all that was, is, and ever will be. It is a process of understanding that takes time, patience, and persistence. To come of age, leave the Anthropocene behind and enter the Age of Understanding.

TO BE ONE

Outposts enable realization. The more we learn, the closer we come to knowing; knowledge in its purest sense. The more we learn, the closer we come to being; being in its purest sense. When we have understood all there is to know, and when we have become all there is to be, *we*, will be One. *We* will be the realization of all there has ever been, all there is, and all there ever will be. *We* will be that which *we* seek. At that moment *we* will have attained our goals and fulfilled our purpose. *We* will have become all that *we* were meant to be and returned to that state from whence *we* came, of One. Outposts enable us to be One.

EMBRACE THE ULTIMATE EXPRESSION OF FREEDOM

Outposts of Change come into existence because we create them. Just as humans have throughout time established villages, towns, cities, nations, systems of governance, commerce, finance, and religion, we establish Outposts. We decide where they will be and what systems to deploy. We may meld the best of past systems into new systems founded upon principles deemed the best for a new way of being. We may choose to meld some of the principles set out herein to serve as guidelines, or we may establish more evolved principles as foundations for a better society.

In the process, you are offered the ultimate expression of freedom: the right to choose which society (old or new) to be a part of. If you choose ours, you gain the freedom to assist in making it the best it can be. All your decisions should be based on reality, on truth. You must seek it out and confirm for yourself the truths about the society you come from, and the one we offer, as only the truth will set you free.

So, choose which society you want to be a part of. We will not force you to join ours, but will yours attempt to deny you the freedom to leave and if so, what does that say about it? Freedom of choice. It is truly a gift. Will you take advantage of it?

WHEN OUR NUMBERS ARE SUFFICIENT

When our numbers are sufficient to operate new structures of governance, commerce, finance, and science, we will use new financial systems to enable the transfer of goods and services necessary to build and operate Outposts as centers of a new way of being.

When our numbers are sufficient, we will use new systems of governance to provide cohesive frameworks within which all other structures and systems can operate to best serve humanity.

When our numbers are sufficient, we will implement new systems of commerce to efficiently conduct our activities.

And, when our numbers are sufficient, we will set out on journeys of discovery of the ways of this universe.

INSTITUTIONS OF CHANGE

Be the change you want to see in the world.
Gandhi.

It begins now, before there are many. Billions of people if given the opportunity will want to help make the world a better place, to create better ways of being for everyone. To be better, we must do things differently than before. That means changing *how* we do most things. Outposts are Institutions of Change. Within, progressive change is a way of life.

ENCOMPASSING UNQUALIFIED GIVING

Outposts begin within the heart and dwell within the soul. It only takes one person to establish an Outpost. From one comes the community and from the community comes humanity. With principals of humanity that are so strong, so righteous, and so profound, we build communities one person at a time by taking actions that benefit those in need first and foremost, without demand or expectation of anything in return. We espouse principals of unqualified giving for the sake of helping another because that is what sets us apart.

BE PATIENT

You, are an Outpost of Change. We all are. They exist within each of us. Outposts begin as a state of mind and materialize through our actions. We make them real and give them presence by uniting with others in pursuit of commonly held goals. Our obligations are to provide for each other. This is especially so during times of great need, which tend to be magnified during periods of transition. Newly built Outposts take time to complete. Lifetimes. So, practice patience. They may start slowly and opposition may delay the development process. But they will take hold and flourish. During these transitionary times, recognize that "patience is truly a virtue." Accept this reality. Be patient as you wait for space within developing Outposts. And join to help accelerate the development process.

ACCEPTANCE

Perhaps the defining characteristic of all Outposts is that they exist to foster a spirit of cooperation thru the pursuit of common goals for everyone's betterment. New rules and regulations are required to enable a fundamentally different and far superior society to emerge from the competitive one you most likely were born into. The decision to change the way you have always done things and adopt new ways of being can only be made by you. You must decide which society is preferable. If you choose to become a Member of an Outpost, you must accept and adopt its ways of being of your own free will.

YOUR OBLIGATIONS

Within Outposts, you will be free to engage in the spiritual practice of your choice, but you will not be free to force your practice on another, whether that other is a spouse, a child, a family member, or another of the community into which you have been granted entry. As with every society that has ever been, as a Member you will be subject to its rules and regulations.

Rules and regulations are established to promote the happiness and well-being of all Members in pursuit of common goals. Within Outposts, rules and regulations are intended to enable unlimited opportunity for self-realization and fulfillment by nurturing the human spirit, stimulating the imagination, and encouraging the mastery of creativity. They are also designed to evolve with us.

Membership has its benefits and its obligations. You and your family will benefit from being a part of the whole; but you may not force past dictates on another. You must embrace the ways of the Outpost even though they may differ vastly from those of the society from which you came. So be it.

LET THE PAST BE

Should you choose to join an Outpost, you must do so wholeheartedly, by embracing their ways as your ways. You will be asked to break with past ways no longer fit for a community of billions, freeing every Member to explore life's possibilities. To break the bonds that hold us all back, you must let the past be just that. You must release hatred. Hatred builds conflict, burdens your soul, and that of your community. You must avoid conflict and acts of aggression, choosing instead to adopt and practice tolerance, compassion, and love. These are the ways of life within Outposts. Ours is a community of one people, of one Earth. We are all of the same species, individually unique but collectively, One. It is time to act as One. To unite to help secure our collective future, you must let the past be.

LIVE IN PEACE

Nothing is perfect. Everything must change. Look to the history of your people to see if the old ways you were born into are best suited for you and your family. If you think they are, stay with them and live in peace. However, should you come to believe that life within Outposts presents better opportunities for you and your family, do not enter an Outpost intending to force old ways upon its Members. You must accept their ways for what they offer, embrace them as your own, and choose to join in peace; for only in peace is a civilized society possible.

HAVE HOPE

Our future will be determined by the predominant actions that *we*, the majority of humans, take over the next few decades. The outcome is not pre-ordained. It will be of our own making. *We*, are responsible for creating our future, and it can be whatever *we* want it to be. That, is the opportunity that has presented. *Now*, is our time of change. No matter how impossible fundamentally changing our ways may seem, with clearly defined goals and dogged determination, *we*, can change the course of humanity. And, it is already happening. As so elegantly expressed by Jeremy Lent in his February 16, 2021 article in *Yes! Magazine*, there is hope for us yet:

A new ecological worldview is spreading globally throughout cultural and religious institutions, establishing common ground with the heritage of traditional Indigenous knowledge. The core principles of an ecological civilization have already been laid out in the Earth Charter—an ethical framework launched in The Hague in 2000 and endorsed by more than 50,000 organizations and individuals worldwide. In 2015, Pope Francis shook the Catholic establishment by issuing his encyclical, Laudato Si', a masterpiece of ecological philosophy that demonstrates the deep interconnectedness of all life, and calls for a rejection of the individualist, neoliberal ethic.

Economists, scientists, and policymakers, recognizing the moral bankruptcy of the current economic model, are pooling resources to offer alternative frameworks. The Wellbeing Economy Alliance is an international collaboration of changemakers working to transform our economic system to one that promotes human and ecological wellbeing. The Global Commons Alliance is similarly developing an international platform for regenerating the Earth's natural systems. Organizations such as the Next System Project and the Global Citizens Initiative are laying down parameters for the political, economic, and social organization of an ecological civilization, and the P2P Foundation is building a commons-based infrastructure for societal change. Around the world, an international movement of transition towns is transforming communities from the grassroots up by nurturing a caring culture, reimagining ways to meet local needs, and crowdsourcing solutions.

Most importantly, a people's movement for life-affirming change is spreading globally. Led by young climate activists like Greta Thunberg, Vanessa Nakate, Mari Copeny, Xiye Bastida, Isra Hirsi, and others, millions of schoolchildren worldwide are rousing their parents' generation from its slumber. A month after Extinction Rebellion demonstrators closed down Central London in 2019, the U.K. Parliament announced a "climate emergency," which has now been declared by nearly 2,000 local and national jurisdictions worldwide, representing more than 12% of the global population. Meanwhile, the Stop Ecocide campaign to establish ecocide as a crime prosecutable under international law is making important strides, gaining serious consideration at the parliamentary level in France and Sweden, with a panel of legal experts convened to draft its definition ...

When we consider the immensity of the transformation needed, the odds of achieving an ecological civilization might seem daunting—but it's far from impossible. As our current civilization begins to unravel on account of its internal failings, the strands that kept it tightly wound also get loosened. Every year that we head closer to catastrophe—as greater climate-related disasters rear up, as the outrages of racial and economic injustice become even more egregious, and as life for most people becomes increasingly intolerable—the old narrative loses its hold on the collective consciousness. Waves of young people are looking for a new worldview - one that makes sense of the current unraveling, one that offers them a future they can believe in.

It's a bold idea to transform the very basis of our civilization to one that's life-affirming. But when the alternative is unthinkable, a vision of a flourishing future shines a light of hope that can become a self-fulfilling reality. Dare to imagine it. Dare to make it possible by the actions you take, both individually and collectively—and it might just happen sooner than you expect.[184]

As awareness of the necessity of fundamentally changing our ways spreads across the lands, the power of each of the millions of movements of progressive change is harnessed and amplified, and its reach and effectiveness is enhanced when joined with others whose most fundamental goals are the same, to help create a more humane humanity. Keep focused on that goal. Unite your movement with others. Become one of many Outposts of Change and create the greatest movement of progressive social change ever. It can happen.

INTEND TO EVOLVE

Evolution takes many forms. For humans to evolve, to become far better beings than we are this day, *we* need to change *how* we do most things. Changing *how* we do most things is simply a matter of intention, a matter of choice. *We* must intend to create a society more humanely human than any has ever been. *We* must intend to create the society we want to be a part of if we are to experience a future of infinite wonder and unlimited possibility. *We* must intend to enable the human life experience to be better than it has ever been. When enough of us have united to create the future most of us want and deserve, we will have evolved. We must intend to evolve.

SO, WHAT WILL YOU DO?

You now possess the knowledge from which transformative change in the ways of being human can be forged. What will you do with that knowledge? Will you stand against change? Will you sit passively on the sidelines and let our evolutionary opportunity slip away? Or, will you do everything within your power to bring about the changes we so desperately need? Should you choose the latter, your actions to help create a more humane humanity will have made our world, a better world. And if *we* possess the collective will to succeed in completing that evolutionary task, oh, what wonders await.

THE CIRCLE THAT IS LIFE

Three simple steps define the circle that is life:

1. Learning enables understanding which leads to Enlightenment, the Earthly embodiment of which is Love, something which we must all learn to do. In the broadest of ways, we must **Learn to Love.**

2. Love is at the heart of all there is, was, and ever will be. For our kind to survive and thrive, in short, to live, we must come to love all living things, including each other. So, we must **Love, to Live.**

3. To experience life in its fullest, to truly live, we must learn all there is to know, so that we may be all there is to be. To complete the circle that is life, we must **Live to Learn.**

It has been said that:

"When the power of love overcomes the love of power, the world will know peace."[185]

Embrace these three simple principles to know peace and become One - One People living together on One Planet whose ultimate life purpose is to explain the unexplainable; to achieve Enlightenment.

- 24 -

THE CONVERSATION CONTINUES

Outposts of Change was written to help galvanize a unifying movement of progressive social change in recognition of the fact that only together will we be able to evolve a civilized society. If you share this belief, and if you want to play a role in creating a future of brilliant possibilities for all human kind, help us unify. Bring your special talents, whatever they may be, to the forefront of change. Engage in the process of fundamentally changing how we do almost everything. The conversation continues at:

OUTPOSTSOFCHANGE.ORG

If you found this work to be educational, thought provoking, or potentially life changing in a positive way, please submit an appropriate review at your place of purchase and on Goodreads. And recommend it to your friends, family members and progressive organizations everywhere.

NOTES

1. Carrington, Damian. (03-11-2020) Polar ice caps melting six times faster than in 1990s. *The Guardian.* https://www.theguardian.com/environment/2020/mar/11/polar-ice-caps-melting-six-times-faster-than-in-1990s Accessed 10-5-2020.

2. WWAP United Nations World Water Assessment Programme/UN-Water. 2018. Nature-Based Solutions for Water. *The United Nations World Water Development Report 2018.* Paris, UNESCO.

3. Crowther, T., Glick, H., Covey, K. *et al.* "Mapping tree density at a global scale." *Nature* 525, 201–205 (2015). https://doi.org/10.1038/nature14967

4. World Wildlife Fund - *2020 Living Planet Report.* WWF, Gland, Switzerland.

5. Serwer, Adam. (July 3, 2019). "A Crime by Any Name." *The Atlantic.*

6. The twentieth-century "Big Bang" theory.

7. Fazekas, Andrew. (October 30, 2014). Mystery of Earth's Water Origin Solved. *National Geographic.* https://www.nationalgeographic.com/news/2014/10/141030-starstruck-earth-water-origin-vesta-science/#close Accessed 11-20-2020.

8. European Commission. (2010). The factory of life. Why soil biodiversity is so important. *Luxembourg: Office for Official Publications of the European Communities.* 22 pp. — 21 x 21cm ISBN 978-92-79-14998-6 doi 10.2779/17050.

9. Wikipedia. *Permian – Triassic extinction event.* https://en.wikipedia.org/wiki/Permian%E2%80%93Triassic_extinction_event Accessed October 10, 2020.

10. Food and Agriculture Organization of the United Nations. *Global Forest Resources Assessment 2015.* (Rome, 2016). ISBN 978-92-5-109283-5.

11. Tree Foundation. *Forest Facts.* https://treefoundation.org/education/forest-facts/

12. Rousseaux, Cecile S., and Gregg, Watson W. *Recent decadal trends in global phytoplankton composition.* AGU100 - Global Biogeochemical Cycles, September 23, 2015. https://agupubs.onlinelibrary.wiley.com/doi/full/10.1002/2015GB005139; https://www.nasa.gov/feature/goddard/nasa-study-shows-oceanic-phytoplankton-declines-in-northern-hemisphere

13. Georgia Institute of Technology. Decades of data on world's oceans reveal a troubling oxygen decline. *Phys.org;* Takamitsu, Ito. Et al. (May 4, 2017). Upper Ocean Trends: 1958-2015. *Geophysical Research Letters.* AGU Publications. Online Library. https://agupubs.onlinelibrary.wiley.com/doi/full/10.1002/2017GL073613; Schmidtko, Sunke; Stramma, Lothar & Visbeck, Martin. (February15, 2017). Decline in global oceanic oxygen content during the past five decades. *Nature International*

Journal of Science. https://www.nature.com/articles/nature21399; Juang, Jianping, et al. (September 30, 2018). The global oxygen budget and its future projection. *Science Direct, Science Bulletin,* Vol 63, Issue 18, Pg 1180-1186.

14. Juang, Jianping, et al. (September 30, 2018). The Global Oxygen Budget and Its Future Projection. *Science Direct Bulletin,* Vol 63, Issue 18, 1180-1186.

15. U.N. Intergovernmental Science-Policy Platform on Biodiversity and Ecosystem Services (IPBES) Report: *Nature's Dangerous Decline 'Unprecedented': Species Extinction Rates 'Accelerating,'* summary approved Seventh session of the IPBES plenary meeting, April 2019.

16. World Commission on Protected Areas. *Grasslands.* https://www.iucn.org/commissions/world-commission-protected-areas/our-work/grasslands Accessed (2020).

17. Daly, Natasha. (April 11, 2019). Earth's grasslands are vanishing. See the wildlife that calls them home. *National Geographic.* https://www.nationalgeographic.com/animals/2019/04/extreme-animals-that-live-in-grasslands/

18. Grooten, M. and Almond, R.E.A.(Eds). (2018) Aiming Higher. *WWF 2018 Living Planet Report.* WWF, Gland, Switzerland. https://www.worldwildlife.org/pages/living-planet-report-2018

19. UN Sustainable Development Goals. (May 6, 2019). *UN Report: Nature's Dangerous Decline 'Unprecedented'; Species Extinction Rates 'Accelerating'.* https://www.un.org/sustainabledevelopment/blog/2019/05/nature-decline-unprecedented-report/ Accessed 10-12-2020.

20. Almond, R.E.A., Grooten M., and Petersen, T. (Eds). (2020) Bending the Curve of Biodiversity Loss. Executive Summary. *WWF Living Planet Report 2020.* WWF, Gland, Switzerland.

21. Ho, Mae-Wan, Dr. (August 19, 2009). O2 Dropping Faster than CO2 Rising – Implications for Climate Change Policies. *Science in Society Archive.* http://www.i-sis.org.uk/O2DroppingFasterThanCO2Rising.php

22. Ho, Mae-Wan, Dr. (August 10, 2009) Warming Oceans Starved of Oxygen. *Science in Society Archive.* http://www.i-sis.org.uk/Warming_Oceans_Starved_of_Oxygen.php

23. EarthSky. (June 08, 2015). *How much do oceans add to world's oxygen?* Earth | Science Wire. https://earthsky.org/earth/how-much-do-oceans-add-to-worlds-oxygen

24. Buis, Alan. (October 9, 2019). The Atmosphere: Getting a Handle on Carbon Dioxide. *NASA – Global Climate Change, Vital Signs of the Planet.* https://climate.nasa.gov/news/2915/the-atmosphere-getting-a-handle-on-carbon-dioxide/ Accessed 11-05-2020.

25. The Ocean Portal Team. (April 2018). Ocean Acidification. *Smithsonian.* https://ocean.si.edu/ocean-life/invertebrates/ocean-acidification

26. Schiermeier, Quirin. (July 28, 2010). A Century of Phytoplankton Decline Suggests That Ocean Ecosystems Are in Peril. *Nature International Weekly Journal of Science.*

doi:10.1038/news.2010.379; Boyce, Daniel G.; Lewis, Marlon R. & Worm, Boris. (July 29, 2010). Global phytoplankton decline over past century. *Nature* 466, 591-596.

27. EarthSky. (06-08-2015) *How much do oceans add to world's oxygen?* Earth | Science Wire. https://earthsky.org/earth/how-much-do-oceans-add-to-worlds-oxygen

28. *Interesting Ocean Facts.* SavetheSea.org. http://www.savethesea.org/STS%20ocean_facts.htm

29. UN Environment Programme. https://ozone.unep.org/ozone-and-you Accessed January 14, 2020.

30. World Health Organization. *Air Pollution.* http://www.who.int/airpollution/en/ Accessed October 5, 2019.

31. Manisalidis I., Stavropoulou E., Stavropoulos A., Bezirtzoglou E. Environmental and Health Impacts of Air Pollution: A Review. *Front Public Health.* 2020; 8:14. Published 2020 Feb 20. doi:10.3389/fpubh.2020.00014

32. IPBES: *Summary for Policymakers of the Assessment Report of the Intergovernmental Science-Policy Platform on Biodiversity and Ecosystem Services on Pollinators, Pollination, and Pood Production.* S.G. Potts, V. L. Imperatriz-Fonseca, H. T. Ngo, J. C. Biesmeijer, T. D. Breeze, L. V. Dicks, L. A. Garibaldi, R. Hill, J. Settele, A. J. Vanbergen, M. A. Aizen, S. A. Cunningham, C. Eardley, B. M. Freitas, N. Gallai, P. G. Kevan, A. Kovács-Hostyánszki, P. K. Kwapong, J. Li, X. Li, D. J. Martins, G. Nates-Parra, J. S. Pettis, R. Rader, and B. F. Viana (eds.). Secretariat of the Intergovernmental Science-Policy Platform on Biodiversity and Ecosystem Services, Bonn, Germany, 2016, 36 pages.

33. Hood, Marlowe. (February 2019). *World Seeing 'Catastrophic Collapse' of Insects: study.* Science X – Phys.org. https://phys.org/news/2019-02-world-catastrophic-collapse-insects.html Accessed February 11, 2019.

34. Sanchez-Bayo, Francisco & Wyckhuys, Kris A.G. (April 2019). "Worldwide Decline of the Entomofauna: A Review of its Drivers." *Biological Conservation,* vol 232, 8-27.

35. Weisse, Mikaela & Glodman, Liz. (June 27, 2018). 2017 Was the Second Worst Year on Record for Tropical Tree Cover Loss. *Global Forest Watch.* https://blog.globalforestwatch.org/data-and-research/2017-was-the-second-worst-year-on-record-for-tropical-tree-cover-loss

36. Lakehead University Faculty of Natural Resources Management. (August 2019). World Boreal Forests: An Introduction. *Borealforest.org.* http://www.borealforest.org/world/world_overview.htm

37. Robbins, Jim. (October 12, 2015). The Rapid and Startling Decline Of World's Vast Boreal Forests. *Yale Environment 360.* https://e360.yale.edu/features/the_rapid_and_startling_decline_of_worlds_vast_boreal_forests Accessed November 7, 2020.

38. WWF Living Planet Report 2020. https://livingplanet.panda.org/en-us/ Accessed October 14, 2020.

39. Carrington, Damian. (October 29, 2018). Humanity Has Wiped out 60% of Animal Populations Since 1970, Report Finds. *The Guardian* - The Age of Extinction - Quoting Mike Barrett, executive director of science and conservation at WWF. https://www.theguardian.com/environment/2018/oct/30/humanity-wiped-out-animals-since-1970-major-report-finds Accessed 11-30-19.

40. *World Scientists' Warning to Humanity.* Sponsored by the Union of Concerned Scientists. https://www.ucsusa.org/about/1992-world-scientists.html#. WnOeFKinGUk, 1992.

41. Ripple, William J. et al. "World Scientists' Warning to Humanity: A Second Notice." *BioScience*, Vol 67, Issue 12, December 2017, Pages 1026-1028 https://doi.org/10.1093/biosci/bix125

42. Daley, Jason. (July 26, 2016)Behold LUCA, the Last Universal Common Ancestor of Life on Earth. *Smithsonianmag.com.*

43. Merriam Webster, s. v. "evolution."

44. Khetani, Sanya. (May 4, 2012). These 14 Countries Are Buying Incredible Amounts Of Foreign Land In Deals You Never Hear About. *Businessinsider.com* https://www.businessinsider.com/transnational-land-deals-india-china-2012-5

45. Schwartzstein, Peter. (April 26, 2016). Gulf Countries Look to Farm Abroad as Aquifer Dries Up. *Nationalgeographic.com.* https://www.nationalgeographic.com/culture/article/gulf-countries-look-to-farm-abroad-as-aquifer-dries-up

46. Diamond, Jared. *Collapse, How Societies Choose to Fail or Succeed.* USA: Penguin Books, 2011, page 119.

47. Ibid, 120.

48. Brown, Lester R. *World on the Edge.* New York: W.W. Norton & Company, Inc., 2011, p. 7.

49. Ibid., p. 6 & 10.

50. Connett, Wendy. (July 7, 2019). Understanding China's Former One Child Policy. *Investopedia.* https://www.investopedia.com/articles/investing/120114/understanding-chinas-one-child-policy.asp Accessed December 8, 2019.

51. Hallmann, Casper A., et al. (10-18-2017). More Than 75 Percent Decline over 27 Years in Total Flying Insect Biomass in Protected Areas. *Plos One.* https://doi.org/10.1371/journal.pone.0185809

52. Ibid.

53. Carrington, Damian. (October 18, 2017). Warning of 'Ecological Armageddon' after Dramatic Plunge in Insect Numbers. *The Guardian.* https://www.theguardian.com/environment/2017/oct/18/warning-of-ecological-armageddon-after-dramatic-plunge-in-insect-numbers Accessed 12-7-2019.

54. Princeton University. (October 9, 2019). Antibiotic resistance in food animals nearly tripled since 2000. *ScienceDaily.* www.sciencedaily.com/releases/2019/10/191009132321.htm

55. Ibid.

56. Cardoso, Pedro, et al. Scientists' warning to humanity on insect extinctions. *Biological Conservation*, Volume 242, February 2020, 108426. https://www. sciencedirect.com/science/article/pii/S0006320719317823?via%3Dihub Accessed 11-8-2020.

57. Doheny, Kathleen. (June 14, 2019). Weedkillers in Cereals: What to Know" *WebMD*. https://www.webmd.com/diet/news/20190614/weedkillers-in-cereal-what-to-know Accessed December 7, 2019.

58. Malkan, Stacy. (October 1, 2020). Glyphosate Fact Sheet: Cancer and Other Health Concerns. *U.S. Right to Know*. https://usrtk.org/pesticides/glyphosate-health-concerns/ Accessed 11-8-2020.

59. Formuzis, Alex. (December 6, 2019). As U.S. Ignores Risks to Kids, E.U. Bans Brain-Damaging Pesticide; EWG: Trump EPA Kowtows to Chemical Ag Industry. *Environmental Working Group*. https://www.ewg.org/release/us-ignores-risks-kids-eu-bans-brain-damaging-pesticide Accessed November 8, 2020.

60. Ibid.

61. Belluz, Julia & Viswanathan, Radhika. (12-4-2018). The Problem with All the Plastic That's Leaching into Your Food. *Vox*. https://www.vox.com/science-and-health/2018/9/11/17614540/plastic-food-containers-contamination-health-risks Accessed 12-7-2019.

62. Kravitz, Melissa. (March 26, 2019). Food Companies Are Making Their Products Addictive, and It's Sickening (Literally). *Independent Media Institute*. https://www.ecowatch.com/food-companies-making-products-addictive-2632845184.html?rebelltitem=1#rebelltitem1 Accessed 11-20-2020.

63. Mitchell, Nia MD, Catenacci, Vicki MD, Wyatt, Holly R. MD & Hill, James O. PhD. (December 2012). Obesity: Overview of an Epidemic. *U.S. National Library of Medicine, National Institute of Health*.

64. Tartof, S.Y., Qian L, Hong V. Obesity and Mortality among Patients Diagnosed with COVID-19: Results from an Integrated Health Care Organization. *Ann Intern Med.* Published online August 12, 2020. doi:10.7326/M20-3742

65. Jamieson, A. J. et al. (February 13, 2017). Bioaccumulation of Persistent Organic Pollutants in the Deepest Ocean Fauna. *Nature Ecology & Evolution 1*, Article # 0051.

66. Common Dreams Staff. (September 14, 2019), German Study: Alarming Levels of Dangerous Plastics in Children's Bodies. *Common Dreams*. https://www.commondreams.org/news/2019/09/14/german-study-alarming-levels-dangerous-plastics-childrens-bodies Accessed 12-8-2019.

67. Cho, Renee. (1-26-2011). Our Oceans: A Plastic Soup. *Earth Institute | Columbia University - State of the Planet blog*. https://blogs.ei.columbia.edu/2011/01/26/our-oceans-a-plastic-soup/

68. Alfred Wegener Institute, Helmholtz Centre for Polar and Marine Research. (August 2019) Microplastic drifting down with the snow: In the Alps and the Arctic, experts confirm the presence of plastic in snow. *ScienceDaily.* www.sciencedaily.com/releases/2019/08/190814144503.htm (accessed November 1, 2019).

69. Zimmermann, Lisa et al. (08-05-2019). Benchmarking the in Vitro Toxicity and Chemical Composition of Plastic Consumer Products. *Environ. Sci. Technol.,* 2019, 53, 19, 11467-11477

70. Loria, Kevin. (October 2, 2019). Most Plastic Products Contain Potentially Toxic Chemicals, Study Reveals. *Consumer Reports.* https://www.consumerreports.org/toxic-chemicals-substances/most-plastic-products-contain-potentially-toxic-chemicals/

71. NOAA. (1-15-2020). 2019 Was 2nd Hottest Year on Record for Earth Say NOAA, NASA. NOAA Finds Ocean Heat Content Was the Highest in Recorded History" *NOAA News.* https://www.noaa.gov/news/2019-was-2nd-hottest-year-on-record-for-earth-say-noaa-nasa Accessed 1-16-2020.

72. Wigglesworth, A, et al. (September 6, 2020). Intense Heat Breaks Records and Fuels Fires. *Los Angeles Times.*

73. Cheng, L., and Coauthors. (January 27, 2020) Record-Setting Ocean Warmth Continued in 2019. *Adv. Atmos. Sci.,* 37(2),137–142, https://doi.org/10.1007/s00376-020-9283-7

74. R. S. Nerem, B. D. Beckley, J. T. Fasullo, B. D. Hamlington, D. Masters and G. T. Mitchum. (2-12-18). Climate-change–driven accelerated sea-level rise detected in the altimeter era. *PNAS,* 2018 DOI: 10.1073/pnas.1717312115

75. Levitus, S.; Antonov, J.; Boyer, T.; Baranova, O.; Garcia, H.; Locarnini, R.; Mishonov, A.; Reagan, J.; Seidov, D.; Yarosh, E.; Zweng, M. (2017). NCEI ocean heat content, temperature anomalies, salinity anomalies, thermosteric sea level anomalies, halosteric sea level anomalies, and total steric sea level anomalies from 1955 to present calculated from in situ oceanographic subsurface profile data (NCEI Accession 0164586). Version 4.4. *NOAA National Centers for Environmental Information.* Dataset. doi:10.7289/V53F4MVP

76. US EPA. Climate Change Indicators: Sea Surface Temperature. https://www.epa.gov/climate-indicators/climate-change-indicators-sea-surface-temperature Accessed 3-7-2021.

77. Surging Seas. (October 29, 2019). New study triples global estimates of population threatened by sea level rise. *Climate Central.* https://sealevel.climatecentral.org/news/new-study-triples-global-estimates-of-population-threatened-by-sea-level-ri/ Accessed 11-22-2020; Kulp, S.A., Strauss, B.H. New elevation data triple estimates of global vulnerability to sea-level rise and coastal flooding. *Nat Commun* 10, 4844 (2019). https://doi.org/10.1038/s41467-019-12808-z

78. Sweet, William V., et al. (January 2017). Global and Regional Seal Level Rise Scenarios for the United States. *NOAA Technical Report* NOS CO-OPS 083.

79. Kahn, Brian. (July 9, 2015). Sea Levels Could Rise At Least 20 Feet. *Climate Central.* https://www.climatecentral.org/news/sea-levels-rise-20-feet-19211 Accessed 11-22-2020.

80. Ibid.

81. Stipp, David. (February 9, 2004). The Pentagon's Weather Nightmare: The Climate Could Change Radically, and Fast That Would Be the Mother of All National Security Issues. *Fortune.* archive.fortune.com/magazines/fortune/fortune_ archive/2004/02/09/360620/index.htm.

82. "El Nino" Event in Viet Nam: Agriculture, Food Security and Livelihood Needs Assessment in Response to Drought and Saltwater Intrusion. *Report from Food and Agriculture Organization of the United Nations,* August 23, 2016.

83. Somalia: Operational Plan for famine prevention (Jan-June 2017). *Report from UN Office for the Coordination of Humanitarian Affairs,* February 17, 2017.

84. Freund, Mandy; Henley, Benjamin J.; Karoly, David J.; Allen, Kathryn J.; and Baker, Patrick J. (11-30-2017). Multi-century Cool-and Warm-Season Rainfall Reconstructions for Australia's Major Climate Regions. Vol 13, Issue 12, *Clim. Past,* 13,1751-1770, 2017; Copernicus Publications.

85. Rosen, Len. (September 4, 2013). Climate Change and its Impact on our World's Major Rivers-Part 1: The Rivers of Asia. *21st Century Tech.* 21stcentech.com/climate-change-impact-major-rivers-asia/

86. United Nations. (03-18-2019). *World Water Development Report 2019.* UN Water.

87. World Health Organization. JMP 2017 Update Report – *Water sanitation hygiene.*

88. World Health Organization. JMP 2015 Report – *Water sanitation hygiene.*

89. Yang, Jo-Shing. (October 5, 2019) The New 'Water Barons': Wall Street Mega-Banks are Buying up the World's Water. *Global Research.* https://www. globalresearch.ca/the-new-water-barons-wall-street-mega-banks-are-buying-up-the-worlds-water/5383274 Original article published 12-21-2012 in Market Oracle.

90. Boesler, Matthew. (July 12, 2013). Bottled Water Costs 2000 Times As Much As Tap Water. *Business Insider.* http://www.businessinsider.com/bottled-water-costs-2000x-more-than-tap-2013-7

91. Wagner, Martin; Schlusener, Michael P.; Ternes, Thomas A.; & Oehlmann, Jorg. (August 28, 2013). Identification of Putative Steroid Receptor Antagonists in Bottled Water: Combining Bioassays and High-Resolution Mass Spectrometry. *Plos|One.* http://journals.plos.org/plosone/article?id=10.1371/journal.pone.0072472

92. Garner, Sarah. (July 14, 2014). LA Smog: The Battle against Air Pollution. *Marketplace.* http://www.marketplace.org/2014/07/14/sustainability/we-used-be-china/la-smog-battle-against-air-pollution

93. World Health Organization. *Ten threats to global health in 2019.* https://www.who. int/news-room/spotlight/ten-threats-to-global-health-in-2019 Accessed October13, 2020.

94. Acemoglu, Daron, and Robinson, James A. *Why Nations Fail.* 2012. New York, Crown Publishing Group.

95. Diamond, Jared. (2011) *Collapse, How Societies Choose to Fail or Succeed.* USA: Penguin Books.

96. Acemoglu, Daron, and Robinson, James A. *Why Nations Fail.* p 83 & 401.

97. Brown, Lester R., Earth Policy Institute. *World on the Edge.* W.W. Norton & Company, Inc, New York. 2011. p 10.

98. Acemoglu, Daron, and Robinson, James A. *Why Nations Fail.* p 75.

99. Wiener, Jacob D. August 25, 2020.

100. Citizens United v. Federal Election Commission, 558 U.S. 310 (2010).

101. U.S. Energy Policy Act of 2005 (Pub. L. 109-58), aka the Halliburton Loophole—exempts oil and gas operations from regulation and liability under CERCLA, Safe Drinking Water Act, Clean Water Act & Clean Air Act.

102. Diamond, Jared. *Collapse, How Societies Choose to Fail or Succeed,* p 438. USA: Penguin Books, 2011.

103. Shah, Anup. (1-7-2013). *Poverty Facts and Stats.* Global Issues.org. https://www.globalissues.org/article/26/poverty-facts-and-stats Accessed 11-11-2020.

104. News Release. (09-11-2018). *Global Hunger continues to rise new UN report says.* World Health Organization. Rome.

105. Shah, Anup. (1-7-2013). *Poverty Facts and Stats.* Global Issues.org. https://www.globalissues.org/article/26/poverty-facts-and-stats

106. Patterson, Jeffrey L. The Development of the Concept of Corporation from Earliest Roman Times to A.D. 476. *Accounting Historians Journal*, Vol 10, Number 1. http://www.accountingin.com/accounting-historians-journal/volume-10-number-1/the-development-of-the-concept-of-corporation-from-earliest-roman-times-to-a-d-476/

107. Clinard, Marshall B. *Corporate Corruption: The Abuse of Power.* Greenwood Publishing Group, 1990.

108. Jacobs, Andrew. Opposition to Breast-Feeding Resolution by U.S. Stuns World Health Officials. *NY Times.* https://www.nytimes.com/2018/07/08/health/world-health-breastfeeding-ecuador-trump.html?rref=collection%2Fsectioncollection%2Fworld&action=click&contentCollection=world&region=stream&module=stream_unit&version=latest&contentPlacement=1&pgtype=sectionfront Accessed December12, 2019.

109. *2005 List: The 14 Worst Corporate Evildoers.* International Labor Rights Forum. https://laborrights.org/in-the-news/2005-list-14-worst-corporate-evildoers

110. Jacobson, et al. (September 6, 2017). 100% Clean and Renewable Wind, Water, and Sunlight All-Sector Energy Roadmaps for 139 Countries of the World. *Joule 1 Cell Press.* pp 108-121. https://web.stanford.edu/group/efmh/jacobson/Articles/I/CountriesWWS.pdf

111. Jennings, Katie, Grandoni, Dino, and Rust, Susanne. (10-23-2015). How Exxon went from leader to skeptic on climate change research. *LA Times*. https://graphics. latimes.com/exxon-research/ Accessed 12-12-2019.

112. Ibid.

113. Oreskes, Naomi, and Supran, Geoffrey. "Yes, ExxonMobil Misled the Public." Op-Ed. *LATimes*, Sep.1, 2017.

114. Ibid.

115. Diamond, Jared. *Collapse, How Societies Choose to Fail or Succeed*, p. 428. USA: Penguin Books, 2011.

116. Ibid, 430.

117. Ibid, 431.

118. Keynes, JM. *A Treatise on Money Volume 2: The Applied Theory of Money*. Cambridge: MacMillan, 1971. 8th ed., p 133.

119. Quoted in "Someone Has to Print the Nation's Money ... So Why Not Our Government?" Monetary Reform Online, reprinted from *Victoria Times Colonist*, October 16, 1996; also quoted in *Web of Debt* (2012), Brown, Ellen Hodgson, J.D., 4. Baton Rouge, Louisiana: Third Millennium Press.

120. *U.S. News and World Report*, August 3, 1959.

121. Tiftik, Emre, et al., *Global Debt Monitor Sharp spike in debt rations*. July 16, 2020. The Institute of International Finance, Inc. https://www.iif.com/Portals/0/Files/ content/Research/Global%20Debt%20Monitor_July2020.pdf Accessed 11-12-2020. Maki, Sydney. *World's $281 Trillion Debt Pile Is Set to Rise Again in 2021*. February 17, 2021. Bloomberg. https://www.bloomberg.com/news/articles/2021-02-17/global-debt-hits-all-time-high-as-pandemic-boosts-spending-need Accessed 6-28-2021.

122. Public Banking Institute. *What Wall Street Costs America*. http://www. publicbankinginstitute.org/what_wall_street_costs_america?utm_ campaign=pbinews2016_5&utm_medium=email&utm_source=pbi Accessed 2-3-2016.

123. Josiah Stamp, 1st Baron Stamp. Wikipedia. ("Said to be from an informal talk at the University of Texas in the 1920s, but as yet unverified"). Accessed 11-14-2020.

124. Tanous, Peter J. (March 6, 2018). *Rising interest rates will be devastating to the US economy for one big reason*; CNBC Commentary. https://www.cnbc.com/2018/03/05/ rising-interest-rates-will-be-devastating-to-the-us-economy-for-one-big-reason. html Accessed 11-14-2020.

125. Definitions: Theft by Deception Law and Legal Definition. Uslegal.com. Accessed 11-11-2019.

126. Rao, Venkatesh. (June 8, 2011). *A Brief History of the Corporation: 1600 to 2100*. Ribbonfarm.com. https://www.ribbonfarm.com/2011/06/08/a-brief-history-of-the-corporation-1600-to-2100/ Accessed 11-12-2019.

127. Brown, Ellen. (06-06-2013). It Can Happen Here: The Confiscation Scheme Planned for US and UK Depositors. *Huffpost*. https://www.huffpost.com/entry/banks-confisc ation_b_2957937?guccounter=1 Accessed 11-22-2020.

128. Sanders, Bernie. (4-15-16). Rome

129. Eisinger, Jesse. (April 30, 2014). Why Only One Top Banker Went to Jail for the Financial Crisis. *The New York Times Magazine*

130. Ibid.

131. November 23, 1933 letter to Colonel Edward M. House.

132. Feds: Payday lender charged 700 percent interest on loans. (April 7, 2016). *CBS/AP News*. https://www.cbsnews.com/news/feds-payday-lender-charged-700-percent-interest-on-loans/ Accessed 11-14-2020.

133. Reich, Robert B. (August 10, 2015). How Goldman Sachs Profited from the Greek Debt Crisis. *The Nation*.

134. Ibid.

135. Ibid.

136. Rickards, James. (2016). *The Road to Ruin*. New York: Penguin Random House LLC.

137. XAT. *The History of Money, Part 2*. XAT.org. http://www.xat.org/xat/usury.html Accessed 11-15-2020.

138. Brown, Ellen Hodgson. (October 13, 2011). *Publicly-owned Banks as an Instrument of Economic Development: The German Model*; Global Research / Brown, Ellen Hodgson, J.D. (2011). *Web of Debt*; Baton Rouge, Louisiana: Third Millennium Press.

139. Monetary Reform in Britain. *Wikipedia*. https://en.wikipedia.org/wiki/Monetary_reform_in_Britain Accessed June 26, 2019.

140. Baumgaertner, Emily. (July 4, 2019). Ebola is Raging, and the World Watches. *Los Angeles Times*.

141. Ibid.

142. Press Release. (October 4, 2015). World Bank Forecasts Global Poverty to Fall Below 10% for First Time; Major Hurdles Remain to End Poverty by 2030. The World Bank.

143. Press Release. (October 17, 2018). Nearly Half the World Lives on Less than $5.50 a Day. The World Bank. Washington, D.C.

144. World Water Assessment Program, *The United Nations World Water Development Report 2018*. United Nations Educational, Scientific and Cultural Organization, New York, United States. www.unwater.org/publications/world-water-development-report-2018/

145. United Nations Conference on Trade and Development. (2013). *Trade and Environment Review 2013, Wake Up Before It Is Too Late*. https://unctad.org/en/PublicationsLibrary/ditcted2012d3_en.pdf Accessed 11-21-2019.

146. Global Happiness Council. (February 12, 2018). *Global Happiness Policy Report 2018.* https://www.happinesscouncil.org/report/2018/

147. Lincoln, Abraham, President. (November 19, 1863). *The Gettysburg Address.*

148. Citizens United v. Federal Election Commission. 558 U.S. 310, January 21, 2010.

149. U.S. Declaration of Independence, July 4, 1776.

150. *Global Happiness Policy Report 2018.* https://www.happinesscouncil.org/report/2018/

151. The Club of Rome. (What do the happiest countries in the world have in common? *https://www.clubofrome.org/2016/03/17/what-do-the-happiest-countries-in-the-world-have-in-common/*

152. Berkley Wellness. (11-09-2015). *What is the science of happiness?* https://www.berkeleywellness.com/healthy-mind/mind-body/article/what-science-happiness

153. Helliwell, J., Layard, R., & Sachs, J. *World Happiness Report 2019*, New York: Sustainable Development Solutions Network, 2019. https://worldhappiness.report/ed/2019/changing-world-happiness/.

154. Willies, Egberto. (03-04-2018). Oprah Got Perfect Response from Danish Woman on Their Social Welfare State. *Daily Kos.* https://www.dailykos.com/stories/2018/3/4/1746440/-Oprah-got-perfect-response-from-Danish-woman-on-their-social-welfare-state?detail=emaildkre

155. Dictionary.com, s. v. "lie."

156. Centers for Disease Control and Prevention. (July 23, 2019). *Smoking and Tobacco Use Fast Facts and Fact Sheets.* https://www.cdc.gov/tobacco/data_statistics/fact_sheets/health_effects/effects_cig_smoking/index.htm

157. Bates, Clive & Rowell, Andy. Tobacco Explained. The Truth about the Tobacco Industry ... in Its Own Words. Adapted for World No Tobacco Day. *World Health Organization.* https://www.who.int/tobacco/media/en/TobaccoExplained.pdf Accessed March 8, 2021.

158. *Merriam-Webster*, s. v. "truth."

159. Leachman, Michael; Masterson, Kathleen; & Wallace, Marlana. (October 20, 2016). After Nearly a Decade, School Investments Still Way Down in Some States. *Center on Budget and Policy Priorities.* https://www.cbpp.org/research/state-budget-and-tax/after-nearly-a-decade-school-investments-still-way-down-in-some

160. Davies, Nicolas J.S. (October 1, 2016). The Record U.S. Military Budget. *HuffPost.* https://www.huffpost.com/entry/the-record-us-military-bu_b_8227820?guccounter=1

161. Amadeo, Kimberly. (June 25, 2019). FY 2016 Federal Budget: President's Request vs. Spending. *The Balance.* https://www.thebalance.com/fy-2016-federal-budget-3882293

162. Collier, Paul. (4-10-1999). Doing Well out of War. *The World Bank.* Paper prepared for Conference on Economic Agendas in Civil Wars, London, April 26-27, 1999, Pg. 5.

163. Leachman, Ibid.

164. Miller, Lawrence M. (May 14, 2013). Transformational Change vs. Continuous Improvement. *Industry Week.* https://www.industryweek.com/change-management/transformational-change-vs-continuous-improvement

165. Gitlin, Todd.

166. King, Martin Luther, Jr. (April 16, 1963). Letter from Birmingham Jail. Reprinted, *African Studies Center, University of Pennsylvania.* http://www.un.org/en/universal-declaration-human-rights/index.html Accessed January 24, 2020.

167. Summary of the advisory panel of the International Monsanto Tribunal. Hearings in The Hague on 15-16 October 2016. *Stichting/Foundation Monsanto Tribunal.* http://www.monsanto-tribunal.org/upload/asset_cache/1016160509.pdf

168. Friends of the Earth Europe. (February 4, 2021). *Coal company sues Netherlands for €1.4 billion for coal phaseout.* https://friendsoftheearth.eu/press-release/coal-company-sues-netherlands-for-1-4-billion/ Accessed 03-01-2021.

169. United Nations General Assembly. (December 10, 1948). *The Universal Declaration of Human Rights.* http://www.un.org/en/universal-declaration-human-rights/index.html

170. United Nations Human Rights Office of the High Commissioner. (January 3, 1976). *International Covenant on Economic, Social and Cultural Rights.* https://www.ohchr.org/en/professionalinterest/pages/cescr.aspx

171. Convention on the Elimination of All Forms of Discrimination against Women – Treaty Adopted December 18, 1979. *UN Women.* http://www.un.org/womenwatch/daw/cedaw/text/econvention.htm#article3

172. US Declaration of Independence. July 4, 1776.

173. Khan, Mehreen. (February 2, 2015). The Biggest Debt Write-offs in the History of the World. *The Telegraph.* https://www.telegraph.co.uk/finance/economics/11383374/The-biggest-debt-write-offs-in-the-history-of-the-world.html

174. Ibid.

175. Arnold, Amanda. (June 21, 2018). What to Know About the Detention Centers for Immigrant Children Along the U.S.-Mexico Border. Family Separation Policy. *The Cut.* https://www.thecut.com/2018/06/immigrant-children-detention-center-separated-parents.html Accessed; Serwer, Adam. (July 3, 2019). A Crime by Any Name. The Trump administration's commitment to deterring immigration through cruelty has made horrifying conditions in detention facilities inevitable. *The Atlantic.* https://www.theatlantic.com/ideas/archive/2019/07/border-facilities/593239/; Family separation under the Trump administration – a timeline. (June 17, 2020). *Southern Poverty Law Center.* https://www.splcenter.org/news/2020/06/17/family-separation-under-trump-administration-timeline Accessed 11-18-2020.

176. Ibid.

177. United Nations. (June 17, 2019) World Population Prospects 2019: Highlights. United Nations Department of Economic and Social Affairs.

178. Taylor, Leslie. (August 2019) About the Rainforest. *Raintree.* http://rain-tree.com/facts.htm#.WKTIALHMyi4.

179. Ibid.

180. Vidal, John. (January 23, 2017) We are destroying rainforests so quickly they may be gone in 100 years. *The Guardian.* https://www.theguardian.com/global-development-professionals-network/2017/jan/23/destroying-rainforests-quickly-gone-100-years-deforestation Accessed 11-18-2020.

181. Juang, Jianping, et al. (September 30, 2018). The global oxygen budget and its future projection. *Science Direct Bulletin*, Vol 63, Issue 18, Pg 1180-1186.

182. 100 People: A World Portrait. A Global Education Toolbox. *100 People.org.* https://www.100people.org/statistics-details/ Accessed 11-19-2020.

183. Coldron, Alice Clubbs. (December 17, 2019) How Rare (or Common) is it to have a Phd? *Findaphd.com blog.* https://www.findaphd.com/advice/blog/5403/how-rare-or-common-is-it-to-have-a-phd Accessed 11-19-2020.

184. Lent, Jeremy. (February 16, 2021). What Does An Ecological Civilization Look Like? *Yes! Magazine.*

185. Jimi Hendrix.

AUTHOR BIOGRAPHY

Benjamin R. Wiener is a naturalist, a humanist, an environmentalist, an adventurer, and a retired attorney. He majored in environmental science before that was a thing, and became corporate counsel to an alternative energy company before that was a thing. He has studied earth processes, as well as how our societies function and their associated impacts on the natural world for over 50 years. Those studies resulted in countless hours of deep thought considering how to fundamentally change our ways to enable humanity to not just survive, but to thrive. *Outposts of Change* is the culmination of his life's work. Ben lives in California with his wife and golden retriever.

9 781736 803509